How to
Balance
Your
Hormones

Dr. Joanne Messenger

BALBOA.
PRESS
A DIVISION OF HAY HOUSE

Balboa Press books may be ordered through booksellers or by contacting:

Balboa Press
A Division of Hay House
1663 Liberty Drive
Bloomington, IN 47403
www.balboapress.com.au
1 (877) 407-4847

Because of the dynamic nature of the Internet, any web addresses or links contained in this book may have changed since publication and may no longer be valid. The views expressed in this work are solely those of the author and do not necessarily reflect the views of the publisher, and the publisher hereby disclaims any responsibility for them.

All information, including techniques, exercises, therapies, medicines, nutrients, and herbs, contained in this publication is general in nature and is intended for use as an educational aid. It does not cover all possible uses, actions, precautions, side effects, or interactions, nor is the information intended as medical advice for individual problems or for making an evaluation as to the risks and benefits of taking a particular substance or doing a particular exercise. The information contained herein has been devised without reference to cultural, dietary, societal, linguistic, prescriptive, or dispensing conditions that might affect the information provided.

Joanne's website: www.drjoannemessenger.com

Printed in the United States of America.

ISBN: 978-1-4525-2518-1 (sc)
ISBN: 978-1-4525-2519-8 (e)

Balboa Press rev. date: 08/14/2014

To the beautiful Candice, who has ridden my waves of misery and mastery and thrived in the face of complexity.

Contents

Physiologically Compatible Nutrients

Mastication

Fresh Air

Natural Clothing

Exercise

Yoga

Meditation

Sex

Self-Love

Love for Others

Gratitude

Being

Relax

Sleep

Foreword

Dr. Joanne Messenger's second book, *How to Balance Your Hormones,* is a comprehensive guide for those who wish to explore the myriad of reasons why their personal health might not be optimal.

The central theme pertains to the balance of the hormone system—an absolute prerequisite for optimal well-being.

Dr. Messenger details how hormones drive our physiological and psychological functions and are required to be in balance for optimal health.

Virtually all cells in the human body have receptors for hormones. Therefore, it can be logically assumed that hormones have an effect on all cells within our bodies. The brain, and the amygdala in particular (the emotional centre), is particularly rich in hormone receptors, so it would be of no surprise to know that fluctuating levels of hormones (sex steroid hormones oestrogen, progesterone, and testosterone) have a profound effect on mood, memory, libido, and sense of well-being. Deficiency in sex steroid hormones leads to mood disorders, failing memory, anxiety, depression, low libido, and symptoms of premenstrual tension. These relate to low levels of progesterone, which leads to symptoms, such as food cravings, anxiety, breast tenderness, fluid retention, bloating, and even catamenial epilepsy in the luteal phase of a woman's cycle (the premenstrual phase).

There is an increased risk of cardiovascular disease, osteoporosis, thinning of the skin, loss of hair, and vaginal dryness when sex steroid hormones are low, as seen in the perimenopause and menopausal period of a woman's life. Ageing is directly related the drop in hormone levels which occur after menopause.

Girls develop into women solely through the effects of increasing oestrogen beginning at age eight and increasing progesterone levels, which begin within a year of menses. It is testosterone in utero (produced by the foetus) that develops the foetus into a male, and without testosterone in utero, despite having an XY chromosome, the foetus will develop into a girl.

Yet the difference between the structure of testosterone and oestradiol is a single hydrogen molecule. This is critically important to remember when considering the effects of synthetic or non-bioidentical hormones and the effects they may have on health. Hormones affect the growth of cells, control of immune function, and control of metabolism and when disordered leads to disease.

As Dr. Messenger shows in her book, disruption or changes of the hormone regulatory system can occur through a variety of environmental mechanisms.

The commonest mechanism for changing hormone profile is taking the oral contraceptive pill. These are analogue or synthetic hormones that suppress the production of oestrogen, testosterone, and progesterone by the ovaries. The side effects of the hormone contraceptive pill are many and can include depression, obesity, blood clots, psychiatric, or mood changes and an increase in immunological disorders.

Dr. Messenger also outlines other causes of hormone perturbation or changes. These include xenoestrogens which are often related to pollutants and other chemicals in our environment.

The world is literally polluted with tens and tens of thousands of novel chemicals and compounds which have been introduced in the last fifty to seventy years. Many can affect oestrogen receptors and are therefore defined as xenoestrogens. These may act by blocking receptors so our own hormones have an inability to trigger our DNA, or they can act by blocking hormone receptor sites from our own hormones. They may similarly stimulate the cell and DNA synthesis in unpredictable ways.

That we can find DDT in polar bears in the Arctic Circle and trace the reduced fertility rates of alligators in Florida to contamination by DDT affecting weakness of eggs means there are no borders for chemical or radioactive pollutants.

It should come as no surprise to us that newborn babies in the USA have up to 250 different environmental chemicals in their bodies. Up to 50 per cent of these chemicals are potentially carcinogenic.

Dr. Messenger's book adds weight to the concept of "the fundamental connectedness of all things" and is a timely reminder of how our health can be affected through exposure to environmental chemicals found in a myriad of different products. Cosmetics, for example, contain more than 10,000 chemicals and only 1,300 have been assessed for safety. Chemicals can also enter our bodies via our diet, through the air we breathe, the water we drink, and even our clothes and furnishings.

Dr. Messenger's book is packed with factual information regarding the adverse effects of our polluted environment in all its forms. Perhaps more heroically, Dr. Messenger's book offers ways and means to optimise health through a variety of different strategies, including avoidance, supplementation, and correction of hormone imbalance, as well as being aware of the energy systems of our body and how this can be altered to optimise energy flow. This includes correction of malalignment of the spine, the use of anti-inflammatory botanicals, aromatherapy, meditation, self-awareness, self-responsibility, and so on.

The holistic nature of Dr. Messenger's theme paints a broad but detailed picture for the reader, providing an opportunity for the reader to choose and reflect on issues and strategies that may be relevant to them.

The broad scope of Dr. Messenger's book includes details of how subluxation of the spine may cause menstrual disorders. She also includes the effects of phylates (plastic pollutants) in maternal blood and how this may cause genital anomalies in male offspring. She discusses new concepts, such as the biology of belief, which means how your thinking will affect your neuro-endocrine system and your own biology. Dr. Messenger's book details how to best optimise health through a number of different strategies.

Dr. Messenger's book will be a welcome addition in any library for those who have an interest in self-determination, health, and taking responsibility for their own well-being. I recommend this book to everyone in these categories.

Dr. Jeremy Coleman
MBBS, FRACP

1

Hormone Hell

Out of Control

If you've ever known the misery of feeling trapped in hormone hell or been around someone who has, you'll welcome these pages with open arms.

When you know that life can be fulfilling, rewarding, and pleasurable, it compounds the frustration and restrictions of those times when hormones dictate another path, demanding you succumb to their plans for you. When normal, sweet, and caring people become raging monsters, all because of an imbalance in biochemistry, it makes sense to try to restore some level of equilibrium and control.

Unfortunately, the knowledge of modern medicine still hasn't knocked this on the head for the millions of women who are still suffering worldwide. And it's not just the women who suffer. Their relationships, careers, and the people around them also pay a high price for what theoretically is a normal body function that, for whatever reason, has run amok.

Emotions Run Wild

Any woman who suffers hormonal symptoms also needs to be aware of the underlying energy or emotions involved. Whenever a woman loses touch with her nurturing, female aspect and takes on a more male-orientated energy, it disrupts the ovaries and breasts, causing menstrual and breast problems.

1

Women need to reclaim their self-nurturing and femaleness. The techniques outlined in this book will help facilitate this.

This step is critical, because if you seek hormone therapy without addressing the underlying emotional imbalances, you'll only improve your bodily function without truly healing and restoring harmony in your body. Restoring function without addressing the underlying energy concerns buries the issues deeper—only to arise again in the future with potentially more severe symptoms.

The Facts

According to the National Women's Health Information Centre (NWHIC),

- 75 per cent of women get premenstrual syndrome (PMS); 35 per cent of women get PMS to the degree that it impairs their daily activities; and 5 per cent have premenstrual dysphoric disorder (PMDD), symptoms so severe that it's debilitating. This represents 40.8 million women in the United States alone.

- 5–10 per cent of women of childbearing age (twenty to forty years) have polycystic ovary syndrome (PCOS) and 30 per cent have some PCOS symptoms. This is another 6.8 million women in the United States alone. 50 per cent of these women are insulin resistant, which can degenerate into type 2 diabetes.

- 10–20 per cent of women of childbearing age have endometriosis. Again, this is 13.6 million in the United States alone.

- There are at least two million *new cases* of female infertility annually.

These are the statistics for women who actually have the hormone conditions. And for every one of these, there's another circle around them who are also affected because of their condition.

Even if they experience only one day per month at less than their best, this means they're compromised for nearly two weeks every year—that equates to a whole year and a half out of their lives.

Unfortunately, most women are affected much longer than that.

Most women feel low an average of three and a half days every month because of their menstrual cycle. This means they're having pain and other hormone-related problems (e.g., irritability, anger, depression, breast swelling and tenderness, skin problems, headaches, backache, insomnia, nervousness, dizziness, fainting spells, lethargy, confusion, bloating, fluid retention, changes in personality, and cravings for sweets) for six weeks a year. That's an alarming four and a half years of menstrual difficulties in a lifetime.

This is not just a personal issue; it's a community issue. It impacts every aspect of life, including relationships, work, family, and society.

If you're suffering for two weeks per month, as many women are, this is nearly six months per year—a horrible eighteen and a half years of your precious life. This is not OK, and changes need to be made.

Symptoms versus Cause

In this era of modern medicine, research, and availability of information, why is this still happening?

So much has been written about hormone issues from both orthodox and traditional medicine, so why is it still rampant in our society? Why are the figures growing, rather than receding?

Logic says, "If you keep doing the same thing, you'll keep getting the same results. If you want a different result, you need to do things differently," so clearly we need to look at what's happening and what to do about it differently.

Most people know the benefits of exercise, nutrition, adjustments, herbs, hormone-replacement therapy (HRT), massage, acupuncture, energy healing, meditation, and so on. Even so, the statistics are screaming. We've been missing something.

Have we spent so long looking at symptoms and how to minimize or cope with them and missed the cause of the problem?

If the old approach isn't working, then doesn't it make sense to take a new one?

In this book, we're going to explore the causes of hormonal imbalances and give a variety of options as to what you can do about them—to manage them, adapt to them, and ideally to heal and resolve them.

You won't need a medical degree, any prior knowledge of herbal lore, or the intricacies of the way what you think, say, and do affects the physical health of your body. It doesn't matter if you've already tried and done everything you've known so far, seen everyone from your medical doctor to shamanic doctors in a bid to ease your plight, or if this is your first port of call; the concepts and information in this book will still be able to help you.

You don't need to be born with a healing gift to heal yourself—just the right information and the initiative to take the right steps. Understanding and accepting your uniqueness will help you find your way with the most direct route.

These keys I'm offering you aren't intended to replace wise medical opinion; however, they are intended to provide you with more knowledge, awareness, practical techniques, and solutions so you can work with your team of professionals to not only manage your condition but also free yourself from it with clear intention.

If you've been on a merry-go-round from one practitioner to another— swallowing vitamins, minerals, herbs, and medications; sucking lozenges; sticking patches; using creams; or imbedding implants—and still have problems, then it's time to look for new keys.

This doesn't mean stop using the medications or therapies you need to support yourself. I'm not saying they're bad. What I am saying is if you're using them and you still have issues, then you need to look deeper. If you stopped using them, would your symptoms come back? If so, then you need to look deeper, because what you're currently doing is merely masking your symptoms and not healing the cause of why you have the symptoms in the first place.

It's time to stop treating symptoms and deal with the real causes of problems. If you're driving a car and the oil light comes on, does it make sense to tape over the oil light so you can't see it anymore? Isn't the light a sign of a deeper issue? Isn't it likely there's going to be a bigger problem soon if you don't deal with that deeper issue?

If your body expresses symptoms, it's telling you something is wrong. If you keep covering your symptoms with pills, lotions, and potions without also dealing with the deeper issues, you too will likely have a bigger problem soon.

If you don't listen to the whispers, you'll get the screams.

For example,

- If you crave carbohydrates, you need to find out why. Is it a chromium or vitamin B6 deficiency causing your cravings?

  If so, why do you have a chromium or vitamin B6 deficiency?

  Are you eating the right foods in the right amounts and combinations for you? If not, why not? What are you going to do about it and when?

  Are you absorbing the nutrients from your food efficiently? If not, why not? What are you going to do about it and when?

  Do you need to eat more protein? Are you not digesting protein efficiently? If not, why not? What are you going to about it and when?

  If you just restrict yourself from eating carbohydrates without resolving why you're craving them in the first place, the cause doesn't get resolved and you'll have to fight the cravings indefinitely—until you either do or you succumb to the consequences of inflammation and diabetes that can result.

  There are a lot of questions here, but that's exactly what's needed. Keep asking questions of "What causes what within you?" until you get to the root of your trouble.

- If you crave chocolate, do you have a chocolate deficiency? Really?

  Do you have a magnesium deficiency? When you're low in magnesium, you'll crave chocolate—in direct proportion to the degree of deficiency.

  What stress have you been under that's chewing up your magnesium? What are you going to do about the magnesium deficiency, and when?

  What are you going to do about the stresses? When?

- If you have a progesterone deficiency, why? What caused the deficiency in the first place?

  If your progesterone building blocks have been used up to make cortisol and other stress hormones, what are you going to do to dissipate that stress and stop more stress and progesterone deficiency in the future?

If you have a spinal subluxation (a misalignment of a vertebra causing interference to the nerve supply to corresponding organs, muscles, and systems) of your third lumbar vertebra interfering with your ovaries and their production of progesterone, what are you going to do to realign your spine? How? When? What are you going to do to maintain the alignment of your spine?

It makes sense to take your vitamins, minerals, herbs, and medications to support you while you resolve the underlying causes, but don't be tricked into thinking they're healing you. They're helping you, while you get on with the business of healing yourself. Covering the oil light in a car does nothing to fix the underlying problem.

It's you that heals you, not external things. If you cut yourself, it'll heal all by itself given the right conditions.

If you cut a piece of steak, it's never going to heal no matter what you inject it with, rub on it, or wrap it in. If there's no life force, it won't heal. It's the life force in you that heals you.

It's your job to remove all the blocks you've put in place that interfere with your life force. What are they? That's what you need to find out—and resolve.

Find Your Path

Everyone is different.

We know that logically because we all look, sound, smell, and think differently. No two people on the planet have the same finger or voiceprint. We're seeing the personal importance of this more and more. A career that is inspiring and fulfilling for one person, such as computer technology, appears boring and equally unfulfilling to another. A food that is essential nutrition for one person, such as dairy and wheat, is allergic poison to another.

It's imperative you seek out the concepts, therapies, and supplements you have a personal affinity with and run a mile from those you don't.

For example, you may need to do things that help your body make more oestrogen, whereas someone else may need to do things that help their body rid itself from an excess of oestrogen.

Most of our imbalances come from simply having too much or too little of something. This book will help you determine where this has relevance for you and what to do about it.

My Story

I'm just the right person to write this book.
I've bitten off more heads than foxes in a chicken yard.
I've gained and lost weight enough times to make Jenny Craig go pale.
I've consumed enough chocolate to keep the economy of Belgium afloat.
I've been focused and lost it. Started projects and stopped them.
I've been gorgeous and inspired and grumpy and lazy.
I've been everything!
The pendulum swing of my hormonal cycle was overriding my life on every level, affecting everything from my mood and motivation to physical appearance and sensuality—until I found the keys to open the right doors.

I know the concepts and methods in this book work because they're the foundations I utilized to restore my own hormonal and life balance.

I was born the youngest of seven children, all of us girls except for six boys, in country Western Australia. It's no surprise I grew up very athletic and competitive. By age ten, I won bronze at the state gymnastics championships. Then at age twelve, seeming disaster struck. I was doing backward somersaults on the trampoline and landed on the frame, fracturing my pelvis. If you've ever fractured a bone, you'll recognize the agony.

The pain was just the beginning. All the organs around the fracture site had to compensate for the injury. Within a year, my period stopped, I had my appendix removed, I gained weight, and my moods took on a life of their own.

At fifteen, I went to boarding school (not renowned for quality nutrition), and my health suffered even further.

At seventeen, I went to Victoria to attend chiropractic college. By now, my body was adapting to the adaptations. I was getting constipated and headaches as well. I had the good fortune to be adjusted by a chiropractor known affectionately as Billy Mac (Dr. Bill McPherson). Billy Mac was one of the forefront teachers in Australia of sacro-occipital technique. He adjusted my pelvis and my period came back. It was a miracle for me.

Even at such a young age, this got my attention. It laid the foundations for a journey into the healing arts. I went into private practice as a chiropractor and craniopath, but my healing and learning journey never stopped. I attended post-graduate courses on nutrition and herbs and added them into my health maintenance regime, as well as using this knowledge to help others.

I was a sponge for knowledge.

I learned about flower essences and essential oils and how they help emotions and biochemistry—and added them in. I studied neurolinguistic programming (NLP), including how we process information through sight, sound, feeling, and logic, and how this affects our experience of the world.

Even so, my hormones were still nagging for my attention.

I was already gifted at being in my head. It became evident I needed to get out of my head and into my body rather than farther into logic. (In contrast to me, if you're a person who "feels" too much, it's likely you'll need to pay more attention to what and how you think or process life, rather than feel even more deeply.)

Every time my hormones screamed louder than what my current regime was holding at bay, I'd learn another modality to add into my self-maintenance program.

I had a patient who was a trance medium and learned Chiron healing through her. This work with the master diamond blueprints of the body's electromagnetic fields fascinated me immensely. So much so that I wrote all the training manuals for this method and became principal of the school. I studied yoga and became a teacher. I studied aromatherapy and cosmetic manufacture. I studied meditation, pranic healing, Pleiadean light work, and delved into everything that expanded my knowledge of how our bodies work and what I could do to enhance their function and quality of life experience.

In the early days, I learned about natural progesterone creams and began importing them from the United States. At this time, a group of clinics in Sydney began testing hormones in more detail and were using troches.

The concept of bioidentical hormones made sense to me. In other words, if your body isn't making enough of a particular hormone to keep pace with the out-of-balance lifestyle you're submitting it to, then at least support it with nature identical hormones rather than those harvested from pregnant horse's urine and the like.

At this stage, my life was extremely out of balance. I was a divorced single parent with three ex-stepchildren and living in relationship with a single-parent man who had two sons—all the while maintaining a busy clinic, running the Chiron healing school and teaching throughout Australia and New Zealand most weekends.

I knew I desperately needed more progesterone (the feel-good hormone) but hadn't learned why I needed so much. Yes, I had a damaged right ovary from the trampoline accident, but the extreme business of my life was chewing up the building blocks I needed for progesterone by using them to make stress hormones!

The new Sydney clinic promised to have the answer. Yes, they gave me the progesterone I needed, but they also insisted on giving me oestrogen, because in their experience, women my age (then fortyish) needed oestrogen as well—even though I told them all the reasons, according to my research, why I didn't need it.

I learned the following big lessons:
- to listen to me. I had done my research and knew from my symptoms I was oestrogen dominant, not deficient.
- the power of hormones. My mood went from being a bit dark sometimes to so black I couldn't override it with positivity with my usual strategies. I was feeling so dark that even mentioning oestrogen to me now makes me shiver.
- to be responsible for my own decisions. If someone isn't helping, no matter how expert they say they are, go somewhere else!

- to never give up. The next step always shows up if you keeping asking and paying attention.

Fortunately, there's precise blood testing available now.

These days, there's no reason for anyone to prescribe inaccurately because the numbers on the page say what's high and what's low. You can see an integrative medical doctor who can test your levels and prescribe bioidentical hormone creams accordingly.

The more I studied the mind-body connection and how the energy field not just affects physical health but even determines it, I began to connect the dots between life events that had caused me to keep going out of balance. It was not enough to try to override the effect of these events and soldier on; rather, I had to accept and release the issues and the people involved, much like is done in a twelve-step program.

This is as continuous as life itself. It can be a wonderful foundation to your life journey rather than a curse or something to try to control. Acceptance of what you've created with intent to find resolution, rather than resistance or arguing against the universe, seems to help rather than hurt.

2

A Natural Response

A Natural Response to Your Life

Progesterone is known as "the feel-good hormone."

Progesterone's building blocks are the same building blocks needed to make your stress hormones, such as cortisol. When you get tired or stressed, the building blocks for your progesterone get used up to make your stress hormones instead. Then you don't feel good anymore because your feel-good hormone is deficient.

This lets you know to change what you think, say, and do. In other words, change what is causing the stress and; hence, the feel-good hormone deficiency in the first place.

This is a natural body response. It is not a disease state.

Diverting feel-good hormone building blocks to stress hormone manufacture is a natural body response to stress. In other words, you feel bad to let you know to change what you're thinking, saying, and doing.

If you want more feel-good hormone, stop spending its building block budget on stress hormone manufacture.

The changes in your body associated with acute stress are essential for your survival in a stressful environment.

The problem is you're not designed to be under constant stress.

The natural, normal, and useful responses to acute fight or flight situations are now being stimulated for days, weeks, months, and even years. Rather than the presence of stress every now and then, people are living in almost constant stress—and we're not designed for this.

Your Body's Natural Response to Stress

- Your nerve system detects a stimulus, such as a lion leaping at you at the water hole. (Hence, the importance of your spine alignment so there's no interference to this detection and message relay system to and from your brain and body.)
- Your sympathetic nerve system increases your
    - heart rate
    - blood pressure
    - blood glucose (Hence, in the long term, you want to eat more sugar.)
    - blood lipids (Hence, in the long term, you want to eat more fat.)
    - cortisol (down-regulates your insulin receptors)
    - catecholamines (This stimulates emotional anxiety so next time you watch out for lions at the water hole. This also decreases your learning ability—you don't need to spell while running from lions.)
    - blood cholesterol (increases LDL; decreases HDL). Cholesterol is an essential building block for your steroid hormones and is required for healing your wounds, should you not totally escape the lion, and mood regulation. This is why some people become depressed or suicidal when on cholesterol-lowering drugs!
    - insulin resistance
    - blood-clotting factors
- Your parasympathetic nerve system decreases your
    - sex-gland function
    - sex drive
    - digestion
    - growth
    - cellular immunity
    - serotonin (Hence, you'll feel tired, depressed, irritable, headachy, and have appetite changes.)

These are intelligent responses by your parasympathetic nerve system because these are not immediately useful responses in a "lion attack" or stressful situations.

These responses to stress are normal and totally essential.

It's the chronically stressful environment that's pathological— not your body's response to it.

If you ignore this and continue to just treat the symptoms, you will cause even more damage than what's happening already.

For example, if you have high blood pressure and rather than recognize it as an intelligent response by your body to stress and eliminate that stress, and you take medication to lower the blood pressure, your body would soon recognize the blood pressure is now inappropriately low given the stressful circumstances it's in and will endeavour to raise it once more.

Often more or stronger medication is then recommended.

Unfortunately, your ability to adapt is now chemically interfered with and you are left feeling even more anxious or depressed, so anti-depressants are often prescribed as well.

What happens if you stop taking the medication?

Blood pressure skyrockets and moods plummet.

It's essential to deal with the stress that is causing this spiral in the first place.

Similarly, if you have high blood sugar, this is an intelligent response by your body to deal with stress. Taking insulin lowers your blood sugar, which your body soon recognizes is inappropriately low given the stressful circumstances you're under. Your body takes measures to increase it once more, causing insulin resistance—then even more insulin is required and there is even more resistance.

Repeatedly, it's essential to deal with the stress that's determining the need for high blood sugar in the first place—and likewise for high cholesterol and everything else on the list above.

Resolve your stress—all of it!

If you insist on thinking, at least think new thoughts instead of the same old same old, over and over.

Everyone and everything that stresses or displeases you in any way is showing you where you need to forgive, release, and let go.

Unforgiveness and resentment physiologically kill you.

Resentment is re-send-ment. In other words, it is thinking the same thing over and over.

Drugs and Health

We've been taught to use symptoms as a monitor for health, but this is limited. Supposedly, if you have symptoms, you are unhealthy, and if you don't have symptoms, you're healthy, yet it's a well-known fact that the absence of symptoms is a poor indicator of health. There are thousands of people who have been riddled with cancer and never had noticeable symptoms even though the disease had been in their body for at least five to ten years.

Make the distinction between health and the absence of symptoms.

Just like some people think they can stand still even though they're standing on the Earth, which is rotating on its own axis, as well as revolving around the sun, which also revolves around something else, there are some who think taking drugs to alleviate symptoms makes them healthier.

Don't confuse alleviating symptoms with health. They're not the same thing.

Covering the oil light in the car stops it shining in your eyes but does nothing to improve the function of the car.

Medication can take away the symptoms of sickness and disease but cause even poorer health because your body now has to deal with the original sickness *and* the physiological incompatible chemical that was used. The less your body has to deal with the side effects of foreign chemicals, the better off you'll be.

If medication or HRT are part of your arsenal to support yourself while you resolve your underlying issues, search out practitioners who can prescribe nature identical hormones.

The Western world spends increasingly more money on medication and has more doctors, nurses, tests, and technical equipment per capita, yet we still continue to have more and more sick people.

Medicine doesn't make people healthy—it just produces people with temporarily fewer symptoms.

The malfunctions that caused the symptoms in the first place still need to be addressed. You still need to stop going to the water hole when the lions are there.

Drugs may make you *feel* better while you're sick, but they'll never make you function better and get you well. That job is for you and your life force.

The Three Phases of Disease

Health is not merely the absence of symptoms. Disease takes time to form and even longer to express itself at a recognizable level.

The three phases of disease are the following

1. Subclinical
   This is when there are changes in your body but you don't know about them yet.
   At this level of disease, you don't recognize any symptoms and medical tests won't show a positive result yet. This can be frustrating for sensitive, tuned-in, and aware people who know something isn't quite right but are told medically that nothing is wrong.
   This is the easiest level to heal from because the adaptation of the body isn't a full-blown disease process yet. This is the level where chiropractors and natural healers excel when they focus on wellness and prevention rather than wait to get sick and try to sort it out later.
2. Symptomatic
   At this level, the body has been trying to adapt to stressors that have been present long enough or severe enough for you to notice symptoms because of it. Medical tests may or may not give enough information at this stage. Best you pay attention to the signs your body is displaying and re-jig your lifestyle accordingly.

3. Pathological

This is when there's a clear and present disease process in progress. This is the level of medical diagnosis, even though there've been two distinct phases prior. By the time a disease process gets to this level, there's been a myriad of changes over time. There's much more work for you to do to resolve an imbalance from this level because you've not recognized or have ignored what was happening or needed changing, and now your destructive patterns of thinking, saying, and doing have been established over time. Nonetheless, do what works.

Make the changes and do more of what takes you closer to what you want. Stop doing what takes you away from it.

You Can't Make New Wine in Old Skins

If you want your life and your health to be different from what it is, you need to think, say, and do things differently from what you currently do. You can't make new wine in old skins.

If you try to squish a new paradigm of health and wellness into an old paradigm of disease and symptomatic care, it's not going to work.

If you desire health and wellness, you need to think the things that promote health and wellness. You can't have health and wellness if your focus is on how to avoid symptoms and disease.

If you focus on disease, you'll get more disease—you can't not.

Disease and hormonal imbalances are the result of the way you live, think, and function. They are not an accident. They are lifestyle diseases.

You can't even blame them on your genes. The eminent scientist Dr. Bruce Lipton has now shown and documented in his book *The Biology of Belief* (Mountain of Love/Elite Books, ISBN 09759914–7–7) how your genes are affected by what you think, say, and do. The genes you suppress or express are directly affected by your lifestyle.

If you weren't born with the disease, you've created it by how you've lived.

If you do nothing to change the way you're living, the hormonal imbalance or disease cannot go away. It has no choice but to get worse or come back as soon as you stop taking the treatments that mask its symptoms.

Your imbalances and illnesses are a guide to what needs changing.

Stop trying to get back to where you were! This is where it all started!

It's essential to look forward to how and where you'd like your life and health to be. As long as you keep focus on the past, you can't move forward.

A Balancing Act

Clearly, hormonal imbalance isn't the true problem. The problem is the lack of balance—the lack of balance in your life.

Cold bacteria and viruses cannot thrive in a healthy body.

Cancer cells cannot thrive in a healthy body.

Hormonal imbalance cannot exist in a healthy body.

Darkness is an absence of light.

Poverty is an absence of abundance.

Cold is a lack of heat.

Hormonal imbalance comes from a balance deficiency.

Disease is a lack of health. Disease is a health deficiency, and it comes from disease, which simply means "a lack of ease." *Ease* is effortlessness with no resistance—going with the flow. When you resist and block the natural flow of your life, you create disease. *Dis*ease is your body's way of telling you you have been resisting and not going with the natural flow of your life. It's your body's way of communicating with you to get back on track.

Hormonal Imbalance Is Not From Bad Luck

It's almost tradition for people to cling to old ideas and paradigms even when they're clearly obsolete. Disbelief in new paradigms seems to be a rite of passage before they become mainstream.

For example,

- The cure for scurvy was known hundreds of years before people listened and ate more fruits and vegetables. Thousands of people had miserable lives and died unnecessarily because they didn't believe something as simple as vitamin C could help such a rampant disease.
- The doctor who suggested surgeons wash their hands in-between patients was ridiculed for his suggestion. Thousands of people died because they didn't believe something so simple could make such a difference.

Just because an old lifestyle, habit, or belief system might be familiar or common, it doesn't make it true.

If what you've done so far isn't working the way you want it to, question and change it, even if the good intentions of other people are contrary to what you're discovering.

Do What Works

When you use a computer, you have to follow its rules to get it to do what you want. If you want to copy and paste, you have to follow the correct commands and steps. Nothing else will work. You can yell at the computer, thump your fist on the desk, or even offer it lucrative rewards, but it still won't copy and paste until you do what works. Follow the correct commands and steps and you'll get the results you want predictably.

If you don't know the steps, you need to find out.

It's exactly the same with your health, life, finances, relationships, or anything else. Doing what works works!

If you're not getting the health, etc. you want, you need to find out what works and follow the correct and predictable commands and steps. There are universal laws that govern how your body works. You can yell, thump, and cajole as much as you like, but if you want results that work, you need to do what works.

3

You'll Never Get Healthy by Fighting Disease

The natural state of your mind and body is health. If you weren't born with the disease, then you created it from your lifestyle—with what you've thought, said, and did.

Illness is not from bad luck. It's a natural result of adaptation to your lifestyle.

You Get More of What You Think About

You get more of what you think about. Your central nervous system (CNS) is wired to facilitate this.

The reticular activation formation (RAF)—some people call this the reticular activation system (RAS)—in your brain helps you notice more of what you focus on. If you recently purchased a white car, you'll begin to notice more white cars. If you've lost or gained weight, you'll start to notice others who've lost or gained weight. When you don't put your attention on it anymore, you will begin to notice more of what you have moved your attention to instead.

Use this to your advantage.

Think about health (rather than what you think is wrong) and you'll see more of it.

Where your health is today was determined by the choices you made in the past that brought you to this point. Similarly, the choices you make now will determine where your health goes in the future.

The choices you make are a result of your beliefs.

To be precise, your health is created according to your *beliefs*. Your beliefs determine your *thoughts*, your thoughts determine your *words,* and your words determine your *actions*. For example, your beliefs and thoughts determine what and how much you eat; whether you meditate, exercise, use positive self-talk; etc. In other words, *you create your health and life by what you think, say, and do.*

Have you ever embarked on a self-improvement campaign by changing your actions, only to revert to your old ways when you got tired or distracted? Maybe you successfully gave up smoking or lost weight only to relapse at a later time. Often the setback happens when you're under stress and the subconscious patterns that you truly believe about yourself get airplay again.

When you make changes at an action or behaviour level, the changes will only be successful as long as you keep up your new behaviours. To have longer-lasting change, you can change your words—not only the words you speak out loud but also the words you speak in your head. You can do this simply by monitoring your language and making sure it takes you in the direction you want to go. For example, say, "I am smoke free" or "I am shedding excess fat" instead of "I am giving up smoking" or "I want to lose weight."

The words you use are a direct command to all the cells of your body to give you what you asked for (i.e., to specifically give you what you asked for, not what you thought you asked for).

If you want something, you get to want something. In other words, rather than actually getting it, you get to keep wanting it.

If you want to lose weight, you get to keep wanting to lose weight. In other words, rather than lose it and keep it off, you'll create circumstances where you'll get to want to lose weight again—as you commanded, whether this was your intent or not.

Wanting something projects it into the future.

Be very selective about where you use the word *want.*

Also, be discerning with how you use the words *I am.*

Remember the words you use are direct commands to all the cells in your body. They have no choice but to obey.

If you declare, "I am gorgeous," then you are.

If you say, "I am smart," then you are.

Whatever you state after "I am" is a self-fulfilling prophecy. It's a direct command. You have no choice but to create it in your life.

If you say, "I am hormonal," you have no option but to create it in your life.

If you think, "I'm too fat," you have no choice but to create it.

Words out of your mouth and words in your head determine your actions. If you think you're stupid, your actions will follow and you won't be able to help but make mistakes. If you think you're too fat, you'll have no choice but to put food in your mouth—even when you've had plenty to eat.

Words and thoughts are affirmations. They are your commands. Choose them wisely!

Your beliefs and values set the template for how you think.

When you believe and know "I am smoke free," "I am gorgeous," "I am successful," or whatever else with as much conviction as you believe and know "I am male or I am female," you will have it simply and easily.

Doubt is the saboteur; it undermines you and prevents you from having what you desire. If you doubt you can have it for any reason, you are directly interfering with your manifestation.

I AM was the Hebrews' name for God and is even on the walls of Egyptian temples (Catherine Ponder, *The Dynamic Laws of Healing.* DeVorss Publications: 1966).

If you habitually state, "I am too young," "I am too old," "I am skinny," "I am fat," or whatever else, you will create it. It is a direct order to the god within you to create this for you.

Your words are constantly building you up or breaking you down, healing you or harming you.

Ensure your language is filled with positive *I am* statements, such as

- I am healthy.
- I am beautiful/handsome.
- I am prosperous.

- I am abundant.
- I am peaceful.
- I am loving.
- I am caring.
- I am strong.
- I am worthy.
- I am fertile.
- I am happy.
- I am successful.
- I am grateful.

Until you train your mind to be peaceful and still, it will chatter away for a large part of your waking hours. If it's going to chatter, then give it something positive to chatter about. Instruct it to say affirmations of your conscious choice. Make absolutely certain your beliefs, thoughts, and actions are working for you and not against you. Deliberately choose what you think, say, and do.

Your Brain Doesn't Recognize *Don't*

Your brain doesn't recognize *don't*. No matter what I say, don't think of a giraffe with brown spots on it. No matter what I say, don't think of a red Ferrari.

What happens?

It's automatic, isn't it? Your brain goes ahead and creates the picture all by itself. Your words—whether you think, say, read, or hear them—are a direct command to create. The more direct the order, the more diligent the response.

Trickily, if you say you don't want to lose your temper, your brain doesn't recognize *don't* and sees it as a royal command to get you to lose your temper.

If say you don't want to spill your drink, it's as good as an instruction to tip the contents.

Change your words to support you.

Think and say precisely what you desire rather than what you don't want.

For example,

- instead of "Don't be a pig and eat all the chocolate," tell yourself something like "I love eating carrots for snacks."
- instead of "Don't forget to buy a gift," find a thought that can be more positively expressed such as "Remember to buy a gift."

Change your wording to suit yourself, such as

- I eat celery for snacks.
- I eat apples in-between meals.
- I only eat at meal times.
- I drink plenty of fresh water daily.
- I have fun exercising every day.

Instead of "Don't lose your temper," try something like

- "I am calm and serene."
- "I am relaxed and at ease."
- "My life is peaceful, and my relationships reflect this."

Create affirmations that suit you. Make them your own. Take your power back, and be your own authority.

You're the adult now.

If you don't like your thoughts, change them to what you wish.

You are in charge of creating your life, so make it according to your ideal self and the life you choose rather than settling for crumbs.

4

What Does Your Body Need That It Lacks?

It's essential to restore your health. Everything you have and do depends on it. It affects you and everyone around you. However, you can't restore health by fighting disease. It never has worked and never will.

Health can only be restored by
- **providing your body with something it needs and is lacking, and/or**
- **removing what is toxic that it's getting.**

What does your body need that it's either not getting or not getting enough of? For example, adequate nutrition (including physiologically compatible vitamins, minerals, enzymes, proteins, carbohydrates, and fats); relaxation; pure fresh air; pure fresh water; physiologically compatible protection (including natural clothing, housing, transport); a state of being as opposed to doing; self-love; love for others; weight-bearing exercise; meditation; time; gratitude; touch; alignment; stretching; thorough chewing on both sides of your mouth; etc.

How, when, and where are you going to give your body what it needs? Make a list so you can refer to it easily.

Alignment

Alignment and function are directly related to each other.

If a heel isn't aligned on a shoe, you can't walk properly.

If a lens isn't aligned on glasses, you can't see properly.

If a skyscraper isn't aligned, everything including the plumbing, doors, electrics, and air conditioning can't work properly.

Likewise, if your body isn't aligned, it can't work properly either. Its mechanics and neurology are organized in a practical way.

The degree and longevity of misalignments often match the corresponding dysfunction; however, even a minor misalignment in a crucial place can have far-reaching and dire consequences for your health and well-being.

You may already know the nerve system controls and coordinates the function of every tissue, organ, and system in the body. There is a crucial relationship between the structure (especially the spine and cranium) and the function (primarily coordinated by the nerve system) and restoration and maintenance of health.

Your cranium and pelvis must be aligned so they can work together to pump CSF (cerebro-spinal fluid) around your brain and spinal cord. Namely, your sacrum (the triangular bone at the back of your pelvis) and your occiput (the bowl-shaped bone forming the base of your skull) have to work rhythmically together so the CSF can adequately nourish, cushion, and conduct nerve energy. If you lose your alignment, you will have symptoms wherever your body has to compensate for it.

The integrity of your nerve system begins with this CSF pump, the stability of your pelvis (which is constantly subject to the pull of gravity), the bones of your skull, and the tension in your spinal cord.

Think of your spinal cord like a harp string. Is it flexible and healthy or stretched and tight?

Anything you do to improve your alignment, posture, and spinal flexibility (chiropractic adjustments, yoga, stretching, appropriate exercise, etc.) will assist your nerve system and overall health.

Karen's Story

Whenever Karen sat at her desk for extended periods, she would repeatedly get uncomfortable in her lower back, neck, and shoulders. When she sat ergonomically correct, it helped but didn't prevent the tension from creeping in. The nerves from these parts of her spine controlled her ovaries, uterus, and thyroid glands.

The constant sitting and resultant tension were not only compressing her organs but directly interfering with the messages to and from her brain via her nerve system.

Sitting is an unnatural position for humans. Indigenous people who are aligned with nature stand, lie down, or squat; they don't sit.

Adequate Nutrition

There's a plethora of information about diet and nutrition available. It can seem a bit of a minefield to find your way through when the information provided is in direct conflict. For example, should you eat eggs or not eat eggs? The pro-egg eaters will tell you they're a fantastic, cheap, and easy protein pill. The anti-egg eaters will say they're high in cholesterol and risky suppliers of salmonella.

Who is right? *You are.*

Your body will tell you what is right for you. If it likes eggs, it will let you eat them, even make you crave them. If it doesn't like eggs, it will make you nauseous at the smell, or even allergic.

The ideal nutrition for you is unique to you.

You look, sound, think, and feel different from everyone else on the planet. Why would you think you need the same foods in the same amounts as anyone else? You don't. *You need what's right for you* and this is likely to vary on any given day because you think, say, and do different things on different days and need different nutrients accordingly. So be flexible in your approach. In other words, your body requires different nutrients when you're active compared to relaxing, thinking, intuiting, growing, or resting, and so on.

Explore what this means for you. If you don't know what's right for you, it's time to find out. Make it fun playing self-detective, rather than turn it into a chore. Enjoy the process of discovering what promotes your health and what demotes it.

Your health affects everything you do and everyone you know.

When you do physical activity, you need high-quality carbohydrates

Be aware that excess carbohydrates, whether high quality or not, cause inflammation and all the modern diseases associated with it (e.g., diabetes, cancer, Alzheimer's, and atherosclerosis).

These include the following:
- fruit
- vegetables
- lentils
- gluten-free whole grains, such as brown rice, corn, quinoa *(keen-wah)*, buckwheat, millet, amaranth, teff, and sorghum

Eliminate all the poor-quality carbohydrates from your diet.

What are these?

Processed breakfast cereals, fruit juices (unless it's freshly juiced), white flour, sweeties, manufactured cakes, and cookies. If you really love desserts, cakes, and cookies make them yourself with real ingredients. In other words, no trans-fats, preservatives, flavour enhancers, colours, or ultra heat-treated, irradiated, or modified components.

As a rule of thumb, if your great grandmother couldn't get it, don't eat it.

Skip eating anything that didn't use to be alive.

Have you ever seen a fizzy drink tree? A Cheerio tree? Or a doughnut animal?

If it was never alive, it's not going to pass any quality life force onto you—because it hasn't got it to give.

Cate's Story

Cate was a vegetarian. She'd been told it was a good idea to avoid eating red meat and began to eat more and more carbohydrates instead. She became more and more confused, lazy, and gained weight. She found she wasn't motivated and focused like she used to be and was diagnosed with polycystic ovary syndrome (PCOS).

To turn it around, she learned to combine her foods to make whole proteins from her plant-based diet and made herself huff, puff, and sweat for a minimum half hour each day.

When you're growing, you need high-quality protein

In other words, when you're physically growing (baby, child, teenager, or pregnancy), mentally growing (self-development or studying), or spiritually growing (meditation or energy healing), you need high-quality protein, such as the following:

- free-range meat (preferably wild game compared to fat and lazy farmed animals)
- eggs
- seeds
- nuts
- legumes

You need protein for bone and muscle growth, plus it's the building blocks for the lines of energy in your aura. In other words, the master diamond blueprints for your body.

Buy the best quality you can afford. It will save you in the long term.

An extra few dollars spent now might save you thousands in so-called disease treatments later.

This is where it can get a bit tricky, but it's important so follow along.

Just because you're eating well (Aren't you? If not, why not? What are you going to do about it? When?), doesn't mean you're getting good nutrition.

If you're not digesting your foods well enough, your body can't get the ingredients it needs.

For example, if you're stressed and making excess HCl (hydrochloric acid) in your stomach, you can burn out your cells and then they don't/can't/won't make enough when you actually need it—when you eat your excellent-quality protein.

Therefore, don't eat when you're stressed. Relax.

Don't eat when you're moving around. Sit, kneel, or stand. Honour the process of eating.

Whenever you eat, ask if what you're doing is an act of self-love.

If you eat foods your body is sensitive to, your bowel will make mucous to prevent these toxins entering your bloodstream.

This is a natural and healthy response by your body to the conditions you have provided it with. However, the mucous also blocks the absorption of the ingredients you do want passing into your bloodstream—setting up the need for more and more vitamin and mineral supplementation to counteract it.

○ Gluten and dairy products are popular starters for this award. In other words, gluten and dairy are two of the most common food groups people are sensitive to and hence trigger defensive mucous production

- Corn is the traditional grain that opens up people's intuition. (The "spiritual people" of the planet typically eat a lot of corn—the American Indians, Mexicans, South Americans, etc).
- Wheat is the traditional grain that closes down your spiritual connection and anchors you into your body. No wonder so many sensitive people are sensitive to gluten—they don't want their intuition shut down.
- Humans are the only creatures on the planet that consume the milk of another species. It's not compatible with our bodies.
Cow's milk is made for baby cows, not for baby people.

Humans are the only species on the planet that continue consuming milk past weaning.

"What about calcium?" you ask.

Grown cows don't drink milk. In other words, they don't get their calcium from milk to put it in the milk people drink. They get the calcium from the grass they eat.

All they eat is grass.

You can get your calcium from a variety of sources, such as salmon, sardines, peas, broccoli, Brussels sprouts, rhubarb, beans, bok choy, and almonds.

As a rule of thumb: don't eat foods that make excess mucous in your body.

How do you know?

If you need to wipe your nose when you're not sad, you've eaten something that has caused your body to make mucous.

Pay attention.

If the mucous is in your nose, it's more than likely in your bowel as well, preventing you from absorbing the good ingredients as well as blocking the irritant or toxic ingredients.

Be your own detective. What did you eat that caused the mucous? The big two are wheat and dairy, so start your investigation here, but don't limit your awareness to these groups.

It's not a punishment to avoid eating what your body reacts to. Rather than focus on what you can't eat, open your eyes to all the wonderful foods you can eat, that promote you rather than demote you. *Plus* remember to resolve the stress that has triggered you to be sensitive to these foods in the first place.

There's no need to feel deprived. If you love bread, find a baker who makes great gluten-free bread.

If you love smoothies, make them with soy, almond, or rice milk—as long as they're non-reactive substitutes for you.

Don't be derailed by what other people can eat or not. Focus on you. What promotes you?

As a rule of thumb, these are foods to eat more of:

- cruciferous vegetables (broccoli, cauliflower, cabbage, kale, bok choy, Brussels sprouts). These contain sulphuraphane and calcium d-glucorate, which remove excess oestrogens from your body.

  Unfortunately, these are also vegetables that readily absorb insecticides, so buy organic or grow your own wherever possible, and rinse them well if they're not.
- fish and eggs. These provide you with
  - essential fatty acids. You need to ingest fatty acids because your body can't manufacture them; hence, they're called "essential."
  - protein which helps your hormones, moods, skin, and hair.
- soy products. Soy is pro-estrogenic for your brain and bones and anti-estrogenic for your breasts and uterus, due to its effect on the beta receptors. This is a clever food match for your body, especially the fermented forms of soy (tempeh, natto, miso, pickled tofu).
- sprouts. Sprouted seeds provide protein, enzymes, antioxidants, and phytoestrogens (oestrogen from plants).
- seaweed. This is high in calcium, iodine, and iron.
- flaxseed: This helps sex-hormone-binding globulin and therefore helps conditions that express high androgen (male hormones) levels and polycystic ovaries.
- cold pressed extra virgin olive oil for essential fatty acids.
- whole grains, such as brown rice for fibre.
- fresh fruit and vegetables for fibre, minerals, antioxidants, and a natural sweet fix.
- clean water. Drink plenty of it.

Eat the Good Fats

Fats are present in every cell in your body and are essential for hormone production and enzyme reactions. You need fats to make new cells, hormones, line your lungs, store vitamins A, D, E, and K, support your immune system, and for optimal brain function.

Your body has to make the best of whatever fats you feed it, so it makes sense to give it the good oil. In other words, saturated fats, such as coconut oil, vegetable oil, and yes, even animal fats, are better than dangerous trans-fats.

A low-fat diet can be a stress on your body when you don't provide it with the raw materials it needs to function at its optimum.

Eat High-Antioxidant Foods

Antioxidants can help counteract free radical damage that results from excess stress.

Antioxidant-rich foods are fruits and vegetables.

If you're under chronic stress, you'll need even more antioxidants and vitamin C than usual; hence, the recommended daily allowance is often inadequate.

Physiologically Compatible Nutrients

Not all supplements are created equal.

If you need to supplement your vitamin, mineral, enzyme, protein, carbohydrate, or fat intake (because it's not in your food in the quantity or quality you need, your body has lost its ability to absorb or assimilate it adequately, or you need extra to balance out a long-standing condition), buy the best quality you can afford. Price is often a good indicator of quality.

Talk to your health-care professional about which ones, how much, how often, when and with/without what. For example, which supplements are best taken with food or away from food, with or away from heat, at night or in the morning?

Mastication

Mastication is another name for chewing. It's the process of making the food on your plate small enough to fit down your oesophagus and increase its surface area enough so your digestive enzymes can break it down efficiently.

If you don't use your teeth to crush and grind your food well enough, it puts an added strain on your digestion. In the short term, you can adapt to this. In the long term, it creates enzyme deficiency, indigestion, and malnutrition.

Digestion begins in the mouth. The food is made softer and warmer here and the enzyme amylase begins to catabolise carbohydrates in the mouth.

Mastication is so important for helping the body to extract nutrients that some animals such as cattle chew their food more than once to maximize the benefits.

If you're a persistent gulper of food, it may be that your cranial bones (in particular your mandible or jaw bone) and neck vertebrae are out of alignment with each other. These misalignments will also exaggerate the impact of dental misalignments and drive orthodontists, who only look at the mouth and not the whole body, crazy.

Chew your food and change your life.

Pure Fresh Water

If you see a wilting plant, what's the first thing you think it needs? Water.

Did you immediately think it needed a drug, surgery, adjustment, herb, vitamin, or supplement? No, because it's natural to think of water first.

The longer you leave the plant without water, the sicker it gets and then it dies.

It's the same for people.

When you see a wilting person, the first thing they're likely to need is more water. The longer you leave the person without water, the sicker they'll get and then die.

Without water, plants die. Without water, people die too. Suicide by dehydration.

Why don't you immediately drink water whenever you feel sick?

Humans have a back-up system. We can get some water from the food we eat. Most plants don't have this.

Many people who don't drink enough water overeat because their body is trying to get water anyway it can.

In the long term, this adds more body weight and therefore increases the requirements for even more water. Not drinking enough water creates a long and drawn-out death.

It doesn't matter how positively you think, how much medication you take, what surgery you endure, or how many acupuncture sessions or massages you have, if you don't drink enough water, you get sick and die. If you drink some water but not enough, you simply get sick and die slower, but the result is the same.

The amount of water in the human body varies from 50–75 per cent, averaging around 60 per cent. Obesity decreases this to sometimes as low as 45 per cent, which begs the following questions:

- Is not drinking enough water a major component of obesity?
- Do obese people have to eat an excess of food to top up the water quantity they're not drinking?

Water is often referred to as the universal solvent because substances, such as salts, sugars, acids, alkalis, and some gases (including oxygen and carbon dioxide) dissolve in it. What may be lesser known is emotions can also dissolve in it too. In other words, water can take on the resonance of the energy or thoughts directed at it. It is claimed that prayer and positive visualization can restore polluted water. If the water content of the body is around 60 per cent, doesn't it make sense to have it store positive thoughts and beliefs rather than negative?

How much water is enough?

As you know, if you don't drink enough water, you dehydrate and you die.

If you have too much water, you drown and die also.

Too much or too little is not good. You need the right amount for you.

As a rule of thumb, human adults need 33 ml of water per kilo of body weight every day. Without this quantity, you'll wilt.

Naturally, if you're in a hot climate, exercising intensely, or breastfeeding, you'll need even more.

You need enough water when you eat food to make it moist and easy to digest. If you have too much water, when you eat, it dilutes the HCl (hydrochloric acid) in your stomach, making digestion hard and slow.

Fresh Air

Most people know they need to breathe fresh air to stay alive. This is not news. The average person only lasts about three minutes without air.

We need to breathe about ten thousand litres of air every day to survive. How well we survive is dependent on the quantity and quality of the air we breathe as well as how well our bodies uses the air we supply it with.

Not all air is the same.

The contrast between the air in an open natural environment and the air in a city street, stuffy, polluted building, or vehicle isn't just academic. We physically experience the difference.

Ancient texts recommend people wanting to hone their body and mind through yogic breathing exercises should practise near a waterfall, in a cave, or better still in a cave under a waterfall. The ancient masters may not have had access to modern research into negative ions, but they were familiar with their benefits.

Invigorating places (such as waterfalls, caves, forests, mountains over five thousand feet above sea level, and the ocean, especially where waves break on the rocks) feel that way because of the abundance of small negative oxygen ions in the air.

Nature has a plentiful supply of both negative and positive ions.

It's the negative ions that make us feel good.

Have you ever noticed how you feel before and after a storm? The air prior to a storm has high levels of positive ions and can feel oppressive and trigger tempers to unravel. The air after a storm has high levels of negative ions and makes you feel recharged again.

Positive ions cause
- lethargy
- low mood
- reduced immunity
- increased blood acidity
- weakened bones
- suppressed urination (and decreased the amount of nitrogen excreted)
- increased heart rate
- high blood pressure
- constricted blood vessels
- prolonged physical recovery time

Negative ions cause
- improved mood
- improved immunity
- decreased blood acidity
- strengthened bones
- more urination(and increased amount of nitrogen excreted)
- decreased heart rate
- lower blood pressure
- dilated blood vessels
- speeded physical recovery

Negative ions can be increased by
- a negative ionizer. Negative ions are electrically attracted to airborne particles (such as the top ten toxins listed below) and drop them onto the nearest surface, cleaning the air of toxins and bacteria.
- salt lamps.
- plants. (They take in carbon dioxide and give off oxygen.)
- sealing off the earth with concrete, etc. In nature, everything is balanced. When the earth is bombarded with positive ions, it responds by producing negative ions. It does this by breaking down naturally occurring radium in the earth's crust, which is

converted to radon gas. This natural radiation causes oxygen ions to form.

When we cover the earth's crust with concrete, highways, and buildings, we cut off our most important natural source of negative ions.

Natural Clothing

Synthetic fabrics demote rather than promote your energy and vitality. The chemicals used in synthetic clothing manufacture have been linked to hormone disruption, cancer, immune system damage, and behavioural problems.

In the early days of Kirlian photography (photographing the electromagnetic energy field or aura around the body), you couldn't see the energy if the person was wearing synthetic clothing.

Exercise

Exercise is like breathing. It's best done regularly.

Even if you do gentle exercise like walking or tai chi, you need to do something aerobic as well. In other words, something that gets you puffing and sweating.

Merely half an hour a day of energetic exercise is ample for most people. If you're not puffing and sweating, it's not energetic enough. Then you'll need to do more to get what your body needs out of it.

If you miss a day, do more the next day.

This half hour per day is as well as, not instead of, your daily essentials like walking to the bus or work.

Use it or lose it.

If you keep doing the same thing over and over, you'll keep getting the same results. If your current level of exercise isn't giving you the results you want, you need to change it. Just because something has been good for you in the past doesn't mean it'll be good for you forever. For example, if your stress levels go up, your exercise levels need to go up to disperse it.

Work with what you've got now, and who you are in the present, rather than hanging onto past ideals.

Make it a pleasure, not a punishment. Go dancing, swimming, mountain bike riding, making passionate love, or doing whatever else. Do what you like, for at least half an hour each day.

If it's something you dread, it'll add to your stress hormone production rather than your feel-good hormone production. Do what promotes you, not demotes you.

If you've not enjoyed exercise in the past, search out a variety of options and keep experimenting until you find what you have an affinity with.

The rewards of exercise outweigh the effort, such as the following:

- "Increased physical activity has been associated with decreased incidence of breast cancer in menopausal women. 1.25 to 2.5 hours per week of brisk walking gave an 18 per cent decreased risk."

(Rice VM. "Effect of Moderate Exercise in Alleviating Menopausal Symptoms." *Menopause.* July-August, 2004: 11(4) 372–4.)

- Exercise releases endorphins from your pituitary gland and hypothalamus. (They're also released during excitement, pain, eating spicy food, sex, and orgasm). They block pain and make you feel exhilarated. They give you the "runner's high" with strenuous exercise.

- Serotonin levels increase when you exercise regularly. Serotonin (or 5 Hydroxytryptamine/5HTP) is a neurotransmitter responsible for happiness, clear thinking, restful sleep, and healthy appetite. It works with endorphins to make exercising a pleasurable activity; hence, the more you do the better you'll like it.

  Serotonin also helps hot flushes. You might get more hot flushes while you're exercising, but it'll decrease the amounts in-between.

  Serotonin is made from tryptophan, which is high in chicken, egg whites, fish (especially salmon and cod), nuts (especially cashews and pistachios), parmesan cheese, spirulina, soybeans, pumpkin seeds, sesame seeds, and sunflower seeds.

90 per cent of Serotonin is made in your gut. This is another excellent reason not to eat mucous-producing foods you're sensitive to. In other words, you don't want your serotonin levels inhibited by mucous caused from food sensitivities.

- Stimulates the production of dopamine, another pleasure chemical. Regular exercise keeps dopamine levels up and weight gain at bay. If you have fewer brain receptors for dopamine, this will result in weight gain and a need for more food to get the same level of satisfaction as people with normal levels of dopamine. Plus dopamine is required for orgasm.

- Exercise can result in coregasm. Many women need a build-up of tension in their legs before they can orgasm. Exercise releases both endorphins and dopamine. Combine this with tension in the legs and a coregasm is born. It happens when women repetitiously connect into their deep core muscles (from pelvic floor exercises, crunches, leg lifts, and backbends). One squeeze isn't likely to get you there. Perhaps I should have mentioned this first so you you'd be a whole lot happier about the exercise thing?

- Exercise increases 5AMP (adenosine monophosphate) levels which take carbohydrates into your cells just like insulin does, without making you insulin resistant. This helps prevent diabetes, polycystic ovaries, and obesity.

- When you exercise before breakfast, you'll burn fat because you don't have any carbohydrates from recent food immediately available. If you eat carbohydrates and then exercise, you'll simply burn the carbohydrates you've just eaten.

- Oestrogen determines whether you burn carbohydrates or fat to fuel your body during intense exercise. The higher your oestrogen levels, the more fat you'll burn; hence, women tend to burn more fat for fuel while men burn more carbohydrates.

This is why women need to exercise more during and after menopause—the drop in oestrogen leads to less fat being burned.

Yoga

Millions of people resort to pills, lotions, potions, and operations to alleviate the symptoms of hormonal imbalances which affect how you look, sleep, feel, and behave, so how can something as simple as getting into a yoga posture be a viable alternative?

Yoga's focus on breathing, meditation, alignment, postures or asanas, and union with your spirit has a beneficial effect on all these aspects. Yoga as a therapy is successful because of the balance it induces in the nervous and endocrine systems which directly influence every organ and system in the body.

The rishis (Indian sages who cultivated insight) understood the effects of a particular posture on hormone secretions. For example, by being in a posture that imitates a rabbit or hare, you can influence the flow of adrenaline responsible for the fight or flight response.

The body and mind are not separate entities. Every muscle or body knot has a corresponding mental knot and vice versa. One of the aims of yoga is to release these knots. It's still up to you to stop creating more.

Yoga postures or asanas are not so much exercise as techniques which align your body in such a way to induce relaxation, awareness, concentration, meditation, and optimum function.

Yoga

- compresses and decompresses the endocrine glands (hormone producing glands) which can help regulate their hormonal secretions.
- aligns the body. The ability of your brain and nerve system to control and coordinate all the functions, systems, organs, and muscles in your body specifically depends upon the alignment of your frame or skeleton.
- When your body is out of alignment, it interferes with the clear and accurate transmission of nerve impulses to and from the brain, causing the organs, muscles, and systems that are controlled by those nerves to compensate by over or under functioning. This is a major cause of disease in general (over

or under functioning due to interference to the nerve system), not only hormone imbalances.

- You may already know this is why chiropractic works so well. In other words, by realigning the spine, cranium, and extremities and removing interference to the nerve system, the messages to and from the brain to all the muscles, organs, and systems can return to homeostasis and their optimum function.

- aligns your energy. When your posture is in correct alignment, the energy can flow uninhibited. Just like when a water hose is unkinked, water can flow more easily than when the hose is kinked. This is also why it's immensely easier to meditate when you sit with your spine straight. The straighter your spine, the easier it is for your energy to flow uninhibited. Correct posture and alignment from birth is essential for health and well-being.

- As the twig is bent, so grows the tree.

- improves moods and eases anxiety. Depression and anxiety are linked to low GABA (gamma-aminobutyric acid) levels. Research at the Boston University School of Medicine shows yoga to be a better reliever and mood lifter than other exercises, including walking.

- reduces hot flushes. Studies show regular yoga practice can reduce hot flushes by up to 30 per cent.

- turbo-charges your libido. Yoga strengthens the pelvic floor. The stronger your pelvic floor, the stronger your orgasms. Plus yoga streamlines the body and improves self-image and self-confidence, which are directly connected to sexual confidence.

- helps your memory. Improved blood flow, mental alertness, and focused breathing help clear brain fog and losing track of your thought.

- disperses stress or distress. Stress can be good because it signals you that something needs attention; however, when it becomes distress, it can be pathological. We often cause our own stress through toxic emotions, thoughts, and beliefs.

- Yoga helps calm your mind so you can free it from your negative instructions.

- Your mind is under your command. It just regurgitates whatever you tell it or allow it to.
- releases tension and anxiety. Stress, tension, and anxiety activate your sympathetic nerve system so you can either fight or take flight. When your sympathetic nerve system is revved up by "fear of lions at the waterhole," everything gets tense and super alert. Yoga promotes inner peace and calmness, helping restore relaxation and balance.
- relieves insomnia. Insomnia can result from a variety of factors, such as anxiety, stress, and plunging progesterone levels due to adrenal exhaustion. Inverted yoga positions, such as downward dog, headstands, and shoulder stands, help resolve this and restore peaceful sleep.
- eases wrinkles on your face. Growth hormone from the pituitary gland causes deepened face wrinkles. Yoga helps regulate pituitary function and can compensate for this.
- reduces thyroid symptoms. The thyroid gland controls your basal metabolic rate (BMR), growth, and temperature. Imbalances here can cause depression, weight gain, cold hands and feet, and difficulty walking in the morning. Shoulder stands and asanas that compress the throat (such as plough) help the thyroid.

Which Postures Are Best?

- adrenal exhaustion: sun salute, cat pose, cobra, camel, extended triangle, bow, locust, forward bend, wheel, standing forward bend, spinal twist, and plough
- anger: hare, psychic union pose, seated forward bend
- anxiety: Pawanmuktasana series 1 (a series of postures which are anti-rheumatic and also release gas, abdominal fat, improve digestion and abdominal tone), sun salute, hare, psychic union pose, intoxicating bliss pose, forward bend, cobra, locust, shoulder stand, plough, corpse

- candida: sun salute, Pawanmuktasana series 2 and 3 (a series of postures which help the digestion and abdomen), thunderbolt or Vajrāsana series
- depression: sun salute; all back-bending, standing, and twisting postures
- fatigue: Pawanmuktasana series 1, mountain, cobra, camel, wheel, bow, sun salute
- impotence: Pawanmuktasana series 2 and 3, sun salute, shoulder stand, plough
- insomnia: Pawanmuktasana series 1, hare, all inverted poses
- menopause: Pawanmuktasana series 2 and 3, sun salute, cobra, bow, shoulder stand, plough, fish, forward bend, and all balancing postures
- menstruation: sun salute, Pawanmuktasana series 2 and 3, cobra, locust, bow, forward bend, bridge, wheel, camel, all inverted postures, except when actually menstruating
- menstrual cramps: thunderbolt, hare, cat, corpse
- miscarriage recovery: Pawanmuktasana series 2 and 3, sun salute
- pituitary and pineal: sun salute, all inverted poses
- thyroid and parathyroid: sun salute, fish, all inverted poses (especially shoulder stand and plough), and all back-bending poses (especially Grivasana or neck pose)

Inverted Postures

- reverse the effect of gravity upon the body.
- can help you shed new light on old patterns, reduce anxiety and stress, improve your confidence and concentration, and help you sleep.
- increase blood supply to the pituitary and hence aid the whole endocrine system.
- transform sexual energy into spiritual energy. They stimulate the chakras, or energy centres, to open in such a way as to enhance psychic awakening.

Nadine's Story

Nadine was good at sports. She had exercised all her life, but try as she may, she didn't like yoga. She found it boring, non-stimulating, and non-beneficial to her metabolism. Even though "everyone" said it would be good for her, she just didn't feel the benefit that was promised her.

She decided to give it one more chance and went to a class where the teacher was particular about breathing, insisting they breathe deeply and in time with the asanas and movements.

The world changed in an instant.

Nadine's heart rate, sense of achievement, and strength went up, and so did the corners of her mouth. By exaggerating her breath, it changed her whole experience, enjoyment, and results. She went on to become a yoga teacher.

Meditation

The word *meditation* is derived from the Latin word *meditation*, which means "to think, contemplate, devise, or ponder."

Meditation is wide and varied like food. Different types appeal to different people and have different effects like proteins, fats, and carbohydrates do.

Meditation techniques can be used for
- relaxation
- concentration, focus, and intelligence
- lower blood pressure
- easing anxiety, anger, hatred, and emotional imbalances
- ease depression
- improving immunity
- improving self-discipline (which is also linked to higher IQ scores)
- promoting forgiveness and releasing old emotional wounds
- increasing attributes like love, compassion, and patience
- developing a spiritual connection and humility

- mind and thought wrangling
- transformation

Types of Meditation

- breathing or pranayama
- progressive muscle relaxation: tensing muscle groups and then relaxing them in a progressive sequence. This technique is especially good for people with extreme anxiety.
- mindfulness: staying present rather than focusing on the past or future to allow moment-to-moment, non-judgmental awareness
- guided: often a narrative taking the meditator on a journey
- active: such as walking
- mantra: reciting a sound, syllable, word, or phrase repeatedly
- chanting: in Buddhism, chanting is the traditional means of preparing the mind for meditation
- prayer and prayer beads. Prayer beads are commonly used in devotional meditation. Different religions have different numbers of beads, but the principle is the same. Often it's a set of ten followed by another bead up to either ninety-nine or 108 beads. Each bead is counted once as the devotee recites a mantra until they have gone the whole way around the beads.
- transcendental: rising above the body and mind travelling

Common Elements of Meditation Techniques

- slower and deeper breathing than normal
- alignment of the spine. The more aligned the spine is, the better the nerve system function and energy flow through the meridian systems and master diamond blueprints or sacred geometry of the aura.
- eyes closed
- body relaxed. Comfort is important. It's easier to relax when your body is comfortable.
- peaceful mind and letting go of expectations
- surrender to a higher power

Sex

It's not just an apple a day that can help keep the doctors away.

A low sex drive is an intelligent response by your body to stress. It's essential to resolve the stress that has caused the low libido or else something else has to compensate to get your attention to make changes.

If you don't listen to the whispers, you get the screams.

The benefits of regular, healthy, and pleasurable sex are well documented; however, it's not a panacea for everything. Sexuality without caring feelings or emotion has limited value.

The extra edge that sex gives may be due to feeling wanted and the hormonal and physiological changes that occur as we express love for another.

A fulfilling sex life with your partner not only gets you physically in shape with better skin, hair, and nails, it burns extra calories, relieves asthma, headaches, depression, and mood swings.

From hairdressers to sexologists and fitness experts, there's a general consensus that a happy and plentiful sex life supports a healthy physical and emotional life.

Dr. Sanjay Chugh, a specialist on sexual issues, states, "Sex contributes to good health. Any sexual intimacy that is enjoyable and pleasurable promotes well-being by providing several physical and psychological benefits. It is believed sex boosts chemicals in the body that protects us against diseases. Research also suggests that sex and masturbation can help ease joint and muscle pain, combat depression, promote heart health, and lengthen one's life span."

A healthy thirst is an indicator of health. When you lose or ignore your sense of thirst or it gets excessive, it's indicative of lack of health.

A healthy appetite is an indicator of health. When you lose your appetite or it gets excessive, it's indicative of lack of health.

A healthy libido is an indicator of health. When you lose your libido or it gets excessive, it's an indicator of a lack of health.

Yes, all of these fluctuate from day to day, but overall, too much or too little of anything is a symptom of disease and will result in disease if the cause is not remedied.

Christine's Story

Christine had lost her libido. Between work, kids, and the kitchen, it had disappeared. Some suggested this was natural, and given the superwoman conditions, it possibly was.

She mentioned it to her chiropractor, who adjusted the base of her spine and pelvis. Bingo! her desire and ability to let go control and enjoy her body returned.

Needless to say, she also had to learn to allocate her time, thoughts, and energy more wisely to prevent relapses.

Self-Love

Some authorities suggest that into order to truly love another person, you need to love yourself first.

Some take this premise even farther and say it's a direct match. In other words, how much you love yourself is the same as how much you can love someone else and how much you'll allow others to love you.

What if how much you love yourself is also a direct match for how healthy you are?

It's well documented that people who worry a lot get stomach ulcers, people who are resentful get gall bladder problems, and people with low self-esteem get pancreas problems, and so on.

Worrying is not an act of self-love.

Resentment is not an act of self-love.

And neither is low self-esteem an act of self-love.

Are you prepared to love yourself enough so you no longer worry? Most of what people worry about doesn't happen or is about someone else and not even their responsibility.

Are you prepared to love yourself enough so you're no longer resentful? Resentment is re-send-ment. In other words, thinking the same thoughts over and over. Are you prepared to stop thinking those revolving thoughts? Are you prepared to let it go? Your health depends on it.

Are you prepared to love yourself enough to raise your self-esteem? Are you ready to start seeing the good in yourself? It's just as easy to notice what's good about you as it is to focus on what you judge harshly.

Your health depends on it.

Loving yourself isn't arrogant, conceited, or egocentric. It includes

- caring about your own welfare. Not just eating nutritious food and brushing your teeth but thinking nice thoughts about yourself, encouraging and lifting yourself up, etc.
- taking responsibility for yourself, including your thoughts, words, and actions. What you believe determines what you think. What you think determines what you say. And these also determine what you do and the actions you take.
- Thoughts are things.
- Take responsibility for your thoughts and consider which of your beliefs are serving you well and which ones are undermining you and your life.
- Are you prepared to change your mind and beliefs in order to restore your health?
- respecting yourself. Hold yourself in high regard and set clear boundaries as to what's OK for you and what isn't.
- If there aren't any boundaries, anyone can rule the land.
- know yourself. Be realistic and honest with yourself about your strengths and weaknesses.

Love for Others

In a tennis club, the common denominator of the members is they like tennis. In a Ukrainian club, the common threads pertain to the Ukraine. In an alumnus, everyone has come from the same school.

It's the things about us that are the same that draw us together. The more we have in common, the more it brings us together.

It's the things about us that are different (race, gender, social standing, religion or beliefs, etc.) that can pull us apart—if we allow them.

The more we hold others in positive regard (the more we love them), the more it brings us all together.

It's just as easy to notice the things you like in others as the things you don't like. Put your attention on what's good and right about them. It builds rapport, creates community, and brings peace.

When you have peace (absence of worry, resentment, and poor self-esteem), you can also have good health.

Gratitude

It's not happiness that makes us grateful; it's gratitude that makes us happy.

Gratitude is the feeling, emotion, or attitude of appreciation for what you have.

It's all too common to focus on what you think you don't have compared to focusing on what you do and appreciating it. You get more of what you think about, so focusing on what you think you don't have can only give you more of it.

Likewise, focusing on what you do have gives you more of it, and hence more to be grateful for.

The direction this spiral goes is totally your choice and under your direct control.

Measurement of Gratitude

Yes, there are three scales to measure gratitude. Apparently, someone thinks this is important. Most of us just look at the person's face and evaluate which way the corners of their mouth are pointing.

1. GQ6 assesses rates: how often and how intensely people feel gratitude.
2. The Appreciation Scale measures eight aspects of gratitude: the appreciation of people, possessions, rituals, the present moment, feelings of awe, social comparisons, existential concerns, and behaviours which express gratitude.
3. The GRAT assesses gratitude towards others, the world, and lack of resentment for what you don't have.

Each of these scales measures the way people approach life, their attitude.

An Attitude of Gratitude Enhances

- mental health. Gratitude is one of the strongest indicators of mental health of all the character traits. In other words, the more grateful a person is, the higher the levels of happiness and the lower levels of stress and anxiety.
- gratitude is also associated with altruism and economic generosity.
- health and well-being. Studies show grateful people
   - are happier
   - are less stressed
   - sleep better
   - are more satisfied with their lives and relationships
   - have more self-acceptance
   - have lower levels of stress and depression
   - are less likely to avoid problems, deny there's a problem, blame themselves, or try to cope through substance abuse

Exercises to Increase Gratitude

- Recall and give thanks for three things you're grateful for every night before you go to sleep. It's even better to write them down in a gratitude journal.
- Say thank-you at every appropriate opportunity.
- Think about a person you're grateful for.
- Write about someone you're grateful for.
- Write to someone you're grateful for.

Being

We are human beings, not human doings.

If we constantly look outside ourselves for fulfilment, it drives us to keep doing, whereas when we look inside ourselves for fulfilment, it allows us to "be." Looking outside yourself for satisfaction invites stress, pressure, and lack of control which then drives a need to try to regain control. This viewpoint is often linked with the mind and the desire to constantly think and plan. In other words, it is achievement based.

Looking inside allows inner peace, internal alignment, and no need for control. This in-look is often linked with the heart—feeling and allowing. In other words, it is love based.

Being doesn't mean be lazy and do nothing. It just means get the order right.

Does it make any difference if you put your shoes or socks on first? Likewise, it makes a difference when you "be" and come from a love-based attitude of allowing compared to "doing" and then trying to insist love and fulfilment go with it.

Relax

Take a deep breath. Hold it. Now exaggerate your breath out. Do you feel more relaxed?

As you relax, your body stops producing the hormones that respond to stress (adrenalin and cortisol).

Relaxation is essential. Without it, your endocrine system runs amok.

When you're stressed, your body uses your progesterone-building blocks to make cortisol in your adrenal glands. As you know, progesterone is known as the feel-good hormone, but it's also needed for successful ovulation and carrying a pregnancy.

An excess of adrenaline and cortisol can interrupt other hormone functions like serotonin, melatonin, and fertility hormones (oestrogen, progesterone, testosterone, luteinizing hormone, follicle stimulating hormone, etc.) and cause issues like anxiety, depression, insomnia, muscle problems, infertility, and menstrual irregularities. Relax and help get your balance back.

Prolonged stress also contributes to weight gain around the midsection of your body. Relax and help thin out your waistline.

Relaxing doesn't mean blobbing in front of the TV. Studies show that people who read, do puzzles, learn languages, or do hobbies rather than watch TV are happier and less stressed. There are also some theories that the blue light emitted from TVs and electronics disturb sleep patterns. You're much better off to trade TV watching time with meditation, prayer, or focusing on what you're grateful for in your life.

Sleep

Historically, we're used to sleeping when it's dark and being awake when it's daylight.

By staying awake after sunset, we interrupt the body's natural time for rejuvenation and removing toxins. This causes a backup of toxins and hormones in the body. This is also exaggerated by staring at screens (phone, computer, TV, and other electronic devices) and having their bright light shine into our eyes. This is especially a problem after sundown when by nature's rhythm bright light should be absent.

Lack of sleep can also interfere with the delicate balance of serotonin and melatonin making your brain foggy during the day and restless at night. This perpetuates a cycle of decreased alertness, brain fog, and memory issues.

Celeste's Story

Celeste liked to get things done. She had a husband and two boys and was studying natural therapies. Add into the mix she liked to push the envelope. If she went for a run, she'd attack it as if she were trying out for Olympics.

At night, she would crash into bed physically and mentally exhausted and not be able to sleep. She used the hormones, took the herbs, and drank the teas for only a partial improvement. She installed thick curtains in the bedroom and slept like a baby.

5

What Do You Need to Remove That Is Toxic?

As you know, you can't restore health by fighting disease. It's never worked and never will.

Whatever you fight gets bigger. Fighting disease, poverty, or your mother guarantees you'll have something to keep fighting because they cannot go away while you keep fighting and feeding them.

Health can only be restored by
- **providing your body with something it needs and is lacking, and/or**
- **removing what is toxic that it's getting**

What do you need to remove that is toxic to you and your body?

- Toxic chemicals from food, drinks, air, water, cosmetics, toiletries, cleaning products, drugs, alcohol, cigarettes, plastics, clothing, cleaning products, medications, recreational drugs, paper, ink, petrol, industry and upholstery materials, etc.
- Physical toxins: subluxations (misalignments of the spinal vertebrae interfering with your nerve system), poor posture, electromagnetic radiation (from computers, televisions, mobile phones, etc.), microwaves (from ovens and telecommunications), and misuse of the body (e.g., habitually using one arm as opposed to being ambidextrous, extended sitting or bending, inappropriate

57

lifting, inappropriate shoes, incorrect breathing, diet, inadequate unilateral chewing, etc.).

- Toxic emotions: fear, anger, bitterness, resentment, blame, stubbornness, jealously, betrayal, unworthiness, revenge, etc.
- Toxic beliefs: not good enough, too old, too young, too short/ tall, too curly/straight, wrong gender, wrong job, wrong partner/ family/location, etc.

Be aware that your beliefs determine what you think, say, and do.

Your thoughts create biological change in your body every time.

How, when, and where are you going to remove what is toxic to your body?

You need to think, say, and do things differently if you want a different result.

If you don't change your direction, you'll end up where you're headed. Is that what you want?

The Top Ten Air Toxins in Homes Are …

1. cigarette smoke and poorly ventilated gas heating
2. cleaning chemicals and aerosols
3. pesticides (are they coming in on your food?)
4. mould and mildew
5. EMR (electromagnetic radiation) from electrical equipment. Everything you plug into a power socket emits EMR.
6. carbon monoxide and other particles from petrol and diesel
7. formaldehyde from composite woods (also referred to as particle board or chip board)
8. solvents such as oil-based paints
9. dust and dust mites
10. synthetics. These are often used in carpets, curtains, furnishings, and clothes.

As well as the top ten, there are air conditioning, air freshener sprays, deodorants, hair sprays, etc.

Simple substitutes for chemical air freshener sprays are
- Open the windows for fresh air (great if you live in the country but not such a great idea if you live in the city).
- Use a negative ionizer.
- Evaporate pure essential oils in an oil burner or diluted in water and atomized.
- Burn incense.

Housing

Products we use in our homes and offices every day emit gases that can disrupt hormone function and harm your health. These gases are called VOCs (volatile organic compounds). It's no surprise the concentrations of VOCs are consistently up to ten times higher indoors than outdoors. New buildings have an average of 20 to 40 mg/m3, which is a big problem since adverse health reactions can occur at only 10 mg/m3. According to the CSIRO (Commonwealth Scientific and Industrial Research Organization), older buildings usually have VOC levels below 1 mg/m3.

Equally no surprise, immediately after using products like paints and paints strippers, the levels can sky-rocket to 1,000 times the regular outdoor level.

Sources of VOCs

- paints, paint strippers, varnishes, and solvents
- wood preservatives
- aerosol sprays
- cleaners and disinfectants
- adhesives
- cosmetics and toiletries
- dry-cleaned clothing
- vinyl

- synthetic carpets
- car exhausts
- cigarette smoke
- pressed wood furniture
- photocopying

Harmful Effects of VOCs

The impact of VOCs depends on
- the toxicity of the chemical
- the amount of time you're exposed to it
- the amount or rate of off-gassing
- ventilation
- temperature: The higher the temperature the higher the off-gassing
- whether it's just one chemical or a cocktail

Symptoms of VOC Exposure

Short-term exposure symptoms include
- headache
- dizziness
- nausea or vomiting
- runny nose
- eye irritation
- hormone disruption
- anxiety
- asthma
- skin allergies
- decreased memory

Long-term exposure symptoms include
- hormone disorders
- cancer
- liver, kidney, and nerve system damage
- decreased coordination

To Chlorinate or Not to Chlorinate?

Chlorine is a potent disinfectant which is often added to public water supplies to kill bacteria in the water or the pipes carrying the water, but it has not come without a price.

Chlorine destroys some of the bacteria that challenge health in people with depleted immune systems, but it can also cause health problems itself. Unfortunately, chlorine reacts with other naturally occurring elements to form toxins called THMs (trihalomethanes). These have been linked to asthma, eczema, cancer, and heart disease.

Carbon-based filters are considered the most effective way of removing THMs and other toxins. Chlorine and related compounds will also make their way out of tap water if left uncovered in the fridge for twenty-four hours. It makes sense to not inhale this air from your fridge.

Many Canadian and European cities disinfect their water supply with ozone instead of chlorine.

Toxic Textiles

Most synthetic fabrics are treated with chemicals both during and after processing. These chemicals can be absorbed and inhaled and also leach into the wash water, environment and affect wildlife.

- Formaldehyde (listed by the International Agency for Research on Cancer as a toxic cancer-causing substance or carcinogen) is often added to prevent shrinkage. It is applied with heat to trap it in the fibre permanently.
- Clothes treated with flame-retardant chemicals emit formaldehyde gas.
- Petrochemical dyes are used for colour.
- Dye fixatives often come from heavy metals which also pollute the waterways.
- Nylon and polyester are made from petrochemicals which make the greenhouse gas nitrous oxide, which is over three hundred times more potent than carbon dioxide.

- Rayon is made from wood pulp that is treated with caustic soda and sulphuric acid.
- Most clothing labelled "non-iron" contains PFCs (perflourinated chemicals), which includes the non-stick additive Teflon. These chemicals are added to clothes to extend their life and make them wrinkle free. The EPA (Environmental Protection Agency) cites these as cancer-causing compounds yet they're in many compulsory school uniforms. Parents are unwittingly exposing their children to chemicals which could have dire consequences on their future health.

Endocrine Disruptors (EDs)

Endocrine disruptors are chemicals that can interfere with the hormone systems. In other words, they interfere with the manufacture, secretion, transport, binding, function, or excretion of hormones.

Hormones work at very small doses; hence, endocrine disruption can occur from low-dose exposures.

The most critical stages of human development occur in utero. Exposure to EDs at this stage can cause irreversible effects. In other words, permanent change and problems.

They can cause hormonal imbalances, cancer, menstrual imbalances, infertility, miscarriage, birth defects, learning difficulties, brain and behaviour problems, early puberty, impaired immunity, masculinising of females and feminizing of males, and developmental disorders.

Perhaps the most famous examples of endocrine disruptors are
- DES. DES is a non-steroidal oestrogen used for vaginitis, lactation suppression, menopause symptoms, premature ovarian failure, and prostate cancer. It was also given to pregnant women in the 1940s to 1970s with the intent to prevent miscarriage. It caused a rare vaginal cancer in the mothers and cancers and gross malformations (such as malformed or missing limbs) in the children. DES was banned in the 1970s.

- Phthalates (thay-layts) are added to plastics to increase flexibility, transparency, and life span. They are used in enteric coating of pharmaceutical tablets and nutritional supplements; emulsifying agents; lubricants; glues; electronics; toys; detergents; waxes; food products (it can especially leach into fatty foods, such as milk, butter, and meats); textiles and building materials.

  High phthalates in the mother is associated with a smaller penis and scrotum and undescended testes in her sons.

Routes of Exposure

1. Food is the carrier for 90 per cent of PCBs (polychlorinated biphenyl) and DDT (dichlorodiphenyltrichloroethane) entering the body.
   - PCBs are used in transformers and electric motors. They've been shown to cause cancer and non-Hodgkin's lymphoma. They readily penetrate the skin, latex, and PVC.
   - DDT was first used as an insecticide and to eradicate malaria. It has been linked to disruption in semen quality, menstruation, gestational length, and ability to breastfeed.
2. Indoor air

   An increase of pollutants in household products and a decrease in ventilation has become a significant avenue of exposure.
3. Cleaning and personal care products

Toxic Thoughts and Beliefs

You get more of what you think about, whether you want it or not.

The brain doesn't recognize *don't*. If you say, "Don't think of a red car," it does it anyway. If you say, "Don't think of a vase of flowers," it does it anyway. If you say, "Don't forget to bring your keys," it'll help you forget to bring your keys.

You will have more success communicating with yourself if you think, say, and do in accordance with what you want rather than what you don't want. Think, say, and do the things that will take you closer to what you desire rather than towards what you don't desire.

Accept Responsibility

Everything that is happening in your life is a result of choices you made in the past. The choices you make now will determine the results you get in the future. Make certain your choices are going to take you closer to, not farther away from, what you want.

If you want to see what you look like physically, you look in a mirror and assess what is reflected back to you, but how do you see your non-physical self?

If you want to see your personality, beliefs, or soul, you can see it reflected back to you from others. In other words, the people around you reflect the qualities of your non-physical self back to you. What you look like emotionally is reflected in the situations, behaviours, and emotions of the people around you. You attract the people you do because you're a match in frequency.

The people you like show you the qualities within yourself you approve of and like.

The people you don't like or the behaviours you judge show you the qualities within yourself you disapprove of, don't like, and possibly don't even recognize—or totally deny. The more we judge or don't like something within us, the more likely we are to hide it and not be able to see it within ourselves; hence, the people around us are doing their job by showing us.

This is how our soul communicates to us what we need to resolve in order to heal ourselves, grow as individuals, and fulfil our life purpose on earth. Hence, your relationships with your family, friends, colleagues, and strangers are compelling, powerful, and important.

The more accurately you can interpret what is being mirrored back to you and make the necessary changes without judging yourself or them, the faster you'll heal, feel fulfilled, and align with your divine presence.

Are You Angry Because You're Hormonal or Hormonal Because You're Angry?

The foundations of our world are based in duality. For example,

- light and dark
- hot and cold
- fire and water
- air and earth
- male and female
- positive and negative
- yin and yang

This guarantees you'll seek out the familiar like a magnet. You'll constantly seek to find yourself in other people—both good and bad. This is one of the reasons your connections with other people are so important. When you connect to another person with love, it connects you more deeply to the love within yourself. When you see positive qualities in others, it connects you to the same qualities within yourself and allows them to grow further.

When you focus on negative qualities within someone else, this also connects you to the negative qualities within yourself and makes them grow.

Doesn't it make sense to "look for good"?

When you fill yourself with positive thoughts and beliefs, you glow from the inside out and healing can manifest.

When you fill yourself with negative thoughts and beliefs, you wither and disease ensues.

This doesn't mean you need to be scared of thinking negative thoughts; it simply implores you to be mindful of where you're putting your habitual attention.

If you desire health and wellness, you need to focus on health and wellness.

Laying Blame

If you need help to see where you judge either yourself or others, look at where you lay blame.

Wherever you are blaming someone or something, this is where you're being shown something within you that you're not looking at with accurate perception, or you have seen it and buried it even farther rather than resolving it.

Blaming others is a method of giving your power away.

If you are more tired than your life warrants, or you feel more ineffectual than you ought to, take a look at whom and where you lay blame because this is where your energy is going.

Every time you blame someone or something, you leak energy. It whittles away in proportion to the degree you're blaming. The more passionate you feel about the alleged offense, the more energy you're giving away.

What's even more alarming, you are giving your energy to the very person you're blaming. Rather than resolving anything, you're actually feeding the situation and making it grow, to your own detriment and their benefit.

The bigger the disagreement becomes, the more you can't ignore it, so sooner or later you'll have to look at the truth behind the situations and resolve the cause.

The earlier you recognize the need for resolution and take appropriate action, the less your life will be a drama.

Furthermore, the less you give your energy to spats and quarrels, the more peace you'll have and the more your energy will be available for the pleasurable things in life.

Blame resolves nothing and perpetuates the problem.

Instead of blaming others, take your power back and accept responsibility for your own circumstances. Make your own decisions and allow yourself to have the life you deserve.

Most people already know that if you worry a lot you get stomach ulcers. Some within the medical fraternity blame the Helicobacter pylori bacteria; however, this is a natural resident in the stomach and only becomes a problem when excess worrying alters the acidity. When the pH is altered, the bacteria proliferates as a natural response to the change in the environment.

The worrying is the cause and the Helicobacter pylori proliferation is the symptom.

The bacteria cannot proliferate in a healthy and balanced environment.

If a rubbish bin is clean, are there any flies? No!

It's a dirty rubbish bin that attracts the flies. The flies didn't cause the dirt—they came to feed off it!

If the stomach is healthy, there is no overgrowth of bacteria. If the stomach gets out of balance, the bacteria thrive. The bacteria didn't cause the imbalance; they're just feeding off it!

Your Issues Are Stored in Your Tissues

You already know if you worry, you get stomach ulcers, but are you aware that every emotion you have is either building you up or depleting your health?

In quick summary, if you are

- fearful, you'll create kidney problems, such as urinary tract infections, stones, or renal failure
- resentful (constantly resending or thinking the same story over and over), you'll create gall bladder problems
- angry, you'll create liver problems
- rigid, you'll create arthritic problems
- disappointed, you'll create thyroid problems
- grieving, you'll create lung problems
- not relating well in your female-male relationships, you'll create female or male problems. in other words, reproductive, hormonal, or genital problems
- ashamed, feel unsuccessful, or feel not good enough, you'll create blood sugar and pancreas problems

Every emotion you have affects you either positively or negatively, according to the positivity or negativity of the emotion. Every emotion affects a given organ, muscle, and energy centre or chakra.

The disease you have tells you loud and clear what you need to resolve in your life—if only you'll take the time to listen. Then of course, you need to take appropriate action to rectify the imbalance.

Just as negativity can undo your health, you can use positivity to rebuild it again.

Barb's Story

Barb would always get a nagging dull backache with her period. Massage and hot packs would ease the discomfort, but it plagued her for years. When she began to meditate and consciously work at resolving her childhood issues, the backache went away. She wasn't focusing on the back pain; it was a bonus that it resolved. She had forgiven her brother for events in her childhood that frustrated and angered her. This released the stored emotions in her muscles and spine and freed her from her monthly dread.

The Tail Is Wagging the Dog

Do you think you're angry because you're hormonal?

What if the tail is wagging the dog?

What if you're hormonal because you're angry?

Hormonal imbalance is a natural body response to your habitual anger. Confronting, I know. I didn't want to hear this at first either.

The blessing of hormonal anger is your body is telling you loudly and clearly what you need to resolve, if you're prepared to accept self-responsibility and listen.

Anger affects your liver, which in turn affects your ability to remove excess hormones from your body, which creates an imbalance. Typically, when you're angry, excess oestrogen isn't removed from your system efficiently enough, so you have too much oestrogen relative to progesterone in your circulation. In other words, too much oestrogen and not enough feel-good hormone. Hence, you feel angrier still. It's easier to think it's the hormones that are the problem, even though deep down your know it's your anger that started the fight.

There are no flies around a clean bin.

There's no hormonal balance in a peaceful person.

In order to truly heal your hormonal imbalance, you'll need to resolve the deep-seated causes of your anger—else you'll hold the legacy of getting spinal adjustments, taking herbs and supplements, or using hormonal creams or troches for the rest of your days.

Plus if karma is real, you'll get to revisit the same issues over gain because you didn't resolve it this time.

Who or what are you angry about?

Resolve that!

Likewise for depression.

Do you think you're depressed because you're hormonal?

What if the inmates are running the asylum?

What if you're hormonal because you're depressed?

There are no flies around a clean bin.

There's no depression in a peaceful person who stays focused in the present.

Depression comes from judging something or someone in the past.

Anxiety comes from looking too far into the future.

When you stay peacefully focused in the present, there is no depression.

In order to truly heal your hormonal imbalance, you'll need to resolve the deep-seated causes of your depression—else you'll hold the legacy of getting spinal adjustments, taking herbs and supplements, or using hormonal creams or troches for the rest of your days.

What or who are you judging from your past?

Resolve that!

The sooner you get started, the sooner you'll harvest the results.

What You Resist Persists

In over thirty years in private practice, I've found this to be true. It's also been true in my own life even though I've argued against it on many occasions. We get what we need, not what we necessarily want.

For our own growth, it will serve you well to pay attention to this. If you resist dealing with something, it will simply persist until you do.

Usually, it will persist louder and stronger until you cannot comfortably ignore it any longer! Even if you medicate it, inebriate it, drug it, or whatever your choice of anaesthetic, it will still be waiting underneath for you, screaming at you for attention.

If you have a persisting problem present in your life, whether it's with your health, relationships, finances, career or otherwise, it is showing you what you're resisting and you'll need to find ways to resolve it. If you don't, the challenging situation will keep growing. This is how your soul communicates with you.

If you follow the trail of the problem back to its source, you will eventually end up with yourself, once again reminding you that you create your own reality. The problem is present because of your resistance somewhere.

Resistance is a lack of flow or you not going with the natural flow. It is showing you where you lack love. **If there's something you do not love in the other person or situation, it is highlighting to you where you do not love yourself.**

This can seem a bit challenging at first, especially if you've been raised to believe that loving yourself is bad, selfish, and ego-driven or any other negative thing.

Even so, some of our tasks on earth are to
- find our own truth
- live by our own philosophy
- reclaim our love of self
- regain our love for others

- express our own uniqueness

If we don't find our self-love and inner peace, how can we ever have world peace?

To give yourself a kick-start on the road to loving yourself without your ego interfering, it may help you to start thinking and treating yourself as your own friend. This means you need to be friendly with yourself instead of judgmental.

Your problems are your gifts. Without them, you wouldn't know there's anything to heal or have any clues how to go about it. Instead of getting frustrated or cursing your challenges, be grateful for them. Often when you soften your energy to gratitude rather than the rigidity of resistance or anger at the person or situation, you find things start to flow your way rather than keeping you stuck.

By seeing your challenges as a gift, it helps you to take your power back and find solutions. Whenever you see your problems as external and irresolute, you are giving your power to it. This feeds the problem and it has no option but to grow rather than be resolved.

Energy is like a budget, and it is best to use it wisely rather than spending it on inappropriate things.

It is far easier to deal with issues when they're small rather than let them escalate into mammoths for you to try to slay later.

If you think your problems are too big to handle now, make sure you attend to them immediately! Because if you don't, they'll grow bigger and bigger until you do!

This is a timely reminder to live in the present because it too is a gift. When you focus on the past, your energy feeds the past and intensifies it—making you feel depressed.

Any perceived wrongdoings will appear even bigger.

It is the same with your future. When you live in the future, you are projecting your energy into things you are only guessing at.

Bring your focus back to the present because the choices you make here and now determine how your future will be. This is where you have the power to make changes.

When you live totally in the present, you automatically become problem free and stress free. All the problems you think you have are only problems when you relate them to something from the past or the future.

For example, if you think you have money problems and you recall when you had money problems in the past, you can feel stressed or depressed all over again. If you predict money problems in your future, this too can make you can feel stressed or anxious.

Right now, in this very present moment, you don't actually have a problem and there is no stress. As soon as you think of the past or project into the future again, you will feel like you have a problem again. It's an illusion. We simply create it in our heads. Stay in the present; it is your gift and it is stress free.

The same principle applies to all areas of your life, whether it's relationship, health, career, physical appearance, or whatever else. They're only a problem if you recall a stressful experience from the past or you project a negative possibility into the future.

If you stay focused right here, right now, you don't have a problem.

Stay in the present; it is your gift.

When you plant healthy, stress-free seeds in the present, it helps ensure the potential of a healthy and stress-free future.

If you plant negative seeds about what is ahead for you in your future, these are the seeds of your future weeds.

If you plant weed seeds, you can only grow weeds.

If you want to grow flowers, you have to plant flower seeds.

Stay focused on planting positive seeds in the present. Plant the seeds you want and then allow your future to take care of itself.

Exercise

Blaming people and situations depletes your energy and creates disease. Ironically, it's the people and situations you blame that receive the energy you need for your own healing.

It's up to you to let it go. Reclaim your energy and restore your balance. Do this exercise thoroughly.

- Make a complete list of all the people you blame for anything at all. Start with your parents and siblings and then include partners, ex-partners, classmates, teachers, and everyone you've given your power and energy to.

  Don't skip over this. Take the time. Be thorough because if you can't name it, you can't change it, and likewise, if you can name it, you can change it.

- Within every situation where you blame, there will be something you are angry about. What is this?

  Don't skip over this. Take the time.

  Write it down. With all the situations you have listed in the first step of this process, what were you angry about? List it. Take your time and be thorough and compassionate as you get to know yourself better.

- Underneath everything you are angry about, there is something you fear. What is this? Write it down.

  Don't skip over this. Take the time.

  For all the things you were angry about in the previous step, what was the fear underneath it? List it. Notice how the more you ask yourself questions, the easier it gets to find your answers. This becomes a self-perpetuating upward spiral because the more answers you have, the more resolution you can allow. This permits healing and peace and frees up your energy to create the life you prefer. Be really honest with yourself, because if you keep denying or lying, either nothing will change or your situation will get worse.

- Take each situation and see what it is showing you. Look for your gift. List the gifts.

  Don't skip over this. Take the time.

  Fear is the opposite of love. When you recognize what your fear is, simply go to the polar opposite of that and grow it so big the fear cannot take hold.

For example,

- ○ If you were blaming others for your situation because you doubted your own abilities, then grow your confidence so the seeds of doubt can't sprout. Grow your confidence so your own dreams manifest and then there's no reason to blame someone else for you not getting what you want.
- ○ If you were blaming others for your situation because you felt too insecure to make your own decisions, then notice what conditions make you feel secure. Create more of these situations, enhance your security, and once again manifest what you want so there's no need to blame anyone else.

- What are the common fears of the situations you have listed? Take a look at your lists and notice the common issues in your relationships and circumstances.

It helps profoundly when you can see your patterns. When you can recognize your patterns, you can change them. It's a natural response to become defensive and defend your patterns. We don't like to admit we're wrong. Get over the defence as fast as you can, because the longer you defend your patterns or try to justify the need to be right, the longer you keep the pattern and the consequences.

For things to change first you must change.

You cannot change anyone but yourself, and this is where you need to start every time.

It's as simple as this: if you don't change your attitude, you will not heal and risk getting sicker because your body's job is to keep telling you where you need to change course. If you don't change course, it will tell you more and more loudly until you listen. Its' to your own detriment if you don't. Listen to the whispers and change course so you don't have to hear the screams.

Adopt and attitude of gratitude.

By taking your power back and germinating the seeds of your dreams rather than your fears, you get the life you aspire to. If you fertilise the weeds, you get more weeds. If you water the trees, you'll get a beautiful forest.

As soon as you make positive changes, you will see positive results, as long as you look for and acknowledge them. Break the habit of looking for negativity and retrain yourself to look for good.

You can't change anyone else. You can only change yourself, so you may as well get started now.

The paradox is when you change, others will change also, but in response to the new you rather than because you were trying to get them to change. The change in you acts as a catalyst for others to make changes also. When you are beaming out a different message, others will accordingly beam new messages back to you.

Easy Tips You Can Integrate Now

Many health-promoting strategies are easy to integrate into your everyday life. The sooner you make the changes you need to make, the sooner you'll feel the benefits.

- Stop eating foods you're sensitive to. If it doesn't work for you, it doesn't work for you.
- Eat raw or conventionally heated foods rather than microwaved.
- Avoid using mobile or cordless phones. Keep usage and talk time to a minimum. Keep the device away from sensitive tissues (e.g., brain, breast, and reproductive areas) as much as possible. Use the loud speaker where appropriate and turn the device off rather than have it transmitting and receiving in your pocket or on your bedside table.
- Minimize exposure to electromagnetic radiation as much as possible. Have short spans on computers with regular breaks in nature.
- Use natural ingredient products, such as
  - natural soap
  - sulphate-free shampoo and propylene-glycol-free conditioner
  - aluminium-free deodorant
  - petrochemical-free skin creams and cosmetics
  - artificial fragrance and petrochemical-free perfumes. Pure essential oils are a natural alternative with therapeutic benefits as well as pleasing aromas.

- ○ ammonia and petrochemical-free hair colourants and treatments
- ○ Grow your own beautiful nails if you like them long instead of acrylics
- ○ chemical-free sunscreens. Wear a hat and long sleeves.
- ○ Sulphate-free and inorganic-fluoride-free toothpaste
- ○ laundry detergents with natural ingredients.
- ○ unbleached and dioxin-free tampons and sanitary liners
- ○ Wear natural fibre clothes wherever possible.

- Live and work where the air is fresh or use a negative ionizer to help counteract air pollutants.
- Use 100 per cent pure essential oils or good-quality incense for air fresheners.
- Invest in a good water purifier and use it for any water you put in or on your body.
- If you live in an area that is free of acid rain, put in a rainwater collection tank.
- Become aware of your habitual thought patterns and notice how they affect you. It's hard to change something when you don't even realize you're doing it, so awareness is a good first step.

  Once you are aware of it, you can stop suppressing what is really at the core of your dilemma. Decide to take your energy back from where you've been allowing it to dwindle. Restore your health and personal power.

It may sound ho-hum, but it's all about balance. Balance within and between your physical, mental, and spiritual self.

- Physically, this includes balancing the scales of your work, play, relationships, exercise, rest, nutrition, supplements, and modalities.
- Mentally, this includes finding positive balance in your thoughts, attitudes, and beliefs.
- Spiritually, this includes being inspired and having faith, confidence, and belief in yourself.

  To be inspired means to be "in your spirit." If you are in your head rather than your spirit, you will be driven rather than inspired.

6

Your Disease Is Your Cure

If you're a female and have issues with males or you're a male and have issues with females, it's a natural response by your body to develop reproductive, hormone, or sexual difficulties or imbalances. If you don't resolve the issues you have between the genders, you will continue to spiral into more and more reproductive, hormonal, or sexual issues.

If you're angry about someone or something, your body will accumulate fat on your thighs and develop liver imbalances or congestion. If you don't resolve the cause and consequences of your anger, your body has no choice but to create thunder thighs (angry as thunder) or liver symptoms (bleep on the liver).

If you are fearful and worry incessantly, it's a natural body response to develop kidney symptoms. If you don't resolve the cause and consequences of your fears and worries, you'll have no choice but to create ongoing kidney problem—until you do. For example, if you don't let go of your emotions, you'll store fluid.

If you worry and don't let things flow, then your fluids can't flow either. If you get pissed off about it, it will also affect your piss. When you have urine symptoms, your body is telling you you're pissed off about someone or something and it's up to you to discover the source and resolve it—even if it's yourself you're annoyed with. Especially if it's yourself you're annoyed with. Kidney and urine problems are the result of being fearful and worrying.

Disease is the cure for the life you are living.

Disease is the result of the way you live, think, and function. Your diseases and illnesses are a clear guide to what you need to change and where you need to change it so you can look forward to where and how you choose your life to be.

Stop trying to restore your health back to where it was! Where you were is where it all started!

As long as you focus on the past, you can't move ahead, and if you don't change your direction, you'll end up where you're headed!

Everyone has a life purpose. In due course, we all have the same purpose of finding acceptance and living in love; however, many roads lead to Rome, and we all get to choose the route we travel to get there.

When you live in love, you can live in peace. Peace has always been your natural state; it just got buried under layers of life experiences.

When you live in love, duality doesn't exist. Nor does separation, judgement of right and wrong, or resistance.

If you fight against duality, however, it can certainly feel like you're separate from everyone and everything. Within duality, there is always more duality, so the more you see yourself as separate, the more separateness you create. I'm sure you've noticed this with religions, governments, companies, and families. Where people disconnect and create separateness, they create factions within factions.

When you live in oneness, ease, and flow, there is no judgement of right or wrong. There is acceptance instead. When you live in oneness, you can see the gift in every experience, such as

- the broken ankle that slows a person down so they don't have a heart attack
- the cancer that tells the person where their bitterness or anger is stored so they can heal it
- the flu that allows a person to rest and release the physical toxins that are counterpart to their toxic emotions, thoughts, and beliefs

Are You Listening to Yourself?

- Are you listening? Do you rest, release, and let go, or do you battle on and hang on to your old patterns?
- Do you let the tail wag the dog?

- Your body is a finely tuned work of art designed to homeostatically steer you through your life and personal mission. When you're on target, on purpose, and doing what is right for you, your body functions smoothly. When you wobble off course, get distracted, or do things that are damaging to your life mission, your body will let you know via its symptoms.

- The question is this: do you listen when your body communicates with you?

- If you need a break, do you take one—or do you wait until you break something? Can you justify the rest then? Why didn't you allow the rest before, when you felt tired and your body told you to stop?

- When your shoulders are tense, do you stop and listen to what your should-ers are telling you? Your shoulders are your should-ers. What is it you think you should have done or not done? Are there things you think you really should have done but haven't got around to yet?

  If you really ought to have done something, then get on and do it. If it's not something you ought to have done, then stop telling yourself you should, let yourself off the hook, and let the tension dissipate from your shoulders.

- If you have a pain in your neck, who or what in your life, do you think is a pain in the neck? Do you monitor what you judge? The judgement pulls you off course and takes you farther away from your mission of acceptance and oneness. It creates pain, and your body tells you so you can resolve the issue, correct your programming, and get back on course.

  If you have hormonal imbalances and don't resolve your deep issues with the other gender, you're not listening.

  If you have high oestrogen levels because your liver is congested and can't remove the excess efficiently, and you don't resolve who or what you're angry with, you're not listening.

  If you have kidney or urinary tract problems and you're still fearful, worrying, or pissed off at someone or something, you're not listening.

Your hormonal imbalances have no choice but to get more severe, your liver becomes even more congested and overloaded, and your kidneys ache even more painfully until you listen and make the changes you need to make.

If you only take hormones to balance out the excess and deficiencies in your body, you're doing the equivalent of covering the oil warning light in the car. If you have a hormonal imbalance, it's a sign there is something wrong. The problem needs to be corrected at its source—else the consequences can be serious.

I'm not saying don't use hormonal supplements. I am saying don't just use the supplements and ignore why you need them in the first place, else you'll just need more and more and something else as well.

Your body has the amazing ability to heal itself within certain considerations. If your engine seized within twenty minutes of your hormones getting out of balance, you would surely get the message—but your body has the remarkable ability to adapt. So rather than you breaking down there and then, you borrow the building blocks for your progesterone (your feel-good hormone) to make more cortisol (your stress hormone), your body raises your blood pressure to either fight or flee from the stress, your muscles tighten ready for action, and so on.

But what are the consequences of your vital resources being used for stress hormones and living in a state of attention rather than relaxation? Your hormonal symptoms are those consequences, as well as the impact this has on your life and those around you

Every time your hormones aren't able to maintain your homeostasis (whether it's from stress; liver congestion; anger; anxiety; ingesting xenoestrogens, volatile organic compounds or hormone-disrupting chemicals), it is signalling you to adjust your course and get back on track. The sooner you correct and put systems in place to not repeat what caused the concern, the smoother your ride and the better your health will be. The longer you take and the more resistant you are to doing what is innately right for you, the bumpier it will get.

If you go past the point of difficult return, your engine will seize!

Exercise

Every time you notice a symptom (a communication from your body regarding its circumstances),

1. Stop.
2. Take inventory.
3. Take a different action or behaviour.

Retrain yourself to listen to your body instead of overriding its signals. Understand that pain and symptoms are your best friends. They are direct communications from your body, telling you that something is not right.

Every time you receive a symptomatic message from your body, *stop*, take inventory, and change your behaviour or the direction you're going. Get closer to living your life from your own centre. Allow the dog to wags its tail again instead of the tail wagging the dog.

7

Oestrogen Dominance

Until recently, accurate information about hormonal imbalances and what to do about them wasn't readily available. Plainly and simply, the research hadn't been done and much of what was released was suspiciously in favour of miracle drugs, which we've since seen people all over the world pay the price for taking.

Much of what I learned about how to manage and heal from hormonal imbalances was from experimenting—basic trial and error.

In previous decades, the doctors who were supposed to have the answers didn't know what to do and some of the things they gave me actually made me worse. I soon realized they were clutching at straws and I had to heal myself.

I took a myriad of herbs, used a variety of modalities and meditation exercises, and swallowed so many different supplements I literally didn't have room for breakfast. Over a long, drawn-out journey spanning more than thirty years, I found some substantial answers. It's been a comprehensive journey of discovery into anything and everything I thought might help me, and I'm really grateful for the help I've received along the way.

What stood out over time was the awareness that most things helped— for a while. And then I'd need higher doses or something else. Nothing seemed to be a cure for all time, reinforcing the concept that no matter what you use to support yourself along the way, sooner or later the source of the problems has to be resolved. In other words, forgive the people or events which triggered the imbalances in the first place and change the beliefs and paradigms that have been holding those issues in place.

In other words, the physical effects are often the consequences of unresolved emotional upsets and memories you still need to tend to regardless of how much attention you give the individual hormones.

Your time and energy are wisely spent forgiving and releasing the causes of why you are the way you are.

Fortunately, a lot of research has been done in recent years and there's a lot more understanding and information regarding biochemistry available now.

When you're reading about hormones and how they work in your body, it's very easy to get lost in the technical facts. I hope I can explain it in simple terms with minimal data so you can get the information you need without bogging you down with information that has little to do with how you can help yourself.

The main actors on the stage of female sex hormones are the
- oestrogens and
- progesterones

The supporting actors are
- DHEA
- pregnenolone, and
- cortisol.

All of these are called *steroid hormones.*

Progesterone is a precursor to most steroid hormones. This means that without progesterone, your body doesn't have the building blocks to make your other steroid hormones. Again, without progesterone, your body doesn't have the building blocks to make your other steroid hormones.

This is important.

This means that when you are stressed, your progesterone gets used up, making stress hormones instead of being available to make you feel happy.

Think of the oestrogens and progesterones as a family. Ideally, they should be balanced and working in harmony. As you are well aware though, theory doesn't always match the reality.

Power struggles between the oestrogens and progesterones will cause you a myriad of physical, emotional, and mental symptoms, just like in any dysfunctional family. This is especially so when you have high levels of oestrogen, in particular estradiol, because this form of oestrogen is toxic to your body.

With many female syndromes, including PMS, pre-menopause, menopause, and osteoporosis, there is more oestrogen relative to progesterone than there should be. This is known as oestrogen dominance.

In the past, it was thought the problems women were encountering at menopause were because of oestrogen deficiency. This assumption was made because oestrogen production can drop by 50 per cent at this time. Giving oestrogen replacement didn't solve the problems though and it has since been found that as well as the drop in oestrogen, there is an even bigger drop in progesterone. This is often the major problem for many women.

Your progesterone production can drop to 1 per cent at menopause, consequently creating a very high level of oestrogen relative to progesterone.

Improving the progesterone levels often significantly improves the symptoms.

The Properties of the Female Sex Hormones

Within the oestrogen and progesterone families, there are a variety of types of oestrogen and progesterone. The characteristics mentioned here are for the overall groups.

Oestrogen

- causes the development of secondary female characteristics at puberty. This includes
    - breast development
    - ovaries moving down into the pelvis
    - pubic and underarm hair growth
    - waist formation
    - menarche or the beginning of menstruation

- regulates your menstrual cycle.
- promotes the division of cells in your body.

Progesterone

- maintains your thyroid hormone function for burning your fat for energy and maintaining your body temperature.
- maintains the lining of your uterus.
- behaves as a natural diuretic and gets rid of excess fluid from your body.
- regulates blood clotting.
  maintains your sex drive.
- builds your bones. This is particularly important with reference to osteoporosis.

Oestrogen Dominance or Progesterone Deficiency and Osteoporosis

As we age, there's a tendency to lose bone density if you aren't doing regular weight-bearing exercise and eating appropriately.

If the loss of bone density becomes extreme, it is called osteoporosis, which commonly involves disfiguring hip and spine fractures.

For a long time, it was thought a lack of oestrogen was a primary cause of osteoporosis; however, it has since been discovered that it is a lack of progesterone that causes the problem. Progesterone re-mineralises bone and restores bone mass. Using natural progesterone has shown to be useful in both preventing and healing osteoporosis.

When you are healthy and not pregnant or pre-menopausal, you will secrete only 100–200 micrograms of oestrogen per day.

On the other hand, you will produce about 20–25 milligrams of progesterone per day and up to 300–400 milligrams per day during pregnancy.

This explains the feeling of calm well-being that many women describe in their third trimester of pregnancy and the postnatal depression that can ensue with the sudden drop of progesterone after birth.

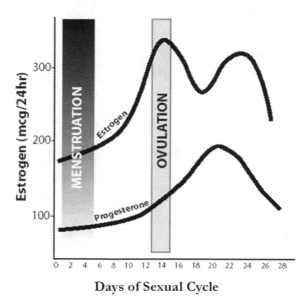

Days of Sexual Cycle

Symptoms of Oestrogen Dominance or Progesterone Deficiency

When you have more oestrogen relative to progesterone than you should (oestrogen dominance), you can experience such problems as

- weight gain
- tiredness
- loss of libido
- depression
- sugar cravings
- headaches
- joint pains
- mood swings
- hypertension
- salt and fluid retention
- abnormal blood clotting
- hypothyroidism
- painful breasts
- fibrocystic breast disease
- menstrual problems

- autoimmune disorders
- uterine fibroids
- uterine erosions and/or dysplasia
- increased risk of uterine and breast cancer
- loss of bone density and osteoporosis

What Are The Main Causes of Oestrogen Dominance?

1. making too much oestrogen or being exposed to it from your environment
2. not making enough progesterone
3. not getting rid of oestrogen out of your body fast enough

Nicole's Story

Nicole was losing the plot. She was getting angry earlier and longer before her period and was being quite difficult to be around.

She exhausted what she knew to do with orthodox treatments and was forced to explore alternative options. She found a practitioner who tested her blood and prescribed a rotation of natural progesterone cream and daily meditation.

She failed meditation 101. She just couldn't get the hang of it, so she attended a Be in One Peace workshop and retreat. It did the trick. She not only mastered how to meditate but also learned how to change her thoughts and brushed up on her nutritional knowledge and life-coping skills.

The progesterone balanced out the oestrogen regime that was running rampant and the daily meditation calmed her and facilitated her body to make more of its own progesterone instead of more and more stress hormones.

Too Much Oestrogen: Oestrogens From Your Environment

Oestrogen-Producing Tumours

A nasty cause of too much oestrogen relative to progesterone can be from an oestrogen-producing tumour. In this case, there would be serious problems from the cancer itself as well as the difficulties from too much oestrogen relative to progesterone.

Fat

Fat cells make oestrogen. That's a good enough reason all by itself to keep your weight under control. If you are oestrogen dominant, the last thing you need is more oestrogen.

Having said that, however, the whole body response can be more complicated than what it appears on the surface. For example, excess body fat can also suppress oestrogen production from your ovaries.

New discoveries in biochemistry are being made all the time, and as new theories come in, often old ones go out. Regardless of current theories, most people know they're healthier and feel better when they maintain a healthy weight range.

Maintain your balance with yourself and nature as much as you possibly can.

Environment

The pollution in our environment is doing more than upsetting the planet; it's also upsetting our bodies. Many chemicals that are used abundantly in manufacture are xenoestrogens, which means they "behave like oestrogens."

Exposure to xenoestrogens has been a large cause of hormonal imbalance in women, men, and children and has even been blamed for the increased incidence of some cancers.

Synthetic industrial chemicals can cause innumerable side effects and can store in the fat of your body.

They can give you
- headaches
- skin irritations
- liver damage
- brain damage
- DNA damage
- nausea
- bowel toxicity

Many chemicals are known to cause cancer. Why are we still using them in the quantities we do almost daily?

I can only assume it is economics, convenience, ignorance, peer pressure, or good marketing on the part of the manufacturers. Why else would we be voluntarily submitting ourselves to poison?

From tampons to plastic food wraps and artificial air fresheners, they contain chemicals which are detrimental to you and your family's health.

Unless you choose pure brands, you are being exposed to a cocktail of chemicals constantly.

As the car industry thrived in the twentieth century, so did the need for fuel. Great quantities of unwanted chemicals are produced when gasoline is extracted from crude oil, so the chemists had to find uses for the unwanted by-products.

Of particular concern with respect to hormonal balance are the xenoestrogens.

Xenoestrogens are chemicals which
- mimic oestrogen. In other words, they behave the same way as oestrogen in the body. Hence, they add to oestrogen dominance and relative progesterone deficiency.
- are highly fat soluble
- don't break down easily
- are hard to excrete

I encourage you to be particularly discerning about what you consume. Some people believe it's cheaper to use common products rather than organic or chemical free. This is false economy. You'll have to pay a much higher fee later to restore the health you are losing now.

Prevention is clearly better than cure.

How do xenoestrogens disrupt your body?

Hormones are the messengers for the regulation of many biological processes in your body.

Hormones relay information to cells about how and when to

- grow
- produce bodily substances
- divide
- die

Hormones bind with specifically tailored cell proteins called receptors in an intricate and precise "lock and key" fit. The hormone-receptor complex then binds to the DNA in your cell's nucleus to activate specific genes.

There are two ways xenoestrogens disrupt the function of your hormone system.

1. They can mimic natural hormones and activate cell activity at the wrong time.
2. They can block the normal biological response by occupying the receptor sites and preventing your own hormones from fitting.

This can cause the inappropriate activation of your genes by incorrect timing or too much or too little cellular activity. This is disruptive and dangerous for adults and even more so for developing babies and children. Children who have been affected by xenoestrogens will grow into adults with inherent hormonal dysfunctions.

Known Xenoestrogens

The following chemicals are considered to have serious reproductive and hormone disruptive effects:

- Pesticides: Many of these pesticides were used regularly in the farming community where I grew up. The local environment had the illusion of fresh country air but it was toxic. Both the ground and water were exposed to chemicals. You may even be familiar with some of these names already: 2, 4, 5-T; 2, 4–D; alachlor; aldicarb; amitrole; atrazine; benomyl; carbaryl; chlordane; cypermethrin; DBCP; DDT; dicofol; dieldrin; endosulfan; esfenvalerate; ethyl parathion; fenvalerate; heptachlor; hexachlorobenzene; lindane; malathion; mancozeb; maneb; methomyl; methoxychlor; metiram; metribuzin; mirex; nitrofen; oxychlordane; permethrin and other synthetic pyrethroids; toxaphen; transnonachlor; tributyltin oxide; trifluralin; vinclozolin; zineb; ziram.

- Heavy Metals
  - Cadmium is used in nickel-cadmium batteries; coatings; pigments; stabilizers in plastics and synthetic products and alloys; and fossil fuels.
  - Lead is used in lead batteries, paints, pipes and leaded fuel.
  - Mercury is used in nickel-cadmium batteries, fluorescent lighting, seed dressings, chlorine production, dental amalgams, immunizations, and fossil fuels.
- Organochlorines
  - Dioxin (2, 3, 7, 8-TCDD) is a by-product of other organochlorine production, use, and disposal. (In other words, it is not intentionally produced.) Examples include incinerator emissions, metal smelting, PVC (vinyl) plastic production, and chlorine-bleached pulping.
    Chlorine bleaches are used in feminine hygiene products, such as tampons and sanitary liners. This is insane. Why do they need to be pristine white instead of beige? Whoever else ever sees them? Even if they did, why would they need to be poisonous white? Aesthetic appeal is not enough to compensate for cancer.
  - PBBs and PCBs. Production is now banned, but PCBs are still used in electrical transformers. PCBs still reside in landfills, toxic-waste dumps, and sediments.
  - Pentachlorophenol is a wood preservative used in the textile industry.
- Plastic Ingredients and Surfactants

o   Bisphenol A is a breakdown product of polycarbonate.
o   Phthalates/ Polycarbons are used to make plastic soft.
o   Styrenes/Alkyl/Nonyl Phenol Ethoxylates are used in detergents; pulp and paper; the textile industry, some plastic products, paints, and pesticides.
- Aromatic Hydrocarbons
  o   PAHs are present in crude oil and most fossil fuels and are products of the combustion of these fuels.

Xenoestrogens are in
- Personal body care products, including
  o   toothpaste
  o   soap
  o   shampoo
  o   conditioner
  o   deodorant
  o   hair colourants
  o   skin creams
  o   sunscreens
  o   shaving treatments
  o   make-up

These products are loaded with chemicals to improve their aesthetic appeal. They include agents that help sudsing, colour, texture, perfume, and shelf life.

- Personal hygiene products, including
  o   tampons
  o   sanitary pads
  o   toilet paper
  o   tissues

These can all contain chlorine and emit dangerous dioxins. If you choose to use cotton tampons, make certain the cotton is organically grown, else they too can contain the toxic sprays used on the crops.

- Beauty treatments, including
  - hair colours
  - perms
  - acrylic nails
  - nail polish
  - nail polish removers.

  You can choose natural hair colourings as an alternative. These are readily available from most health food stores. Most of these use ingredients, such as henna, lemon, and chamomile.

- Household cleaning products, including
  - detergents
  - laundry products
  - window cleaners
  - oven cleaners

  There are now many environmentally aware companies that produce eco-friendly cleaning products you can use instead.

- Clothing (synthetic fabrics) including,
  - rayon
  - Lycra
  - spandex
  - nylon

  Cotton, linen, hemp, and wool are all natural fibres that are generally readily available. Be aware that chemicals may also have been using in their farming and production processes.

- Shoes
  - vinyl
  - synthetic fabrics
  - synthetic soles

Natural leather has traditionally been used for its durability and comfort properties; however, synthetic soles have better traction, which is more suitable for most sports.

- Furnishings
  - vinyl
  - synthetic fabrics. Leather and natural fabrics are generally readily available.

- Cars
  - vinyl
  - synthetic interiors
  - exhaust emissions

You can avoid this by getting leather seats, but the rest of the internal upholstery is often still artificial.

You can purchase a negative ioniser which plugs into the car cigarette lighter. This can dramatically help balance the positive ion emissions from the interior of cars. They are also available for use in houses, offices, and classrooms to help counteract synthetic furnishings. They give you a similar feeling to when you are in the fresh, negative-ion charged air at the beach.

- Food
  - artificial colourings
  - flavourings
  - preservatives
  - humectants
  - emulsifiers

Xenoestrogens accumulate in fat so foods from animals at the top of the food chain are more likely to contain large quantities. This means that meat from animals which eat contaminated food or water probably contains more xeonoestrogens than a plate of vegetables carrying residues of estrogenic pesticides.

Theories don't always translate into practice, so choose organic foods as much as possible and grow your own as much as you can.

- Food containers
  - plastic bottles
  - packaging
  - storage containers
  - liners of food cans and drink cartons

The higher the fat content of the food such as cheese, the more it will absorb the chemicals out of the plastic it is stored in. Hence, cheese wrapped in wax is probably better than cheese wrapped in plastic (even though I'm not an advocate for dairy).

Use glass and ceramic storage containers rather than plastic.

You can easily use dinner plates as lids for bowls rather than use plastic wrap.

- Plastic: Drs. Ana Soto and Carlos Sonnenschein discovered a link between plastics and breast cancer in 1992. They found the breast cancer cells they were working with were multiplying faster than they expected. Research showed that nonylphenol was leaching out of the plastic dishes they were using and affecting the cells. This is a xenoestrogen or oestrogen-mimicking chemical that is used to make plastics more flexible.
- Air pollution. If you live in a city and don't notice the dirty air anymore, use this as an indicator as to how much you've shut down in order to survive, because the pollution is there you just aren't sensing it anymore.

Transport now accounts for 50 per cent of oil use worldwide. Generally speaking, the more cars and industry you are surrounded by, the more air pollution you are being exposed to.

Oil pollutes when
  - we explore for it

- ○ when it is drilled
- ○ transported
- ○ spilt
- ○ refined
- ○ dumped

Notice what happens when a country person comes to the city. They cough and complain. You are breathing the same air they are, only you have gone into coping and denial so that you can focus on other things. Take a trip to the country and come back with new awareness.

This is not to say you can assume country air is necessarily pure either. Many insecticides and fertilizers used in farming are air borne and winds can carry them huge distances.

- Water pollution
  - ○ Heavy metals. Our waterways are now so polluted the fish even contain heavy metals and toxins, which we then absorb when we eat the fish.
  - ○ Chlorine: is often deliberately added to city water supplies along with an assortment of other substances.
  - ○ Fluoride is a waste product from aluminium smelting and is disposed of by being dumped into our water supplies. A large campaign has even been waged in an effort to convince us that it is good for us.

    The fluoride from industrial waste is not "nature identical" to the organic fluoride which is essential for healthy teeth and bones.

    Water filters that remove heavy metals, chemicals, and bacteria have virtually become a necessity in industrialized countries. If you haven't got one, perhaps it's time you did.

- Microwaves. Change the structure of the fats in what you are defrosting, heating, or cooking into the toxic version. In other words, it changes "cis" structured fats to "trans" structured fats. Don't eat them.

Use conventional heating sources.

Microwaves also burn the lines of energy in your aura (or more specifically, the master diamond blueprints for your physical body, emotions, and beliefs), which can cause psychological problems.

Can you see why it's so imperative to be vigilant with what you surround your body with and take into it?

It's becoming more and more important to detox your body, home, and work place than ever before. Do it thoroughly and regularly.

These chemicals store in your body, and unless you intentionally remove them, they will continue to accumulate and wreak havoc with your health and that of future generations.

Food and Phytoestrogens

Phyto means plant; hence, phytoestrogens are simply oestrogens that come from plants.

Phytoestrogens are still technically xenoestrogens because they mimic the functions of the oestrogens your body produces; however, unlike chemical xenoestrogens, they are easily degraded and can be very beneficial if you have either an excess or deficit of oestrogen.

- **When there's an excess,** the plant oestrogens bind to the receptor sites of your cells and take up the sites, preventing your stronger body-made oestrogens from taking effect.
- **When there's a deficit,** the plant oestrogens again bind to the lock and key receptor sites, providing a weak estrogenic effect. This is not as strong an effect as you get from your own body-made oestrogen, but it's better than no oestrogen at all.

Current theory is there's "good" and "bad" oestrogen.

The "good" oestrogen (2-hydroxyestrone) activates the oestrogen receptor only weakly.

The "bad" oestrogen (16-alpha-hydroxyestrone) strongly increases interaction of the receptor with growth-promoting genes, enhances breast-cell proliferation, and possibly damages DNA. Hence, it has been suggested the so-called bad oestrogen is linked to breast cancer.

Food Sources of Phytoestrogens
- soy products
- cabbage
- cauliflower
- brussels sprouts
- broccoli
- alfalfa
- pulses
- dark-green, leafy vegetables

Make certain you choose organic vegetables so they are pesticide free because as well as being excellent at providing you with phytoestrogens and other wonderful nutrients, they are also good at absorbing pesticides and insecticides when they are being grown.

Raw versus Cooked Food
Ideally, raw foods are better than cooked foods because a lot of nutrients can be lost in the cooking process. However, theory doesn't always match reality because many people have such depleted stomach, pancreas, and liver functions they don't have the ability to digest a totally raw diet of fresh wholesome foods any more.

If your body has good digestion, eat a large percentage of seasonal fresh raw fruits and vegetables. When you do cook, lightly steam them rather than boil them to a soggy death.

If you like to stir-fry, use good-quality cold pressed virgin oils with a high smoking point, so you get the maximum essential fatty acid content.

Olive oil is wonderful; however, it has a low smoking point so it isn't ideal for stir-frying at high temperatures.

Utensils
Don't cook in or with aluminium utensils, because they leach into your food and are a major problem with Alzheimer's disease.

Iron cookware is OK in small doses but can cause iron-overload osteoporosis when used extensively.

If your grandmother couldn't get it, don't eat it.

As a rule of thumb, the more hybridized, genetically modified, processed, refrigerated, and interfered with a food is, the less you should eat it.

Time has marched on and the era of our grandmothers may be different, but the intent is still there. Eliminate the manufactured, processed, and frozen and heat-treated items, such as cereals, cakes, biscuits, breads, sweets, candies, prepared meals, and fast foods. Eat local foods that are appropriate for you and your environment.

8

The Importance of Digestion

Clearly, good nutrition is important to your whole hormonal health. Without it, you cannot enter and reside in hormone heaven. You not only need to consume nutritious foods, you also need to be able to assimilate them efficiently within your body.

Many people have been so toxic for so long they have lost the ability to assimilate their food.

People who have worried excessively over time often burn out the cells that make hydrochloric acid in their stomach, making it difficult for them to digest proteins.

This shows up as
- slow digestion time
- constipation
- ridges, breaks and splits in the nails
- dry, rough skin

People who have low self-esteem and judge themselves harshly often deplete their digestive enzymes from their pancreas that are required to assimilate carbohydrates, proteins, and fats.

This shows up as
- indigestion cramps after eating
- large amounts of gas
- foul-smelling gas or stools
- frequent stools
- loose stools

- deficiency of required fats
- deficiency of fat-soluble vitamins (A, D, E, and K)
- diarrhoea
- fatty stools (ones that float)
- formation of toxins
- allergies
- bowel infections

The Pancreas Key

The pancreas is famous for its role in sugar metabolism and the manufacture of insulin; however, it also plays essential roles in protein, carbohydrate, and fat digestion.

The three main pancreatic enzymes are

1. lipase. Lipase works with bile from the liver to break down fat molecules so they can be absorbed and used by the body. A deficiency of lipase causes a deficiency of required fats and fat-soluble vitamins (A, D, E, and K).
2. protease. Protease breaks down proteins and helps keep the bowel free of parasites, such as bacteria, yeast, and protozoa. A deficiency of protease causes allergies and toxins from incomplete digestion.
3. amylase. Amylase is also found in saliva. It breaks down carbohydrates (starches) into sugars so they can be more easily absorbed by the body.

Pancreatic enzyme products are available in both over-the-counter and practitioner-only forms. Different brands are not identical. Price is sometimes a good indicator of quality. Best you ask a trusted health-care professional which brand is best for your situation.

The recommended dosage of pancreatic enzymes needs to be individualized for each person. As a rule of thumb, most people start by taking 8,000–12,000 lipase units with snacks and 16,000–36,000 units with meals. Naturally, start with the smallest dose necessary and then adjust accordingly.

And remember to resolve the emotional issues (self-judgement, criticism, shame, feeling not good enough) that have created the imbalance in your pancreas in the first place.

For Best Results,

- Take the enzymes at the beginning of the snack or meal. They usually don't work as well when forgotten or only taken at the end of the meal.
- Swallow the tablet or capsule whole with water at mealtime. Most will have an enteric coating on them so they can traverse through the stomach without getting broken down before they get to the small bowel, where they are needed to do their work. Hence, don't crush or chew the tablets.
- Don't eat dairy products. These foods have a higher pH, which can dissolve the enteric coating and destroy the enzyme activity before it reaches its destination.
- Don't hold them in your mouth, else they can cause irritation.
- Don't take at the same time as magnesium or calcium supplements, as these reduce their effectiveness.
- Use the enzymes prior to the expiry date because they lose their potency with age.

Enzymes from the Small Intestine

The three main enzymes from the small intestine are

- lactase (breaks down milk sugar)
- DPP IV (breaks down milk protein and other protein bonds)
- disaccharides (breaks down some carbohydrates and sugars)

Anything that interferes with the function of the small intestine may also interfere with the production and release of these enzymes. If you have leaky gut, inflammation, yeast overgrowth, or food sensitivities, you're also likely to have trouble digesting the foods these enzymes work on.

Whenever the gut lining becomes injured, these enzymes may not be readily available to digest your food. An injured gut often becomes "leaky," and this makes undigested food a problem. The malfunction of the bowel and disruption of digestion are often the problem rather than the food.

A common strategy is to remove all triggering foods from the diet. Typically, this means a gluten-free and casein-free diet (GFCF). However, when there is disruption to function, anything you eat becomes a problem because the new foods may be inadequately digested as well. This is why people who start GFCF end up taking out twenty-eight other foods as well. This is a strategy of the specific carbohydrate diet. This means removing all foods requiring these enzymes for a time, giving the gut a chance to heal, and then returning to eating those foods again.

This works well when people also eliminate the negative thought patterns and paradigms that set up the malfunction in the bowel to begin with. If this isn't changed, how can anything else change?

Another approach is to try to proactively heal the gut and support the system with digestive enzymes. Once the gut lining heals, your own digestive enzymes are produced again and the problematic foods aren't a problem anymore.

9

Food Cravings

When you crave something, it can be from a physical need or an emotional need.

Food is often used as anaesthetic for emotional pain, possibly stemming from it being used as a treat or reward when we were children. For example, if you were given sweets as a reward for doing well, then you may have a tendency in later life to eat sweets when you feel you aren't doing so well, in the desire to feel good again. Also, if you were given food to stop you crying if you were in pain or upset, you may have a tendency to eat when you're in pain or upset as an adult.

Often when people are stressed, they'll eat while they're working instead of taking breaks for meals. This can lead to eating more than necessary simply out of not realizing how much is being consumed. Lots of snacks can add up to much more than a few proper meals.

Stay conscientious when you eat. If you find yourself thinking about work or other things while you are eating, bring your focus back to the present.

If you are focused in the past or the future, you may find yourself not feeling satisfied with what you've eaten and therefore eat to excess or begin to snack later on.

Notice the difference between countries where food preparation is often considered a chore, such as Australia, England, and the United States, and countries where food preparation is a passion and an honour, such as France and Italy. Thankfully, Australia seems to be re-finding its passion for well-prepared nutritious and delicious food.

Generally speaking, native French and Italians in their own countries are healthier and slimmer than other Westerners. They even eat foods that many nutritionists have banned as health no-nos, yet they thrive on them.

They eat meat, wheat, and dairy; drink wine; and have far less heart disease and diabetes. They don't eat anything low fat or artificially sweetened. They take pride in their local produce and they have a great time with their cooking.

Clearly, there is more to nutrition than just the food.

The manner in which it is prepared and eaten plays an important role. Yet again we are being shown that what we believe about things influences the results we get.

The foundations of good eating remain true.

- Take your time.
- Enjoy your meal. Actually taste your food, and enjoy the company of the people you are sharing your meal with.
- Chew your food well. Your stomach doesn't have teeth, so the more chewing you do in your mouth, the easier it will be for your stomach.
- Don't eat to excess. Stop when you've had enough and totally eliminate unnecessary snacks.
- Don't drink to excess. There's a difference between a glass and a bottle of wine with your dinner.
- Don't consume large amounts of water with your meal. Water will dilute your digestive juices, so only have enough to moisten your food.
- In between meals, however, drink enough so you get your 33 ml per kilo of body weight per day.
- Don't eat when you're stressed. Eat when you're relaxed. If you think you would never get to eat because you are always stressed, then perhaps it is time to deal with the cause of your stress and emotional issues and became more diligent with your time management. Remember you are worth it. Meditation is probably the best place to start, even if it is simply learning to use your breath to help you relax.

- Eat a balanced diet. Current theory suggests a ratio of 40:30:30 is good for maintenance: 40 per cent carbohydrate, 30 per cent protein, and 30 per cent fats.
- It's just a theory. Discover what is best for you and eat accordingly.
- Eat seasonal local foods. It makes sense that foods which naturally grow in your local environment are the ones that are most appropriate for your current needs. If you travel a lot, you may find the local food helps you to adapt to your present circumstances. However, it may be the foods you are used to that help keep you grounded.
- Discover what is best for you and eat accordingly.
- Eat a variety of foods. There is such a plethora of recipe books and TV cooking shows available to prevent you getting stuck in the routine of just rotating your five or six easiest meals. If you've never been adventurous with foods, maybe this is an opportunity to start a new hobby and experiment. Make food preparation fun rather than a chore.

There can be a physical need underneath your food cravings.
When you crave
- sugar, it's likely you're deficient in protein or chromium or are simply overtired and need to sleep.
- chocolate, it's likely you're deficient in magnesium.
- salt, it's likely you're adrenally exhausted and need more sleep and stress management.
- ice, it's likely you're iron deficient or anaemic.
- peanuts, it's likely you're vitamin B6 deficient.

One thing always seems to lead to another, so the more you keep a simple approach, the easier it will be for you.

For example, high-carbohydrate consumption increases insulin, which increases androgens, which increases testosterone, which causes polycystic ovary syndrome (PCOS) and obesity, which causes insulin resistance, which causes carbohydrate cravings.

Hence, the keep-it-simple philosophy is: to break the cycle by not gorging on carbohydrates in the first place.

High insulin levels increase the theca cells in the ovaries and increase testosterone production. The keep-it-simple philosophy is to have flaxseed oil. This helps sex-hormone-binding globulin and therefore helps high androgens and PCOS.

Low serotonin levels also cause carbohydrates cravings. For example, 100 mg/day of vitamin B6 helps the production of both serotonin and GABA (gamma amino benzoic acid), which helps control depression, pain perception, and anxiety. However, only one-third of women with PMS can activate B6 in their liver.

High levels of estradiol can cause depression. It causes a relative deficiency of progesterone, which causes a reduction of corticotrophin-releasing hormone. When your hypothalamus doesn't secrete enough corticotrophin-releasing hormone, it upsets the pathway between your pituitary and adrenals and can cause depression, including seasonal depression, because it upsets your serotonin balance.

Oestrogen (as compared to estradiol) increases serotonin levels and makes you happy. The herb hypericum or St. John's wort also increases serotonin levels in your brain and makes you feel happy.

Happy is a good thing!

It's an intricate dance, isn't it?

Can you see the importance of having a foundation of a balanced and healthy lifestyle?

Rather than overindulging in the foods you crave, look beneath it and deal with the underlying issues.

Resolve the stress, unresolved emotional issues, and outdated beliefs.

Margo's Story

Margo loved chocolate. Margo also loved to look good. The two didn't seem to naturally support each other. The more chocolate she ate, the more weight she gained and the more headaches she endured.

By increasing her intake of leafy greens and taking a magnesium supplement daily, she lost her craving for chocolate. She dropped a couple of kilos through nothing else other than ditching the chocolate and its sneaky sugar content.

Now Margo loves magnesium and looking good. These two do naturally support each other.

10

Spinal Subluxations

When your body doesn't make enough progesterone, you will have relative oestrogen dominance and all the problems that go with it. It's a reasonable question to ask, "Why isn't my body making enough progesterone?"

A major cause of your body making insufficient progesterone is your brain not sending and receiving the correct messages from your body as to what its current requirements are.

A subluxation in your spine is when one or more of the spinal joints or vertebrae becomes out of alignment with the ones above or below. A subluxation occurs when your body is unable to adapt to stress or imbalance to the degree needed for equilibrium.

A subluxation in your cranium or pelvis is when the subtle movement of your sacrum (the triangular bone at the base of your spine) and the occiput (the bone at the back rear of your skull) are out of balance. This causes aberrations to the pumping of CSF (cerebro-spinal fluid) around the brain, spinal cord, and nerves. Any interference to your CSF flow can have far-reaching effects.

When you have subluxations or misalignments in your spinal vertebrae or cranial bones, they cause interference to your nerve system. Hence, the messages which are communicated by your nerves get distorted or even nullified.

Your skull or cranium is made up of a system of moveable bones. The vertebrae in your spine should be freely moveable. They are specifically designed to provide you with the ability to move and be flexible as well as housing and protecting the soft nervous tissue of your brain, spinal cord, and nerves.

When you have a subluxation of any of these bones, you will have problems because it tractions the protective coverings of your brain, the spinal cord, and nerves and upsets the communication links between your brain and the rest of your body.

Think of your spinal cord like a harp string. Is it flexible and healthy or stretched and tight?

You have twenty-four vertebrae in you spinal column.
- seven in your neck or cervical spine
- twelve in your thorax or thoracic spine
- five in your lower back or lumbar spine

The nerves that exit between your vertebra control different parts of your body just as the wiring in your house controls different parts of the house. Wiring is specific to whatever is at the end of the wires and nerves are specific to whatever is at the end of the nerves.

Just like the wires in your home, your nerves need to be fully functioning in order for what they supply to work properly.

For example, if you have a subluxation at L3 (misalignment of the third lumbar vertebra near the base of your spine), there'll be a problem with the nerves that exit at this level. This impedes the messages that are communicated along those nerves between your brain and your ovaries (between the brain and testes in males).

Subluxation at this level can cause your ovaries to malfunction and hence
- not make enough progesterone
- grow cysts
- not produce and release viable eggs causing infertility problems
- wither

If you have a subluxation at L5 (misalignment of your fifth lumbar vertebra near the base of your spine), you will have problems with your uterus (or prostate gland in males).

Subluxation at this level can cause
- light or heavy bleeding
- fibroids

- painful periods
- improper implantation of the foetus
- miscarriages

Subluxations can be caused

- **In Utero**
  There can be inappropriate cranial and skeletal moulding due to
  - compensating for torsion in the mother's pelvis
  - large baby in a mother's small pelvis

- **By Physical Trauma**
  When you have physical injuries, you will often get problems in other areas of your body as well. This is because when you compensate for damage, you put other regions under strain and then they have to adapt too.

Common physical causes of subluxations are

- birth
  - long labour
  - fast labour
  - caesarean delivery
  - breech delivery
  - forceps delivery
  - suction
- falls
  - off change tables
  - learning to walk
  - off bikes
  - off trampolines
  - off horses
  - out of bed
  - off the couch
  - down stairs

- o   up stairs
  (It's miraculous we even survive childhood!)
- posture
  - o   slouching
  - o   sitting in chairs that aren't a good ergonomic fit for you
  - o   sitting for extended periods (no indigenous person on the planet sits at all. they stand, squat, or lie down)
  - o   talking with the phone tucked on your shoulder
  - o   carrying things inappropriately
  - o   falling asleep on the couch
  - o   non-supportive mattress
- sports
  - o   injuries
  - o   using one side of the body more than the other
- accidents
  - o   car
  - o   misstepping off a curb
  - o   workplace injuries
- junk food
  - o   junk food (excess sugar, salt, and fats cause an overload in the nervous system and the vertebrae misalign to compensate)
- fashion
  - o   high shoes
  - o   carrying bags
  - o   carrying bags repetitively on the same side
  - o   tight clothing (especially tight neckties for men)

By Chemical Trauma

The chemicals and poisons you imbibe, inhale, or smear on your body affect every tissue and cell including your nerve system, organs, and muscles—and the effects can be cumulative.

Your body has a delicately balanced biochemistry. Anything that upsets this chemistry can upset muscle tone and cause subluxation.

Toxins can be in

- food

- air
- water
- prescription drugs
- recreational drugs
- pesticides
- preservatives
- colourings
- flavour enhancers
- cosmetics
- toiletries
- petrochemicals
- plastics
- synthetics
- furnishings

By Emotional Trauma

It's no secret that emotional changes create physical changes in your body. Reputed authors, such as Louise Hay and Candace Pert, have written extensively on this topic.

Emotional situations cause muscles to tighten then the muscle tension causes subluxation.

How does it feel across the back of your neck and shoulders right now? Is it totally relaxed, or is there tension?

What is it from?

- job stress
- family stress
- relationship issues
- financial concerns
- cultural differences
- commuting to work
- running late
- being too busy
- being overwhelmed
- fear of failure
- phobias
- guilt

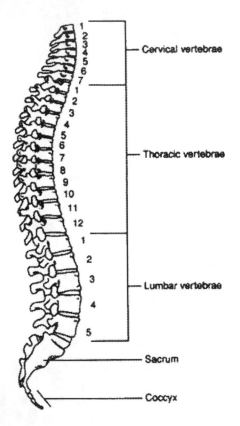

— Cervical vertebrae

— Thoracic vertebrae

— Lumbar vertebrae

— Sacrum

— Coccyx

**SIDE VIEW
OF THE SPINE**

- regret
- shame
- embarrassment
- responsibility

These causes are all widespread and very common. Is it any wonder people have so much trouble with their spines and the consequences of subluxations? The sooner the subluxations are corrected or adjusted, the sooner you can restore your equilibrium. This is why it's essential to have children aligned. Healthy, well-adjusted children have the potential to become healthy, well-adjusted adults.

It may help you to understand that there are specifics involved. In other words, your emotions specifically affect different areas of your body.

For example, when you are

- worried, confused, and don't feel good enough, you will create a subluxation at your *first cervical vertebra* and this will affect your eyes, ears, and brainstem (which is responsible for all your basic brain stem functions, such as breathing, appetite, and libido).
- indecisive, resentful, and blaming you will create a subluxation at your *second cervical vertebra,* and this will affect your eyes, ears, and tonsils.
- being a martyr and biting off more than you can chew will create a subluxation at your *third cervical vertebra,* and this will affect your face and teeth.
- feeling guilty, bitter, and bottling up your emotions, you will create a subluxation at your *fourth cervical vertebra,* and this will affect your diaphragm, breathing, and arms.

- overburdened and not expressing yourself, you will create a subluxation at your *fifth cervical vertebra,* and this will affect your vocal cords, neck glands, and arms.
- inflexible and resistant, you will create a subluxation at your *sixth cervical vertebra,* and this will affect your thyroid and arms.
- constantly worried, especially about the future, you will create a subluxation at your *seventh cervical vertebra,* and this too will affect your thyroid and arms.
- feeling bitter or unforgiving, you will create a subluxation at your *first and second thoracic vertebra,* and this will affect your heart and coronary arteries.
- grieving and feeling the loss of something or someone, sad or anguished, you will create a subluxation at your *third thoracic vertebra,* and this will affect your lungs.
- resentful, frustrated, stubborn, or indecisive, you will create a subluxation at your *fourth thoracic vertebra,* and this will affect your gall bladder and digestion of fats.
- overly sympathetic, obsessive, egotistical, or in despair, you will create a subluxation at your *fifth thoracic vertebra,* and this will affect your stomach and digestion.
- low self-esteem, living your life through others, feeling unsuccessful or ashamed, you will create a subluxation at your *sixth thoracic vertebra,* and this will affect your pancreas and blood sugar balance.
- low self-esteem, insincere and difficulties in your relationship with your mother or children, you will create a subluxation at your *seventh thoracic vertebra,* and this will affect your spleen and immune system.
- angry, irrational, and difficulty in your relationship with your father, you will create a subluxation at your *eighth thoracic vertebra,* and this will affect your liver.
- muddled or emotionally unstable, you will create a subluxation at your *ninth thoracic vertebra,* and this will affect your adrenal glands and ability to handle stress.

- feeling lost, vulnerable, insecure, or abandoned, you will create a subluxation at your *tenth thoracic vertebra,* and this will affect your small bowel.
- fearful or dreading, you will create a subluxation at your *eleventh or twelfth thoracic vertebra,* and this will affect your kidneys.
- feeling stuck, you will create a subluxation at your *first lumbar vertebra,* and this will affect your ileo-caecal valve and can even mimic appendicitis.
- holding back, you will create a subluxation at your *second lumbar vertebra,* and this will affect your caecum, which is the first part of your large bowel.
- hating yourself, you will create a subluxation at your *third lumbar vertebra,* and this will affect your ovaries (testes in males).
- dogmatic, defensive, or feeling powerless, you will create a subluxation at your *fourth lumbar vertebra,* and this will affect your large bowel.
- insecure and angry, you will create a subluxation at your *fifth lumbar vertebra,* and this will affect your uterus (prostate in males).

It's essential to maintain a flexible and strong spine to ensure the nerve system carries the correct messages to and from all your organs, muscles, and systems.

This is particularly vital for optimum hormone function.

Your local chiropractor can correct your subluxations; however, it's up to you to stop creating them.

How often do you need to be adjusted to correct your subluxations? It's as simple as the more you misalign yourself, the more you need to be realigned again.

If it takes two years of constantly wearing dental braces to realign teeth, is it really such a surprise to know you need regular adjustments to realign your spine?

Clearly, it is in your best interests to have your subluxations adjusted as soon as possible, because the longer they are left there, the more your nerve system is affected and the more long-term damage happens.

You can help yourself by rebalancing with such things as meditation, yoga, and tai chi. The more balanced you are, the less likely you'll be to keep creating subluxations repetitively.

It is a good idea to have children adjusted so the imbalances they create in childhood don't get a chance to manifest into diseases and difficulties later on. Plus just as your children look like you on the outside, they're a lot like you on the inside as well.

Cathie's Story

Cathie had never had a normal period. It was always exceptionally light, short, and with really dark blood. Her heavy-period girlfriends were jealous, but this didn't help Cathie's stagnation in anyway. The function of her body was sluggish, and so was she.

She had landed on her rear end when ice skating in high school, damaging her coccyx and lumbar 5 vertebra at the base of her spine. She fell again in a gym class as an adult and went to a chiropractor for the first time. After her adjustments, not only was her recent injury attended to but her period became normal. She didn't know chiropractors helped with such conditions, else she would have gone years earlier.

11

Post-Ganglionic Reflexes

Most people already know the brain and nerve system control and coordinate the functions of all the organs, tissues, and systems of the body. When there's no interference to the nerve system and its messages, there can be 100 per cent health—all of the organs, tissues, and systems working 100 per cent correctly 100 per cent of the time.

However, when there is interference to the nerve system, whether from subluxation (misalignment of a vertebra, cranial bone, or other osseous structure), toxic thoughts and beliefs, toxic emotions, permanent surgical change, chemicals, radiation, or the like, this causes malfunction and disease and can even lead to an untimely death.

There's nothing you can do about permanent surgical change but accept it and deal with the adaptations and consequences that result as best you can. However, there's a lot you can do to free yourself from toxic thoughts, beliefs, emotions, chemicals, radiation, etc. We've discussed some of these options already. You can also see a chiropractor regularly and have your spine adjusted to remove your subluxations and interference to your nerve system to help restore your health.

Most chiropractors work by removing interference to the spinal cord and spinal nerves by adjusting the corresponding spinal vertebrae. Many contemporary chiropractors also work by adjusting the cranial bones and removing interference to brain function.

This can be miraculous, especially with babies whose cranial bones aren't solidified yet. For example, if there's asymmetry of the cranium from birth, especially from forceps and other assisted deliveries, the sooner this can be skilfully remoulded, the better the brain function will be. Once the bones have solidified, they're more limited to adapting to "what they've got" rather than truly maximizing their potential.

Yet another group of chiropractors work with post-ganglionic reflexes to specifically affect the organs, organ functions, and organ systems.

Let's backtrack a little.

Your body has seven main ganglia (masses of nerve cells clumped together much like a lymph node): the ciliary, spheno-palatine, submandibular, otic, celiac, superior mesenteric, and inferior mesenteric. The ganglia provide relay points and intermediary connections between all the different nerve and neurological structures in your body.

The nerves that come from the spinal cord and go to the ganglia are called *pre-ganglionic*.

The nerves that go from the ganglia to the organs they affect are called *post-ganglionic*.

All chiropractors are trained to remove interference to pre-ganglionic nerves. This is chiropractic spinal adjusting 101. Many contemporary chiropractors do further training to extend their skills and remove interference to the post-ganglionic nerves as well.

What has this got to do with you?

I can't teach you how to do everything a chiropractor knows and does in the space of a few chapters—besides which, registration boards have been known to become very upset when people practise without a license—but I can show you the basics of a few post-ganglionic techniques which are specifically related to hormone function and balance.

This does not replace the need to have your spine adjusted and aligned to remove interference to the pre-ganglionic nerves; however, these are wonderful techniques you can integrate into your self-help regime with confidence. Much like you can't replace your dental fillings yourself but you can brush and floss at home each day, and it's highly recommended you do.

Post-Ganglionic Reflex for Your Right Ovary

You can use this technique in the comfort of your home to remove interference to the post-ganglionic nerves that connect to your right ovary.

- Lie comfortably on your back.
- Rest your *left hand* high on your *right shoulder* where your shoulder meets your neck.
- With your *right hand,* gently seek out the tender telltale reflex nodules on the *right* half of your pubic mound or pubic bone— either on the skin or through your clothing; it doesn't matter. There's likely to be a few and they are likely to be surprisingly tender.

  How can they be so tender and you not know they were there?

  If you didn't know to listen to the discomfort when they were originally set up, your brain soon dulls the messages down so you don't continuously feel pain. This is just like if you apply perfume. You smell it for a while and then you don't notice it anymore. It's still there, but the brain dulls the messages so you're not consciously bombarded all the time.

- Gently stimulate or massage the nodules on the right half of your pubic mound, one at a time, while still resting your left hand on your right shoulder where your shoulder meets your neck. Your left hand rests in place to complete a circuit. There are specific corresponding points in the trapezius muscle, but it's just overkill to go into those here.

  Be gentle. There's no need to make yourself sore.

- For best results, repeat daily. Definitely repeat whenever you're "hormonal."

  You can also use this technique regularly when you're not so hormonal, to prevent yourself getting hormonal in the first place.

Reflex for the right ovary.

Post-Ganglionic Reflex for Your Left Ovary

Simply swap sides and hands to use this technique to remove interference to the post-ganglionic nerves that connect to your left ovary.

- Lie comfortably on your back.
- Rest your *right hand* high on your *left shoulder* where your shoulder meets your neck.
- With your *left hand* gently seek out the tender telltale reflex nodules on the *left* half of your pubic mound or pubic bone—either on the skin or through your clothing; it doesn't matter. There's likely to be a few and they are likely to be surprisingly tender.
- Gently stimulate or massage these nodules one at a time (you want them to function better, but there's no need to make yourself sore) while still resting your right hand on your left shoulder where your shoulder meets the neck, to complete the circuit.
- For best results, repeat daily. Definitely repeat whenever you're "hormonal."
  Again, you can use this technique regularly even when you're not symptomatically hormonal to prevent getting so hormonal in the first place.

Reflex for the left ovary.

Post-Ganglionic Reflexes for Your Uterus

You can use this technique in the comfort of your home to remove interference to the post-ganglionic nerves that connect to your uterus.

- Lie comfortably on your back.
- Rest your *right hand* high on your *left shoulder* where your shoulder meets your neck.
- With your *left hand,* gently seek out the tender telltale reflex nodules on your *left ilio-inguinal ligament.* Either on the skin or through your clothing; it doesn't matter. This ligament goes *from* where your left hipbone sticks out at the front (the ASIS: anterior superior iliac spine) *to* your pubic bone. There's likely to be a few nodules and they're likely to be surprisingly tender.
- Gently stimulate or massage these nodules one at a time (you want them to function better, but there's no need to make yourself sore) while still resting your right hand on your left shoulder where your shoulder meets your neck to complete the circuit.
- *Repeat on the other side.*
  Even though you only have one uterus, it has nerves going to it from both the left and right sides of your spine so it is more thorough to *do this post-ganglionic reflex on both sides.*
  Simply swap sides and hands.

In other words, rest your left hand on your right shoulder where your shoulder meets the neck and use your right hand to gently stimulate the reflex nodules on the right ilio-inguinal ligament.

- For best results, repeat daily. Definitely repeat whenever you're "hormonal."
- Again, you can use this technique regularly even when you're not symptomatically hormonal to prevent getting so hormonal in the first place.

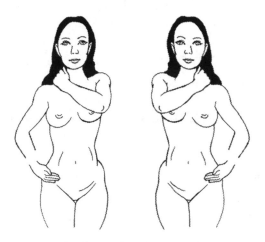

Reflexes for the uterus.

12

The Significance of Your Liver

The name of your liver gives you a clue as to its importance. *Live-r.* Simply put: with it, you live. And without it, you die.

Your liver is the number one hormone regulator in your body and the quality of how it functions largely determines the quality of your overall health. If you have hormonal imbalances, you can reasonably assume you also have issues with your liver.

The liver often contributes to hormonal problems in the first place. In other words, different organs are affected by different emotions and anger largely affects the liver. Hence, if you're angry a lot, it will affect your liver, which also affects the regulation of your hormones.

If your liver is overloaded or congested and can't detoxify your hormones fast enough, then you will have excess hormones circulating in your bloodstream and be constantly be out of balance.

The Caffeine Hit That Hurts You

What you may not realize is your liver metabolizes caffeine through what is known as the cytochrome 34–50 3A4 pathway. The problem is hormones and many other things, including drugs, are metabolized through this pathway as well, so when you consume caffeine, your liver will be busy detoxing this at the expense of being available to detox your hormones (i.e., removing the tired and surplus hormones from your circulation, which can cause oestrogen dominance).

Caffeine also upsets the conversion of oestrogens into their non-cancer causing forms by disrupting methyl donation.

Caffeine also increases homocysteine levels in the body, which leads to dementia and heart disease.

Liver Congestion

If you have an overloaded liver and then subject yourself to further toxins from the likes of alcohol, additives, preservatives, insecticides, and metabolic waste, you'll have an ever-increasing negative spiral.

You liver is situated under your right rib cage and if you feel any tenderness, discomfort, or swelling in that area, you've definitely got work to do.

How do you know if your liver is congested or not?

By the time blood tests show a positive result, there's already an extreme imbalance in place. You can learn to read the messages your body is communicating to you well before there's enough disease happening to show a positive blood test. Far better you turn things around well before this.

Symptoms of Liver Problems

- Hormone problems include
    - irregular periods
    - painful periods
    - absent periods
    - PMS
    - dysmenorrhoea
    - endometriosis
    - lumpy breasts
    - infertility
    - menopausal problems
- coated tongue

- brown saliva. If you drool on your pillow at night and it goes brown or your toothbrush bristles go brown, these are indicators of liver problems.
- brown circles under your eyes (compared to the black circles of kidney issues or food sensitivities)
- yellowish skin
- distressing pressure on top of your head
- pain between the shoulder blades that gets worse when you are stressed
- stiff muscles when you're resting. In other words, you need a warm-up to get started again
- body odour even when you bathe regularly
- fatigue
- headache and migraines
- food sensitivities and allergies
- superficial veins visible on the chest
- varicose veins and haemorrhoids
- chronic fatigue syndrome
- skin disorders
- bad breath
- bloating
- indigestion
- diarrhoea
- constipation
- angry disposition
- sensitivity to alcohol
- sensitivity to chemicals
- sensitive to life. In other words, a short fuse

Practitioner Tests for Liver Issues

Medical blood tests for liver function have limited sensitivity and often only show positive when there's actual liver damage. Best you pay attention to what your body communicates to you, because there can be quite significant problems long before medical tests show positive.

Many practitioners now use other tests, such as
- hair analysis
- saliva
- urine
- live blood
- stool testing

These tests can give comprehensive results and information about the state of your liver and many other organs and functions in your body.

Your liver has to detoxify the by-products of your regular body functions as well as the noxious things that are introduced into your body from the external environment, such as
- food additives including
    - colourings
    - flavourings
    - preservatives
    - humectants
    - emulsifiers
    - foods you are sensitive to
- water additives
    - chlorine
    - fertilizers
    - pesticides
    - industrial waste, such as inorganic fluoride
- air pollution
    - industrial emissions
    - car fumes
    - cigarettes
    - synthetic air fresheners
- prescription drugs
    - medications
    - general anaesthetics
    - immunisations
    - antibiotics
- recreational drugs

- o alcohol
- o cigarettes
- o drugs
• toiletries and cosmetics. Many toiletries and cosmetics contain a cocktail of toxic chemicals aimed at improving shelf life, sudsing, texture, and aesthetic appeal.
  - o shampoos
  - o conditioners
  - o soaps
  - o deodorants
  - o toothpaste
  - o make-up
  - o skin care
  - o sunscreens

In today's so-called civilized world, your liver is working overtime all the time. When you consider the contents of the products that many people use daily, is it any wonder there are rampant hormonal imbalances, immune system problems, behavioural problems, and cancers?

It is essential to cleanse your liver and the whole of your physical body regularly because there is a direct link between how toxic your physical body is and how toxic your emotions, thoughts and behaviours are, and vice versa.

Cleaning the negativity out of your mind will help you release the clog from your liver and bowel, and cleaning your liver and bowel will help release the obstructions from your mind and emotions.

Most things are connected so it often doesn't matter where you start as long as you do—and follow through until you get the results you desire. Then maintain it.

All aspects of your healing journey are important (physical, emotional, and mental) so you may find it easier if you address them all simultaneously so you support yourself in all areas of your life.

Do your meditations, forgiveness, and releasing exercises at the same time as you do your liver and bowel cleansing. This will help prevent you from sabotaging yourself and falling back into patterns that don't support you, that may well have caused your imbalances in the first place.

If you only focus on your physical cleansing without releasing the habitual faulty thoughts that made you toxic in the first place, you will naturally recreate the same congestion over again.

If you're trying to convince yourself it's OK to consume things you know aren't appropriate for you, stop immediately! This is an excellent time to do a meditation to integrate your unresolved aspects because self-sabotage stems from an unresolved memory or issue from the past. By integrating your aspects, you won't feel the need to sabotage yourself and hence deny yourself your well-deserved rewards.

Phase 1 and Phase 2 Liver Detoxification

When your liver is overloaded and doesn't detoxify as fast or thoroughly as you need, you get a build-up of toxins which continue to circulate through your body.

Eventually, the toxins are stored in your fat, including the fat in your brain and central nerve system—not just your thighs. Be aware: your brain is 60 per cent fat, so when you get toxic, your brain gets extra toxic. No wonder we get confused and distorted thoughts and indecisive when we are toxic.

And don't you just love cellulite? This is an easy and obvious indicator of your toxicity levels. Quite simply, the more cellulite you have, the more toxic you are.

It may help you to understand a little about how your liver works in order to get the most out of your self-help programs.

Your liver has two phases of detoxification.

1. **In phase 1** (oxidation), your body enzymes activate the toxins to make them more available for phase 2.

2. **In phase 2** (conjugation), other enzymes, such as from food, convert the toxins to a water-soluble state so you can excrete them through your bowels and kidneys.

It is essential for phase 2 to follow phase 1 because phase 1 oxidizes toxins like benzene (from petrochemicals and cigarettes), which can make them even more toxic.

Hence, it's essential for your liver's phase 2 detoxification to keep up with phase 1, else you've got big problems.

Phase 1 Liver Detoxification (Oxidation)

Most environmental toxins are fat soluble and hard to eliminate without the liver's help. In phase 1 detoxification, the liver makes the toxins more soluble in water so they can be excreted more easily via the kidneys in urine.

Individual medications can increase or decrease phase 1 activity.

Foods That Increase Phase 1 Liver Detoxification
- cruciferous vegetables (cabbage, broccoli, and brussels sprouts)
- oranges and tangerines
- caraway and dill seeds
- foods high in zinc (pumpkin seeds, oysters, beef, lamb, nuts). Zinc deficiency allows the formation of cancer-promoting chemicals.

Phase 2 Liver Detoxification (Conjugation)

In phase 2, the oxidized toxins from phase 1 combine (conjugate) with sulphur or amino acids so they can be excreted in the bile.

Phase 2 is inhibited by
- acetaminophen (Paracetamol or Tylenol)
- nutrition deficiencies. The most important amino acids required for phase 2 are cysteine and methionine, which are the main diet sources of sulphur. This comes from meat, fish, poultry, eggs, and dairy products.

- alcohol
- low protein intake. You need protein to be able to make glutathione from its three building blocks: cysteine, glycine, and glutamine.
  You need glutathione to detox Paracetamol or Tylenol.

Phase 2 helpers are
- bioflavonoids which come from fruits, vegetables (especially peppers, celery, carrots, and herbs) and tea
- the herb St. Mary's thistle or silymarin is high in bioflavonoids. A standard adult dose is 70–120 mg three times per day
- protein
- onions
- citrus fruits
- cruciferous vegetables (the cabbage and broccoli family)
- S-adenosinyl methionine (SAMEe)

Bleep On The Liver

Remember the importance of how your emotions affect your physical body?

As you know, different emotions have a propensity to affect different organs.

Anger in particular affects the liver. In order to stop making your liver emotionally toxic, you need to stop being and feeling angry. This means right now as well as stopping yourself recycling habitual angry responses to people and events from your past or projecting any current angry thoughts into the future.

If you continue to perpetuate angry feelings, it doesn't matter how many detox programs you go on or how much dandelion tea you drink; you will keep overloading your liver and maintaining your problems, including hormonal imbalances.

It is essential to attend to all levels of your physical, emotional, and mental being in order to have optimum health and balance.

It may sound like a challenge that's too hard, but the results of being true to you and doing what needs to be done to support yourself are worth it. As well as improved physical health, you will also grow emotionally and spiritually.

Support For Your Liver

There are simple and easy things you can do every day to help support your liver.

1. **Post-ganglionic reflex for your liver.**
   - Lie comfortably on your back.
   - Rest your *left hand* high on your *right shoulder* where your shoulder meets your neck.
   - With your *right hand,* seek out the tender nodule halfway between the top of your shoulder and your right nipple (the fourth rib space in line with the right nipple). Massage it gently either on the skin or through your clothing; it doesn't matter. Notice how this point gets even tenderer if you drink alcohol or expose yourself to things that congest your liver.
   - You can extend this by leaving your left hand on your right shoulder where your shoulder meets your neck (to maintain the circuit) and moving your right hand down to also gently massage your liver under your right rib cage.
   - For best results, repeat daily. Definitely repeat whenever you're "hormonal."

It's far better to repeat regularly when you're not so liverish or hormonal, to prevent yourself getting so hormonal in the first place.

You only have one liver, and it's on the right side of your body so you only need to do this reflex on your right side.

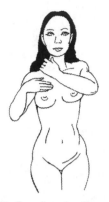

Reflex for the liver.

2. **Meditations:** forgiving and releasing exercises. These will release your stored anger and help you prevent perpetuating your anger from the past, the present, and into your future. This is essential for changing your habitual patterns, else you won't get the depth and long-lasting results you are hoping for.

3. **Stop exposure** to all the things that stress your liver, including alcohol, drugs, cigarettes, pollution, toxic food, chemical cosmetics and personal products, city water, bad attitudes, unnecessary medications, and so on.

4. **Spinal Adjustments.** If your mid-thoracic vertebrae (especially around thoracic eight region) are subluxated and interfering with the nerves from this level of your spinal cord, your liver will not function at its optimum and you will have to take an excess of vitamins, herbs, and minerals to maintain yourself. This is not healing; this is coping. Keeping this area of your spine mobile and your nerve system firing properly will enable your liver to repair itself and function as best it can.

5. **B vitamins** are essential for your liver, proper digestion, absorption of your food, and energy production. If your liver isn't working properly, you can get an accumulation of old hormones in your body. When your liver is working well, it deactivates these hormones and you pass them out of your body. B vitamins help carry out this process.

If this process isn't happening efficiently, you may not be getting enough B vitamins from your food or not absorbing them into your body. If you have congestion or inflammation in your small bowel, this will hinder vitamin B absorption. This inflammation can come from candida overgrowth, food sensitivities, or constant negative thinking or pessimism.

When you take vitamin B supplements, it's best to take a good-quality B complex which contains all the B vitamins in synergistic ratios rather than the individual vitamins, because if you have too much of one and not enough of another, you could be creating an imbalance rather than helping yourself.

What Depletes Your Vitamin B Levels?
- stress
- cigarettes
- alcohol
- excess exercise
- contraceptive pill
- pollution
- caffeine

This means if you are exposing yourself to any of these, you will need even more B vitamins than usual.

Symptoms of Vitamin B deficiency include
- anxiety (B1)
- poor memory (B1)
- depression (B1, 6)
- insulin resistance and diabetes (B1, 3, 6)
- tiredness (B3, 5)
- adrenal exhaustion (B5)
- hormone imbalance (B6)
- mood swings (B6)
- fluid retention (B6)
- irregular periods (B6, 12)
- acne (B6)

- infertility (B6)
- skin and hair problems (biotin)

Foods that are good sources of B vitamins are
- brewer's yeast
- wheat germ
- lean meat
- liver
- botanical royal jelly
- whole grains

It is best to work with a skilled practitioner to determine how much you should take and for how long; however, around 100 mg of B complex per day is a good foundation.

When you take vitamin B, your urine can go a nice bright yellow. Don't think that something is wrong; just keep drinking plenty of pure, fresh water.

If you aren't absorbing the B vitamins properly from your small bowel, taking organic green barley powder in water each day can help. This helps heal inflammation and is actually a good supplement to have in-between meals as a snack substitute that is therapeutic and satisfying.

As always, you need to look at why you aren't absorbing the vitamins properly in the first place. Are you stressed? Do you have food sensitivity? Are you drinking too much alcohol? Are you not absorbing and resolving your life lessons?

Contra-indications

If something is contra-indicated, it means it's recommended you don't do it or use it. In other words, there are probably risks or undesirable consequences associated with it. It's important to remember that just as a deficiency of a nutrient can cause problems, so too can excesses.

Taking supplements is a therapy and is not a substitute for a well-balanced diet and lifestyle.

There are components in B complex that have the potential to interact with some drugs, and if you take extremely high doses of B6 (more than 2,000 mg/day) for a long time, you can develop problems with your nerves. Number one, it would be silly to take such high doses. And number two, it would be unnecessarily expensive for no reasonable gain.

6. **Vitamin C and bioflavonoids** are often present in fruits and vegetables together. The bioflavonoids enhance the action of vitamin C and vitamin C is required for
   - bile production
   - liver detoxification
   - immunity
   - collagen production
   - wound healing
   - preventing the release of histamine
   - reducing inflammation

When you don't have enough vitamin C, your LDL cholesterol (low-density lipoprotein) gets damaged, which leads to atherosclerosis and heart disease.

Symptoms of Vitamin C deficiency include
- bruising easily
- bleeding gums: take note when you brush and floss your teeth
- colds and infections
- acne
- insulin resistance
- diabetes
- cataracts
- hair loss
- irregular or absent periods
- mood swings
- heavy metal toxicity
- obesity
- sleep problems

Foods that are good sources of vitamin C are
- Fresh fruit
- Fresh vegetables

You will get loose bowels if you have too much vitamin C, so the rule of thumb is to take 1,000–3,000 mg per day, spread throughout the day rather than in a single dose. If you get diarrhoea from this program, back off the dosage until you don't.

Be aware vitamin C can sometimes give false positives in urine tests for glucose.

Many "off the shelf" preparations have artificial sweeteners in them to make them taste better, but this adds to the toxicity. If you like it to be sweet and palatable, get a supplement that is sweetened naturally with something like the herb stevia.

7. **Vitamin E** (alpha tocopherol) is a fat-soluble antioxidant that protects your cell membranes and LDL (low-density lipoprotein) from damage. LDL is also known as "bad cholesterol" so vitamin E is essential for helping prevent it from causing heart disease, as does vitamin C.

Vitamin E works in conjunction with selenium to protect all cell membranes so sufficient levels are essential to maintain whole body health. It also
- reduces blood clotting
- reduces scars
- helps wounds to heal
- helps protect you from environmental pollutants
- assists the metabolism of fats

Even if you are doing something beneficial like taking flaxseed or fish oils, if you don't take vitamin E with it, they will go rancid in your body. This means more degeneration and more cellulite.

Taking vitamin E will make a huge difference to breast tenderness and cellulite. The more fatty foods you eat, the more cellulite and breast tenderness you will have. This correlates to the more fatty foods you eat, the more vitamin E you will need. Fatty foods means the likes of chocolate, cream, cheese, and chips, not the good oils, such as olive, salmon, and flax.

Symptoms of vitamin E deficiency are
- breast tenderness
- cellulite
- slow wound healing
- excess scar formation
- atherosclerosis and heart disease
- circulation problems

Foods that are good sources of vitamin E are
- wheat germ
- nuts
- seeds
- cold pressed vegetable oils (processing and bleaching of oils destroy the vitamin e)
- whole grains
- egg yolks
- leafy green vegetables

How much vitamin E you need to take depends on how toxic you are. A therapeutic dose is 500 to 1,000 IU daily. Start with a lower dose and build up.

Natural vitamin E has a *d* in front of it like d-alpha-tocopherol. This is the most potent or bio-available form.

Synthetic vitamin E will have *dl* in front of it.

A blend of alpha, beta, gamma, and delta tocopherols will give you far better results than one by itself and this is how it exists in foods. If you have a tendency to not absorb nutrients well, get a water-soluble product.

Contra-indications

Vitamin E can upset people who take anticoagulant drugs, such as warfarin, so it's essential to consult your health-care practitioner before adding this into your regime.

8. **Selenium** is a mineral that works with vitamin E. It is needed to
   - activate your thyroid hormones
   - stimulate your white blood cells

- prevent cancer. it has been shown to reduce the risk of breast cancer.
- play a vital role in your detoxification pathways

Selenium is known to be deficient in soils in Australian, New Zealand, and China, so even if you are eating well, you may not be getting enough. Rather than taking so many supplements that you haven't got room for breakfast, you may want to get a good combination that has the relevant ingredients in a synergistic ratio for your body.

Foods that are good sources of selenium are
- Brazil nuts
- yeast
- seafood
- meat and organ meats
- whole grains

This is as long as they were grown in regions where the selenium content in the soil or growing environment is high.

Be especially mindful to take selenium if you have abnormal Pap smears or low thyroid function, unless the thyroid problem is caused by an iodine deficiency.

Therapeutic doses are 200 to 600 mcg per day.

Contra-indications

Don't exceed 1,000 mcg per day and don't give it to children under fifteen years.

9. **Essential Fatty Acids (EFAs).** "Essential" means you have to supply it from your diet because your body doesn't make it.
EFAs are fundamental for healthy hormone function and are needed by every cell in the body. The two main types are omega-3 and omega-6. EPA and DHA are omega-3s, and GLA is omega-6.

They help with
- acne
- appetite control and food cravings

- ADD
- breast tenderness
- depression
- fatigue
- fluid retention
- hair loss
- nails
- hormone balance
- infertility
- inflammation and joint pains
- insulin resistance
- mood swings
- obesity
- sugar balance and diabetes

There is some debate about it, but some biochemists say you need to have omega-3 and omega-6 in a 1:4 ratio because the omega-3's have a four times more effective enzyme system which converts them to prostaglandins. Others say to ignore this and eat as much fish as you want. Always use your own common sense and eat a simple balanced diet because theories will come and go and it's the practical results you need rather than an elaborate theory.

Just because you eat, it doesn't mean your body can use it. If your digestive system is below par, often from years of worry and stress, you may not digest your food properly and assimilate its contents well. If you don't digest protein well, you can take a betaine hydrochloride supplement with your meal and make sure you are relaxed when you eat and chew your food. Betaine hydrochloride is a supplement which helps your body to do what your stomach acid should be doing.

Remember your stomach doesn't have teeth so you need to chew with your mouth. Indicators that you aren't digesting protein well are

- a need to take excess EFA supplements to get a minimal result
- Protein "sits in your stomach" and takes a long time to digest.
- your fingernails keep splitting and chipping

Foods that are good sources of omega-3 EFAs are:
- cold-water fish
- salmon
- tuna
- mackerel
- sardines
- herring
- anchovies

Most of today's oceans contain pollutants like pesticides, herbicides, and heavy metals; therefore, purification of fish oils for supplements is essential. They can be detoxified by molecular distillation. Eating the fish also makes you susceptible to these pollutanso you can see the dilemma from polluting our planet and the increased need for regular detoxing.

- Flaxseed (linseed) oil contains omega-3 ALA, which is converted into EPA. Therefore, this is a particularly good substitute for people who really don't like to eat fish. The only thing is you need a lot more of it to be equivalent to fish oil and it tastes disgusting. However, disgusting taste is better than disgusting health so hold your nose and swallow it if you need it.

  Immediately biting into a piece of fruit after consumption can take the edge off the "unusual" taste.

  You'll get well fast just so you never have to taste it again.

  7.2 g of flax oil is equivalent to 1 g of fish oil. Flaxseed oil helps sex-binding globulin and therefore helps high androgen levels and polycystic ovaries. Remember to take vitamin E with this as well to prevent it going rancid in your body.

  You cannot cook with flaxseed oil because this too will make it go rancid.

  You can pour it over your salads.

  Here's the thing: it works. I find most people have amazing results when they take flaxseed oil regularly. Their moods improve, cholesterol goes down, and cramps ease.

  If it has a tendency to go straight through you take digestive enzymes at the same time.

Do not use the linseed oil that is for oiling wood under any circumstances. It is not food grade and is not fit for human consumption.

Plant-based foods that are good sources of Omega-3 EFAs are:
- hemp seeds
- pumpkin seeds
- walnuts

Foods that are good sources of omega-6 EFAs are:
- evening primrose oil
- nuts
- seeds
- legumes
- vegetable oils (olive, sunflower, sesame, peanut, coconut)

Symptoms of EFA deficiency
- dry skin and hair
- excess wax in your ears
- menstrual pain and cramps
- fatigue
- depression
- mood swings
- insulin resistance
- high cholesterol and atherosclerosis
- learning and concentration problems
- ADD

Without enough omega-3 (EPA and DHA) and omega-6 (GLA) fatty acids, you cannot make enough ovarian and stress hormones and this will affect your cycle. Be aware that your innate hormonal cycle is present your entire life regardless of whether you are menstruating or not. It is your natural connection with the earth and the moon. This is why a natural cycle matches the lunar cycle of twenty-eight to twenty-nine days. Hence, it is important to maintain good life style habits your whole life, not just when you are menstrually evident.

The two types of EFAs are not interchangeable so you need to eat a supply of both. If you're taking EFAs as a supplement, it is best to take vitamin E with them, else they will go rancid in your body.

Dosage

If you are taking an omega-3 or fish oil supplement, choose one that has been detoxified by molecular distillation to remove any heavy metals and contains vitamin E.

1–2 g per day is a substantial dose.

10. **St. Mary's Thistle** (Silybum marianum, silymarin, or milk thistle)

When I recommended a patient take St. Mary's thistle to cleanse and support her liver, she promptly answered, "Oh! I used to take that years ago before a big night out. If I took St. Mary's thistle, I didn't get hangovers." Apparently, even university students know the benefits of St. Mary's thistle on the liver.

Taking St. Mary's thistle will help your liver to detoxify your excess hormones faster (as well as alcohol on big nights out). By removing excess oestrogen in particular, it often alleviates many hormonal problems.

Benefits
  • more powerful as an antioxidant than vitamin e
  • prevents toxic and foreign substances from entering liver cells
  • stimulates protein synthesis so that new liver cells can grow and damaged liver cells can be replaced

Helps with
  • hot flushes
  • hormone imbalances
  • skin problems
  • hangovers
  • detoxing
  • liver problems
  • gall bladder problems
  • fatigue

Dosage

It is poorly absorbed so you need to take a lot, even 1,000–3,000 mg with meals per day.

11. **Green Tea** (Camellia sinensis)

Besides the therapeutic benefits, I'm a fan of green tea because you can drink it all day without tiring of it. Especially if you have a tendency to keep snacking, have a cup of green tea to help you not give in to temptation.

One of my brothers used to refuse to drink green tea because it made his sweat stink. I pointed out that this was wonderful because his body was now removing these toxins rather than storing them inside. I think after his initial alarm he got the idea it was good.

Green tea is not fermented whereas black tea is. Therefore, it is especially good for people with candida overgrowth problems who need to avoid fermented products.

Green tea helps with
  * digestion
  * liver disease including fatty liver
  * It contains antioxidants which help the liver as well as all cells in your body.
  * gas
  * eyesight
  * regulates body temperature
  * diarrhoea: the longer you brew the tea, the more tannins it will contain and the more effective it will be.
  * atherosclerosis and heart disease

Drink one to three cups of green tea a day.
More than five cups per day can give you
  * too much caffeine and the side effects that go with that, such as restlessness, insomnia, and anxiety
  * reduce iron absorption
  * decrease the effectiveness of warfarin

12. **Globe Artichoke.** Artichokes help with
- stimulating bile flow—so they are especially good to eat with high fat meals. Perhaps it is better you don't eat such high fat meals to begin with though?
- lowering your blood fat
- lowering your cholesterol
- protecting your liver from toxic damage
- bloating
- constipation

A standard dosage is up to 500 mg three times per day, but you may prefer to eat the artichokes as delicious antipasto.

13. **Dandelion Root**
- stimulates your liver to make bile
- is a mild diuretic so it also helps ease fluid imbalances which upset your cells, kidneys, and brain
- helps your hormones by supporting your liver and digestion
- is a mild laxative which helps move waste through your bowel, which in turn also improves the appearance of your skin

Many people use dandelion root as a coffee substitute to help wean them off caffeine addictions. Use two teaspoons of dried root per cup of boiling water. It takes about five to ten minutes to steep and tastes fine, as long as you're not expecting it to taste like coffee.

14. **Nettle Tea** is a well-known liver cleanser and also helps to keep bowel movements regular. It actually tastes better than you might think and it gives a bit of a "pick me up." You can easily drink a few cups daily including as a cold tea.

Helen's Story

Helen liked a nice drop of red at the end of the day. She was a giver and she worked hard. A glass or two of Shiraz was a simple pleasure and reward for good deeds done. Over time, a glass or two expanded into the best part of a bottle or sometimes two.

Helen became hormonal, tired, grumpy, and not her previous sociable self. A discerning practitioner helped her trade red for green tea and gave her herbs to decongest her liver. It took some months, but it was all worth it to get her bright flame glowing back in the world again.

13

How to Recover From Adrenal Exhaustion

Most hormonal females seem to get exhausted, and rather than rearrange their schedule and get some extra rest, they often
- drag themselves around, forcing themselves to keep going, or
- consume sugary or caffeinated products to get a quick-fix burst of energy so they can complete their tasks.

There's often a "soldier on at all costs" mentality.

Neither of these approaches is very useful in the long term because they lead to burnout and insulin resistance, as well as the other underlying hormonal imbalances.

The premise that "if you work hard, you must be a good person" is flawed. Perhaps it's time to work smarter, not harder?

If you're burning yourself out being superwoman—the daughter, friend, mother, lover, worker, committee member, and achiever of other people's goals—when do you think it'll be a good time to stop?

If you're emotionally and mentally exhausted and taking it out on your immediate family while keeping a smiling public face on, when do you think it's a good time to stop?

The type of person most prone to adrenal fatigue is the people pleaser, the yes person—the person who wants to please everyone even if it's at their own expense.

Do you habitually put everyone else first?

It's common for women have strong and restrictive beliefs about what it is to be a "good" mother, wife, or partner. Many mothers live in total disregard of their own desires and put their children and husbands first. They look to be a good mother, wife, etc. but give their power and lives away to this paradigm. If women responded from their own inner impulses and what their bodies told them, they wouldn't give their power away to an external belief telling them how to act.

Men can also give their power away to ideals and beliefs. Society has taught them what it is to be a "good" husband and father. Often they put being a good provider and protector (spending long hours doing something they don't necessarily enjoy) ahead of their own dreams and desires. They'll often put a mask on their face and hide any signs of vulnerability or fragility because that is "not how men are supposed to act."

We give our power away to try to gain acceptance and recognition from others. We want others to like us and love us from a place of neediness. Whenever we look to someone else to "fill us up" with the love we don't give ourselves, it sets us up to give our power away. When we're self-loving and reconnected to the innate love inside ourselves, there's no need not seek it outside from someone else.

The more we ditch old patterns of self-abuse, self-criticism, self-indulgence, disregard, and lovelessness, the sooner we turn adrenal exhaustion and disease around.

If you are stressed and unhappy, you are probably low in dopamine, which is the precursor to adrenalin. This means you won't have enough adrenalin and you will feel tired. More than likely, you won't feel excited by life anymore, which leads to your enthusiasm dwindling even further.

It's like a perpetuating downward spiral that's imperative to break.

Reorganising your priorities and exercising regularly are two essential places to start. If you haven't got the energy or enthusiasm to exercise, then take Vitex and 5HTP to give yourself a kick-start, then the exercise itself will improve your moods.

Exercise increases 5-adenosine monophosphate and takes glucose into cells independent of insulin and therefore also helps insulin resistance.

Your adrenal glands might be small, but they are incredibly important. You have two which sit on the top of each of your kidneys; hence, they are also known as supra-renal glands. In other words, they are above the renal glands or above the kidney glands. They are made up of two parts: the medulla, which is inside, and the cortex, which is around the outside, similar to the arrangement of your brain.

Adrenal Medulla

Your adrenal medulla is responsible for making adrenalin (and noradrenaline) which responds to stress by raising your

- heart rate
- blood pressure
- blood sugar

Adrenal Cortex

Your adrenal cortex produces other steroid hormones that are necessary for your fluid and electrolyte (salt) balance, such as cortisone, aldosterone, DHEA, and the sex hormones testosterone and oestrogen.

However, the two main players with adrenal exhaustion are DHEA and cortisol. These two hormones are continuously secreted in response to long-term chronic stress.

- Cortisol

The normal adrenal glands of a healthy person make about 20 mg of cortisol each day. This can skyrocket to 200 mg a day in times of stress.

During the early stages of adrenal stress, cortisol levels are high, which can increase obesity, cholesterol, blood pressure, and osteoporosis; alter brain chemistry, causing depression and anxiety; cause insulin resistance; and disrupt thyroid hormone metabolism.

In late stages, cortisol levels drop too low to function properly. In other words, too much or too little of anything can cause disease.

- DHEA

An average healthy woman makes about 20 mg of DHEA a day (30 mg for men); however, this can plummet in times of stress. DHEA helps your immune system and prevents atherosclerosis; however, its main influence is when it is converted into oestrogens and testosterone.

If DHEA levels drop, a hormonal cascade can result with a deficiency of other sex hormones, such as oestrogen, progesterone, and testosterone. If these hormones drop, PMS, menopause, andropause, and hypothyroidism come into play.

In times of stress when adrenal function decreases, the thyroid responds by making more thyroid hormones to compensate for the underactive adrenals. This is where you get the "tired yet wired" feeling. Normally, the adrenal and thyroid glands work together, making their corresponding hormones to control and maintain metabolism and energy levels. As time goes by, the thyroid eventually burns out, making less thyroid hormones causing hypothyroidism. This exacerbates adrenal symptoms even further.

The purpose of your adrenals is to maintain

- salt levels in your blood
- blood pressure
- help control kidney function
- control overall fluid concentrations in your body

When you have been stressed for a long time, you can exhaust your adrenals just like you can exhaust any other part of you. This can be from physical, emotional, or environmental stress.

When this occurs, too much cortisol is produced, which can also trigger the production of testosterone, which amongst other things can lead to problems with aggression.

Testosterone is also the precursor to estradiol, which can then add to oestrogen dominance problems.

Both testosterone and estradiol can cause depression in women. The response is different in men.

As you can see, everything affects everything else.

When it is said that balance is important, it is really important. Your mental, emotional, and physical well-being depend on it, and it determines whether you live in hormone heaven or hormone hell.

Common symptoms of adrenal exhaustion
- fatigue, lethargy, exhaustion
- constant emotional problems
- depression
- increased susceptibility to infections, chronic sore throat, or other infections
- hypoglycaemia (low blood sugar levels)
- sugar cravings
- salt cravings
- muscle weakness, exercise intolerance
- headache, brain fog, memory loss, depression, inability to cope
- increased effort to do everyday tasks
- allergies
- food sensitivities
- dark circles under the eyes
- eyesight problems
- trouble sleeping
- trouble getting out of bed
- decreased ability to handle stress
- skin problems, such as rashes and eczema
- weight gain
- inability to lose weight
- low body temperature
- lightheaded when standing up
- low libido
- PMS and other menstrual problems
- difficult menopause transition
- arthritic type pains
- lowered immunity and propensity to colds and flu

If you are a workaholic or stressaholic, you are unwittingly pushing your adrenals to the max and exaggerating any pre-existing imbalances.

This virtually means that every time you get overtired, you will get hormonal, and you may find yourself getting tired more and more easily.

Stop falling into the trap of the apparent quick fixes, such as consuming more sugar and caffeine, to keep you going. You and your ongoing health and well-being are far more important than your real or imagined deadlines.

Have you noticed that when you get tired and stressed your vision drops? If your eyesight is sometimes better than at othertimes take note, because it can be an important clue for you. If you are feeling tired or stressed and are having trouble reading without moving the page to find a point where you can focus on the words, this is your body telling you your adrenals are under too much stress.

As well as problems with your eyesight, you may even get flare-ups with your skin. This is another clear sign you're exhausting your adrenals.

It's imperative you listen to your body, else you will exhaust yourself even further and risk developing even more imbalances in the long term, such as diabetes. Take the time to stop, rest, meditate, and rethink what you're doing, why you're doing it, and how you're doing it.

Do you need to change what you're doing?

Do you need to change how you are doing it?

Do you need to change who you're doing it with?

Do you need to change how long you're doing it?

Do you need to give it a miss altogether?

As always, what you eat is important too. Adrenaline and noradrenalin are both derived from the amino acid tyrosine which you get from protein. Hence, if you're not eating enough protein regularly, you won't have the building blocks for adrenalin which will make you feel exhausted and perpetuate a largely unnecessary spiral.

How much protein is enough?

As a rule of thumb, you need protein the size of the palm of your hand with each meal. In other words, three of your own palm sizes of protein per day.

What causes adrenal exhaustion?

An easier question might be this: what doesn't cause adrenal exhaustion?

An excess of anything stressful or stress over a prolonged period can lead to adrenal exhaustion.

1. **Physical Causes**
   - spinal misalignment
   - disease
   - excess exercise and overtraining
   - not enough exercise
   - excess sugar
   - junk food
   - dehydration
   - caffeine
   - alcoholism
   - drugs
   - over medication
   - high-heeled shoes
   - long-distance travelling
   - crossing time zones
   - shift work
   - over weight
   - inadequate nutrition
   - heavy metals
   - bacteria or virii overgrowth

2. **Emotional Causes**

Doing things you know aren't good for you, such as consuming inappropriate foods and drinks, taking drugs, smoking, staying up late, ignoring your need to rest and relax, and giving you power away to other people or high ideals energetically causes more stress and depletes your adrenals.

If you say yes and you don't want to do it, you're giving your power away to the other person.

When you do anything you know isn't your truth, you're giving your power away. For example, sacrificing yourself to be a good parent, provider, boss, employee, lover, friend, volunteer, neighbour eventually harms you and the relationship.

This kind of disregard for self leads to biochemical and emotional imbalances as your body tries to homeostatically compensate for your compromise or sacrifice.

- workaholism
- unemployment
- relationship difficulties
- learning difficulties
- fear
- worry
- anxiety
- anger
- lust
- deadlines
- negative thinking

3. **Environmental Causes**
   - electromagnetic fields
   - electrical fields
   - microwaves
   - constant bombardment of city life
   - noise
   - petrochemicals
   - food additives
   - air pollution
   - water pollution
   - plastics

I think it is quite reasonable to add such things as full ironing baskets, phone bills, young children, sick children, aging parents, sick parents, sick anybody, and too much to do in too little time.

All of these circumstances are opportunities to make better decisions about how you run your life.

The Three Stages of Adrenal Exhaustion

Stage 1

The first stage of adrenal exhaustion is called hyper-adrenalism. It typically exhibits abnormally low levels of DHEA and high levels of cortisol.

Typical symptoms of high cortisol are
- poor sleep
- sugar cravings
- glucose intolerance
- confusion
- weight gain
- hot flushes
- fluid retention
- muscle loss
- decrease in serotonin levels which can cause depression
- decrease in melatonin levels which can cause insomnia
- suppression of your immune system which can then result in frequent infections and illness
- inhibition of the metabolism of T4 (a thyroid pro-hormone) into its active T3 form. This can create the thyroid hormone imbalance known as "Reverse T3 Dominance." This can further add to adrenal symptoms.

Stage 2

In stage two, DHEA levels stay low and cortisol levels move in the low to normal range, leaving you feeling tired and stressed but able to function.

Stage 3

During stage 3 adrenal exhaustion, cortisol eventually falls to levels too low (just like DHEA) to adequately maintain normal biochemical function. Hence, it's really important that cortisol levels are maintained at an optimal level for normal function. In other words, if levels are either too high or too low, they both cause problems.

HPA Axis (Hypothalamic Pituitary Adrenal Axis)

The HPA axis gets a lot of airplay when adrenal fatigue is mentioned. Basically, it's a complex feedback mechanism between the hypothalamus in the brain, the pituitary gland, and the adrenal glands with the job of responding to stress and regulating body functions as best it can during the time of stress.

The interactions of this feedback loop influence everything from blood pressure, digestion, immunity, mood, emotional sensitivity, sexual response, and fat storage and mobilization.

Worry and stress activate both the sympathetic nervous system and the modulating systems of the HPA axis. The hypothalamus secretes corticotropin-releasing hormone (CRH) which causes the release of adrenocorticotropic hormone (ACTH) from the pituitary gland into the bloodstream, which stimulates the secretion of cortisol and other glucocorticoids from the adrenal glands. This cascade of events is called the HPA axis.

When you're under constant stress, the adrenals become exhausted and the sympathetic nervous system stays overstimulated; hence, anxiety, insomnia, inability to relax, nervousness, and racy mind get worse. A constantly stimulated sympathetic nervous system decreases the production of digestive juices and gut motility which is what causes the digestive and gut problems that go along with this cycle.

Testing for Adrenal Fatigue

There are blood, saliva, and urine tests that can be done to test the level of adrenal fatigue.

Typically, saliva testing is done four times during the day to measure DHEA and cortisol levels, or alternatively blood test for DHEA and a twenty-four-hour urine test for cortisol.

Thyroid function, heavy metal, food allergy, and parasite testing are often done at the same time to get a more global idea of what's going on.

The thing is you already know what's going on! You know what is stressing you and why.

Regardless of test results, you need to decide to resolve the cause of your stress and your response to it. Otherwise, it doesn't matter what is tested and how many supplements you take; the feedback loop has to perpetuate.

Resolve Adrenal Exhaustion

What can you do about it?

Obviously, you need to stop doing the things that are causing the problem in the first place. This is essential, else you are just going to go around in circles and end up frustrated that all your other good efforts and intentions aren't working.

It's insane to keep doing the same things over and over and expecting a different result.

If nothing has changed, then you need to.

You can see the best practitioners; take the highest quality herbs, vitamins, and minerals; get regular adjustments and massages and the like; but if you're still working or worrying as if it's an Olympic event, then nothing substantial is going to change. Nothing substantial can change under these conditions. This can be an expensive, drawn-out, and difficult lesson, but eventually you'll get it.

Stop Being a People Pleaser

It's essential to change how you run your life. Walk it instead of running it. This is the principle of the hare and the tortoise story—it's the tortoise that wins.

Treating the symptoms of your life will only hold them at bay to greater or lesser degrees. For the symptoms to go away and never come back, you have to stop doing what is causing them.

If your life isn't balanced, then you won't be balanced.

Stop being a people pleaser! Practise saying no!

In order to truly resolve adrenal exhaustion, it's essential to stop giving your power away to others and your ideals and beliefs. Until you do this, you cannot get well and risk getting even worse than you already are.

Live your life according to your truth and by how you feel rather than by what you've been taught to believe and what is expected of you.

Stop being in disregard of yourself. Do everything you can to build yourself acceptance, self-love, and esteem. From this point on, be more self-loving and stop doing the things you know are bad for you.

Meditate

Most people have all the trouble in the world when they first begin to meditate. They can't sit still, get the fidgets, and constantly think things over in their head. At worst, they can even have arguments in their head, even about the fact they're trying to meditate and can't. Instead of relaxing, they beat themselves up that they can't relax.

Some even find friends who have the same difficulty to help justify their lack of progress.

Then one day, someone in the group will break free and get it. Someone will master their mind rather than allowing it to master them and then everything changes. If one can, everyone can.

It's not a case of if you can meditate, it's a case of how. Find the ways that suit you the best and the easiest.

I recommend you experiment safely. By safely, I mean do meditations that use positive words that are aligned and work within the universal white light. Go by the feeling. If doing the meditation gives you a good feeling, then keep doing it. If doing the meditation gives you a bad feeling, then it's not for you. Different people will resonate with different styles. Get a variety of meditation recordings and find out what you like and don't like. Ditch the ones you don't resonate with.

With this in mind, I've recorded a variety of meditations for beginners and experienced meditators alike. You can choose from the range of options and diversity. They are really easy to follow and as well as the relaxation benefits; they're a positive step towards your self-healing.

It's usually easier to use earphones to begin so the sound is inside your head rather than something you have to listen to from outside. This will minimize getting sidetracked by wandering off thinking about other distractions.

Narrow the meditation recordings down to the ones you find easiest and hence like the best, and persist. Persist until you can relax and go to the place within you that has no bounds. It has always been there waiting for you to get through the gate of your mind chatter.

Commit to your daily meditation practice because your life will be better when you meditate regularly compared to when you don't. You'll be healthier, happier, and certainly a whole lot more fun to be around.

You'll be able to respond instead of react in situations that stress you, more often than not.

Try This:
- Sit quietly with your eyes closed.
- Breathe deeply down your body for a count of six.
- Hold for a count of two.
- Breathe out for a count of six.

Don't focus on the numbers as you are counting. Focus on your breathing and allow yourself to relax.

This is called pranic breathing. Even if you do this for a few minutes each day or a few times a day, it'll get you well on the way to more focused practices.

Even committing to twenty minutes meditation each day might be a big step if you are used to running around and being busy all the time. So maybe start with five or ten minutes and work your way up.

A rule of thumb is this: you need the at least the same amount of minutes' meditation each day as you need hours of sleep at night. In other words, if you're a person who needs eight hours sleep each night, then you also need eight minutes of meditation each day. If you need ten hours per night, you need ten minutes per day. It's not much, is it? But just like you need to sleep every night, you also need to meditate every day.

The reward is it's an upward spiral. The more you meditate, the better the results, the better you feel, the more your health and demeanour improve, and hence the more you'll want to meditate.

Notice people who meditate regularly. There's something different about them, and it's good.

Adjustments

Spinal subluxation of your ninth thoracic vertebra interferes with the nerves that exit at this level and impedes the nerve messages between your brain and adrenal glands.

This can cause less than optimal functioning of your adrenal glands, resulting in the signs of adrenal imbalance, such as exhaustion, hormonal imbalances, skin and immune system problems, and blood pressure problems.

Having your spine adjusted regularly will correct the negative spiral you have created between your spine and nerve system.

It's still essential, however, to stop creating the stresses that cause the subluxations affecting the adrenal glands in the first place.

Exercise

It's a pretty simple concept: move it or lose it.

Exercise should be a core treatment for hormonal disorders because regular, moderate exercise improves moods. Blanchl-Demichell F, Lucas H, Chardonnens D. "Premenstrual Dysphoric Disorder: Current status of treatment". *Swiss Med Weekly*. 2002 Nov 2: 132(39–40): 574–8.

You know you need to exercise so if you haven't started already, get going. In our modern world, there's a huge range of activities you can choose from. If you're not sure what to choose, just go for a walk. Don't only go once though. Treat yourself to at least three or four times a week and preferably daily.

Walk at a pace; don't dawdle. If you're not puffing and sweating, you're possibly not doing enough.

You don't need special gear and it's free.

Regular exercise means regular sessions close together, not regular as in once a month.

Herbs

There are a variety of herbs that are used to help adrenal hormones. Don't underestimate their potency.

Rather than wading through the minefield of multiple options yourself, it is probably in your best interests to seek out a qualified and experienced practitioner to guide you. Skilled practitioners can make supportive blends tailored to your circumstances and condition rather than swallowing a range of different ones individually.

Siberian Ginseng (Eleuthrococcus Senticosus)

Most good anti-stress formulae will have ginseng in them. It is a medicinal herb that has traditionally been used to improve overall energy and vitality, particularly during times of fatigue or stress. Siberian ginseng is considered to be weaker and is therefore cheaper than Korean ginseng.

Korean Ginseng (Panax Ginseng)

Korean Ginseng helps the adrenal glands and their controlling mechanisms in both short- and long-term stress. Ginseng appears to help the adrenals respond to stress and also helps the stress hormone levels return to normal faster once the stress has gone. During prolonged stress, ginseng has a growth effect on the adrenals improving their capacity to respond. Fulder S. "The Root of Being: Ginseng and the Pharmacology of Harmony". 1980. pp 156–85. Hutchinson London.

Panax gets its name from panacea because it has been credited with the ability to help with so many things, such as

- boosting energy
- sharpening the mind
- reducing stress
- treating frigidity and impotence
- enhancing the immune system
- controlling blood pressure
- regulating blood sugar levels
- strengthening the cardiovascular system

Dosage recommendations vary between different ginsengs and according to the individual and their condition. Please seek the advice of your qualified health-care practitioner.

Contra-indications: high blood pressure. Ginseng should not be taken with caffeine or guarana or used by children or pregnant or breastfeeding women.

Withania *(Withania Somnifera)*

Withania (also known as winter cherry and ashwaganda) is traditionally used for

- nervous exhaustion
- debility associated with stress
- improving energy

It also has a reputation as an aphrodisiac.

Contra-indications: withania is best used only when you need it and should not be used for long periods of time.

Cat's Claw

Cat's claw is a Peruvian herb *(Uncaria tomentosa)* which helps

- alleviate fatigue
- assist in recovery from illness

Schizandra *(Shizandra Sinensis)*

Schizandra is a creeping vine native to China. As well as providing numerous health benefits, it is another natural choice for helping to reduce fatigue and boost general energy levels. It has adaptogenic and immune enhancing properties similar to ginseng and is sometimes referred to as "Chinese Prozac."

General dosage is a substantial 2 to 6 g per day. Please seek the advice of your health-care practitioner.

Liquorice *(Glycyrrhiza Glabra)*

The glycyrrhizin content of liquorice has a cortisol-sparing action which feedbacks to reduce excess adrenal activity associated with stress. *Soma R, et al. Endocrine Regulations 1994; 28:31–34.*

Contra-indications: hypertension, kidney problems, oedema, and pregnancy.

Liquorice is sodium sparing, which means you will retain sodium and hence water, and lose potassium. You should not take liquorice for longer than four to six weeks at a time. Please seek the advice of your health-care practitioner.

Generally recommended doses range from 1 to 5 g of dried root as an infusion (leaving the plant in water that has boiled) or decoction (boiling for eight to ten minutes) three times per day.

Astragalus Membranaceus

Has been used to
- increase endurance and stamina
- increase resistance to infection
- enhance immune function
- lower blood pressure
- enhance heart function
- protect heart muscle from oxidant damage
- increase sperm motility and male fertility
- increase diuresis or the elimination of fluid
- protect the liver from damage

The commonly utilised dosage range for Astragalus is equivalent to 3 to 6 g of dried root per day as a decoction, tablet, capsule, or fluid extract. Please seek the advice of your health-care practitioner.

Supplements

Finding and taking the right balance of supplements specific for you is important because too much or too little of anything can cause further problems.

Also, different manufacturers have a wide range of quality and dosage. Read your labels and get good advice.

Tyrosine
Tyrosine is a precursor to dopamine and the catecholamines which can reduce the fatigue that is associated with prolonged stress. *Neri DF, et al. Aviat Space Environ Med 1995; 66(4): 313–319.*

Vitamin B Complex
Vitamin B complex is a group of water-soluble vitamins, including
- thiamine (B1)
- riboflavin (B2)
- niacin (B3)
- pantothenic acid (B5)
- pyridoxine B6)
- biotin
- folic acid
- cobalamine (B12)

In summary
- B1, 2, 3 and biotin are involved in energy production.
- B6 is essential for amino acid metabolism.
- B12 and folic acid are essential for proper cell division.

A Simple Test for Vitamin B6 Deficiency
Stand with your arms outstretched to each side with your palms facing up.

Keeping your palms flat, curl your fingers in to touch your palms (not into the middle of your palm but where your fingers first meet your palms), without bending your wrists or palms. You should be able to do this easily. If you can't, you need B6.

Good food sources of vitamin B6 are
- brewer's yeast
- meat
- liver
- botanical royal jelly
- whole grains
- wheat germ

Contra-indications: high doses of B6 (over 2,000 mg/day) over an extended period of time can cause problems with your nerves. This is a ridiculously high dose. Who would do that?

Please seek the advice of your health-care practitioner.

Vitamin C (ascorbic acid)

Vitamin C deficiency is one of the main early indicators of adrenal exhaustion. Early signs of deficiency are
- fatigue
- bruising easily
- bleeding gums

Smokers need a higher daily intake to maintain normal levels.

Vitamin C is a water-soluble vitamin, which means it dissolves in water. This also means that when you cook in water you lose a certain amount of vitamin C because it will dissolve into the water. Better to lightly steam for a short time.

Vitamin C is an antioxidant which helps recycle the fat-soluble antioxidant vitamin E. (The fat-soluble vitamins are A, D, E, and K).

Even people who think they consume large amounts of vitamin C through a diet high in fruits and vegetables can have surprisingly low levels in their blood. There may not be high levels in the food if it is picked before it is at its peak, transported, or stored; you may not be digesting and assimilating the food efficiently and you may be burning it up with your physical, emotional, or mental stress.

If you have excess stress in your life, you will have a need for higher doses of vitamin C and most vitamins and minerals in general.

As a rule, if you have any sign of blood when you brush or floss your teeth, or you are bruising easily, you too need more vitamin C on a regular basis.

A therapeutic dosage can be 1,000 mg up to 3,000 mg. It is probably best to spread this dosage out over your day rather than in one big dose.

Too much vitamin C will cause diarrhoea so if your bowels are getting loose then cut back your dosage or spread it out farther during the day.

Please seek the advice of your health-care practitioner.

Magnesium

Magnesium is a mineral needed for

- bones
- protein, cell, and fatty acid formation
- vitamin b activation
- muscle relaxation
- blood clotting
- energy production
- insulin secretion

Stress, caffeine, alcohol, and sugar all increase the loss of magnesium from your body.

Magnesium helps with

- relaxation
- anxiety
- headaches
- preventing adrenal exhaustion
- lowers blood pressure
- reduces hyperactivity with add
- improves glucose tolerance
- cramps
- abnormal heart rhythms
- depression
- chocolate cravings. If you have chocolate cravings, this is a strong clue that you need more magnesium. You will crave chocolate in direct proportion to how deficient you are in

magnesium, so if you've got the urge to eat the whole box, you know you're extremely depleted. Save the extra kilos and subsequent mood changes and simply have more magnesium instead. Fill up on leafy greens whenever you can.

Good sources of magnesium are
- nuts
- grains
- dark-green vegetables
- fish
- meat

Magnesium is contained in chlorophyll so the darker green the plant, the more magnesium it contains.

A therapeutic dosage is 500–1500 mg per day.

You can use your chocolate cravings as a rough guide. If you are craving chocolate, you need more, and when you lose the craving, you can back off the dosage.

Too much magnesium will cause diarrhoea, so if this is happening, you also need to cut back.

People with kidney disease should seek advice before taking magnesium supplements.

Vitamin B6 enhances your ability to use magnesium. Can you see how interconnected everything is and how important balance and variety are in your diet?

Please seek the advice of your health-care practitioner.

Zinc

Zinc is another essential mineral for your body. You need it for your
- enzyme systems
- immune function
- wound-healing fertility and libido
- growth
- protein metabolism

Zinc deficiency is very common, and by the time you get the telltale white zinc spots in your nails, you are very low.

If you are very depleted in zinc, it will cause what is called a *zinc blockade,* which means you won't absorb your other nutrients adequately through your bowel because of the zinc deficiency.

Symptoms of zinc deficiency are
- fatigue
- acne
- insulin resistance
- infections
- obesity
- loss of taste
- loss of smell
- frigidity and impotence
- white flecks in your nails

Good sources of zinc are
- oysters
- meat
- eggs
- seeds
- wheat germ
- seafood

Therapeutic doses are 15 to 30 mg a day.

Too much zinc over long periods can deplete your immune system rather than boost it.

And of course, remember the importance of dealing with and finding resolution for your life issues because it doesn't matter how many supplements you take, if you don't resolve the problems that are causing your imbalances in the first place, you won't heal. You will just keep things under control or get worse more slowly—and expensively. Long-term supplements aren't cheap.

It will also hurt your hip pocket if you are constantly paying for supplements over an extended period of time. It's money well spent to help you cope in the interim, but it's important that you heal not just cope and keep a status quo.

Once more, just in case you're tempted to ignore it, the most powerful treatment to heal adrenal exhaustion (better than any DHEA, cortisol, adrenal extract, or vitamin supplement) is the ability to say no!

Every time you give your power away, you contribute to adrenal fatigue.

Rachael's Story

Rachael was exhausted. She was busy but no busier than any of her friends. Even so, she was dragging herself around and consuming more and more caffeine and sugar to keep the fire stoked. She was diagnosed with chronic fatigue syndrome (CFS) and spent a large percentage of her days on the couch spiralling into self-judgement and depression.

A friend referred her to an energy-healing practitioner who cut off the energy cords from her solar plexus that were going out to a number of people. It was an instant miracle. She immediately got some energy back. Then she had to learn how to cut the cords herself and also to not allow herself to be drained in the first place.

14

The Impact of Your Thyroid

Make friends with your thyroid. It's the VIP gland located in the front of your neck near your Adam's apple.

The three main hormones that play on the thyroid stage are

- T3 (tri-iodothyronine). T3 does most of the work, but it is made from T4.
- T4 (thyroxine). T4 is considered a pro-hormone because 80 per cent of T3 in the blood comes from T4. The normal ratio of T4 to T3 is 3.3 to1.
- RT3 (reverse T3). RT3 has only 1 per cent the activity of T3 (In other words, it's virtually inactive.) and is a T3 antagonist, which means it binds to T3 receptors and blocks the action of T3. Hence, even if there's plenty of T3 and T4, if there's an excess of rT3, you'll get hypothyroid symptoms.
- Reverse T3 has the same molecular structure as T3; however, its atomic arrangement is a mirror image of T3 hence; it fits into receptor sites upside down. This blocks or antagonises the active T3 from binding to the receptor and activating the usual response.

These crucial hormones are responsible for regulating
- the metabolism of every cell in your body
- body temperature
- heart rate
- your weight
- cholesterol levels
- promote growth and development

- influencing nerve, skeletal, and reproductive system function

In a normal healthy person (do you know any?), the thyroid makes about 90 to 100 mcg of T4 per day.

The T4 circulates through the blood and is converted into about equal amounts of T3 and reverse T3.

The amount of hormones the thyroid makes is influenced by TSH (thyroid stimulating hormone) from the pituitary, which is influenced by TRH (thyrotropin releasing hormone) from the hypothalamus in the brain—another feedback loop.

Hypothyroidism

When the thyroid doesn't make enough hormones, or their ability to act is reduced, it's called hypothyroidism.

Symptoms of Hypothyroidism

Hypothyroidism is generally characterized by a reduction in metabolism which shows up as a slowing of physical and mental functions. For example,

- cold hands and feet
- lowered body temperature
- weight gain
- tired
- sleepy
- depression
- anxiety
- low libido
- hair loss
- loss of the outer third of the eyebrows
- facial hair
- swollen eyelids
- constipation
- headache
- poor memory and concentration

- insomnia
- fluid retention
- dry hair, skin, and nails

If you hate the cold and refuse to live in a cold climate like me, that's an indicator of low thyroid function. I hate the cold and thrive in the warm. It's my body's way of communicating to me. If I live in the cold, it adds more stress which is the opposite of what my body is asking for.

What Causes Hypothyroidism?

- Overstimulation of the nerve system. In other words, stress. (High cortisol levels depress TSH and blocks T4 being converted into T3, the worker.)
- Disappointment. Just as people who worry a lot get stomach issues and people who get angry a lot get liver issues, people who feel disappointed a lot get thyroid issues. Hence, you need to release all your disappointments if you truly want to break the negative feedback loop and restore proper function.
- Subluxation of spinal vertebrae affecting function of the nerve system and brain that control thyroid function. Especially the mid-low cervical vertebrae and lumbar 3.
- Nutritional deficiencies
    - iodine
    - tyrosine
    - selenium
    - zinc
    - iron
    - vitamin B6, B12, D, E
(Deficiencies in vitamin D and iron can cause receptor uptake problems.)
- Insulin resistance
- Heavy metals and environmental toxins

What Is Reverse T3 Dominance?

Reverse T3 dominance used to be called Wilson's syndrome. It's when tests show T4 and T3 to be within normal limits but function isn't normal. In other words, when there's excess rT3 relative to T3.

In times of prolonged stress, the adrenals make more cortisol. As you know, cortisol inhibits the conversion of T4 to T3 (the worker). This is a natural body response. It is not pathology. This is your body slowing you down. Making you do less. In other words, telling you to do less and lower your stress.

Standard blood tests, such as TSH, T4, and T3, won't show up this condition. However, rT3 levels can be tested separately. It's the ratio between rT3 and T3 that's the tell rather than the respective levels.

Thyroid Resistance

Some people show thyroid symptoms even when their blood tests say everything is fine.

Everything is not fine! If they're not letting go their disappointments, things will not and cannot be fine!

Plus if they have high levels of oestrogen (because the progesterone building blocks have been used up to make the stress hormone cortisol) or liver congestion, there can be high TBH (thyroid binding globulin) which minimizes the free roaming T3 and T4—all messages from your body to do less and reduce stress.

If you continue to ignore these messages, your body has to yell at you more loudly, and it does this with symptoms.

Cortisol's Role in Thyroid Imbalance

Your digestive tract is lined with lymph or immune tissue called gut-associated lymphoid tissue (GALT).

Stress to the GALT can be caused by

- food sensitivities
- undigested proteins

- leaky gut
- infections from bacteria, yeasts, or parasites.

These GALT problems can trigger a major stress response which raises cortisol production by your adrenal glands.

Cortisol causes a shift in thyroid hormone metabolism. It increases the amount of the inactive form of T3 and causes an imbalance. Chronic elevations in cortisol due to stress suppress the immune system in the GI tract. This leads to dysbiosis, parasites, yeast, and leaky gut, creating a vicious cycle that disrupts thyroid function even more. Hence, a healthy, balanced GI tract is essential for optimal thyroid hormones and function. Many people have their thyroid function normalise after resolving their GI tract issues. Hence, wheat sensitivity should not be ignored in thyroid conditions.

Oestrogen's Role in Thyroid Imbalance

Excess oestrogen can bind to thyroid hormone receptor sites and therefore suppress thyroid hormone function.

The GI tract contains an enzyme called beta glucuronidase. This can reactivate oestrogen that has been metabolized in the liver.

Oestrogen that has been metabolized by the liver is normally excreted in the faeces, but when there's an excess of beta glucuronidase, it can be reabsorbed into the bloodstream.

This enzyme is dependent on optimal nutrition and healthy gut-bacteria ratios. Once again, you can see how essential healthy gut bacteria are to the health of the thyroid.

What Causes Abnormal Gut Bacteria Ratios?
- poor diet
- spinal subluxation
- stress
- toxins
- toxic thoughts and emotions from unresolved psychological issues

- inadequate stomach acid production
- inadequate digestive enzymes

The Liver's Role in Thyroid Imbalance

Toxins and hormones are normally metabolized in the liver and excreted in the faeces via the GI tract.

As you know, the majority of thyroid hormone is converted into its active form in the liver. When the GI tract is out of balance (from medication, anger, dysbiosis, subluxation, inflammation, leaky gut, infections, excess alcohol, or too many food allergies), this puts a massive strain on the liver's ability to metabolize hormones and thyroid-disrupting chemicals. This causes the liver to become congested and toxic, reducing its ability to activate thyroid hormone.

This situation also increases the possibility of thyroid-disruptive chemicals recirculating and hindering thyroid function. This perpetuates the vicious cycle of beta glucuronidase enzyme, undoing what the liver has done (reactivating and reabsorbing into the bloodstream hormones the liver had already metabolized).

Testing for Hypothyroidism

Testing TSH is only a screening test and will not give a true picture of what's going on.

Remember that you already know what's going on, however: too much disappointment that's been rehashed too many times. It is essential to resolve this if you want lasting change and health promotion rather than getting by and living on supplements eternally.

The normal range for TSH has been debated and re-jigged in previous years, begging the question of what is normal and what isn't.

A better picture can be seen by assessment of TSH, T4, T3, reverse T3, anti-thyroglobulin, anti-microsomal antibodies, twenty-four-hour iodine urine excretion test, and vitamin D.

A rule of thumb is T3 and T4 should be in the upper third of the normal range with a 1 to 3.3 ratio, with rT3 and T3 appropriately balanced.

Anti-thyroglobulin and anti-microsomal antibody tests will show if there's an immunity problem causing thyroiditis or Hashimoto's disease. Low iodine levels can be responsible for low thyroid hormone production.

Plus blood tests measure the levels of thyroid hormones in the blood, not in the tissues where they have their effect.

Hashimoto's disease is hypothyroidism due to an autoimmune reaction. In other words, the body is reacting against itself. This happens when the people are disappointed in themselves.

Testing Body Temperature

Thyroid function can be estimated by measuring underarm body temperature. If your underarm temperature is consistently below 36.5 C for three or more days, your thyroid function may be low.

Adrenal exhaustion can also lower your body temperature, so adrenal function also needs to be considered if you have low body temperature.

Treatment for Hypothyroidism

- Let go all disappointment in yourself, others, and events.
- Speak your truth rather than hold back and block energy in the throat chakra.
- Take old man banksia. This is a flower essence from the Australian bush flower essence range which has anecdotal reports of assisting letting go blocked emotions and helping thyroid function.
- compounded (tailor-made combinations of bioidentical T4 and T3 to suit your individual need) thyroid replacement allows for avoiding fillers, such as lactose, which inhibits absorption.
- Spinal adjustments to remove subluxations in the neck and also lumbar 3 near the base of the spine have a huge impact on improving thyroid function.
- nutritional supplements according to the deficiencies
- Remove heavy metals.
- Remove any foods that are causing sensitivity, such as
  - gluten
  - dairy
  - yeasts

Rosie's Story

Rosie would just fall asleep sometimes. She seemed to be normal and then she'd get confused and sleepy for no apparent reason.

She was sensitive to gluten. It was a minor miracle that her symptoms were resolved, but there was nothing discrete about Rosie. Everyone and every café, restaurant, and bake-house knew that Rosie couldn't eat wheat anymore and would get the whole story whether they wanted it or not. Many people became educated as to the perils of the scourge of our generation.

In a routine check, it was picked up that she was also low in iodine, which was affecting her thyroid function. She started supplementing with iodine and her gluten sensitivity went away. Her friends came closer.

15

Bioidentical Hormones

Hormone imbalances can show up at varying ages and stages, including
- PMS (premenstrual syndrome)
- PCOS (polycystic ovary syndrome)
- endometriosis
- infertility
- perimenopause
- menopause

Whenever there's an imbalance in the person's life, there will be a corresponding hormone imbalance in accordance with the degree of imbalance.

I was a people pleaser. I am the youngest of seven children and my mother wanted peace at any cost, so we learned to stay out of trouble by doing whatever we were told. Naturally, this sets up an imbalance. What we're told by someone else is not a direct match for what we innately know is right for us.

Were you ever forced to eat something you didn't want?

Were you ever made to get out of bed when you wanted or needed to stay longer?

Were you ever forced to use your manners and be nice to people just because they were more senior even if they were arrogant or domineering?

Your internal feelings are a direct monitor for what is right for you or not. And the problem is when you consistently ignore them (even if it's from the good intent of staying out of trouble or not rocking the boat), you can get to where you don't recognize what they're saying anymore.

If this is you, it's time to start paying attention and getting it back.

Oestrogen Dominance and PMS,
Perimenopause and Infertility

PMS, polycystic ovarian syndrome, endometriosis, cysts, and infertility are usually a result of oestrogen dominance. In other words, when there is too much oestrogen relative to progesterone.

It is often written that progesterone production decreases with age or perimenopause, anytime from midthirties to late forties. The menstrual cycle can become erratic in this phase of decreased progesterone production.

Is the tail wagging the dog?

Is progesterone production decreasing with age? Or is it decreasing because the building blocks are being used up to make the stress hormone cortisol to deal with the ongoing stress that's evident in these age groups?

If age was the problem, then wouldn't all women of those ages have imbalances?

Time is going to march on whether you want it to or not. There's not much you can do about that. But there's a lot you can do about the stress in your life.

Menopause

As the natural fertility phase fades with menopause, oestrogen levels eventually decline as well. This can be good news for some because it can even out the discrepancy between oestrogen and progesterone levels.

Unfortunately, a new list of symptoms can now show up because of lowered oestrogen.

- hot flushes
- night sweats
- decreased libido
- dry vagina
- brain fog
- urinary tract infections
- dry skin

In an ideal world, you just need to resolve your imbalances and your hormonal balance will also be on its way to restoration as well.

Restoring balance in a world where we either consciously or unconsciously create imbalance makes this not only difficult but in many cases unlikely. For example,

- turning lights on and stay up instead of going to bed with the sun
- eating foods from all over the world and out of season
- eating foods from cold storage or contain colours, flavours, and preservatives
- travelling across time zones
- doing roles traditionally suited for the opposite gender
- using caffeine, nicotine, sugar, or other stimulants to drive ourselves to keep going long past when our brain and body said stop
- wrapping our bodies in unnatural fibres
- using toiletries and cosmetics which contain chemicals
  You get the idea.

Individualised bioidentical hormone replacement therapy can be a godsend by artificially restoring balance to overcome many hormone symptoms. At least it was for me.

Even though I had done my best to restore balance within myself, my environment, and my mind, I was still far from my true centre.

What Are Bioidentical Hormones?

Traditional HRT (hormone replacement therapy) uses synthetic or animal-derived hormones.

Bioidentical hormones have a molecular structure the same as the hormones in the human body; hence, they're called bioidentical. Because bioidentical hormones are structurally identical to the hormones produced by our body, they are more compatible with our bodies' biochemistry.

Bioidentical hormones are made from a hormone precursor called diosgenin. This is extracted from either soy or wild yam. Diosgenin is extracted from the soybeans or wild yam and then its molecular structure is modified to convert it into the appropriate hormone: estriol, estradiol, estrone, progesterone, testosterone, DHEA, or cortisol.

The bioidentical hormone is made then purified according to pharmaceutical standards, then micronized to maximise absorption.

Although these hormones are synthesized, they are not synthetic.

Synthetic means the molecule does not exist naturally. Synthetic hormones are man-made. In other words, they have not come from nature.

Can you eat wild yam and soybeans to get the same effect? No, the body doesn't have the enzymes to convert the diosgenin into the hormones you need.

Blood tests are usually taken so combinations can be tailor made to suit the individual.

Ongoing monitoring makes basic good sense to ensure doses continue to match your changing needs.

How Do You Use Bioidentical Hormones?

Bioidentical hormones can be administered in different forms.

Creams
This is considered to be the best and safest method largely because
- When the hormones are absorbed, they are stored in the fat under the skin and get released into the blood over time like a slow release. This release of hormones into the blood is fairly consistent over time; hence, it helps keep the blood levels stable. In other words, they don't have the fluctuations like capsules and troches often do.
- The creams are used on the skin and not swallowed so they're administration is not affected by the stomach and liver. This means lower does can be used compared to capsules or troches (lozenges).
- When oestrogens are swallowed via capsules or troches, they can be metabolized by bacteria in the bowel to form oestrone

which increases the possibility of blood clots and thrombo-embolism. This doesn't happen with the creams.

- It's easy to adjust the dose. For example, more or less amount of cream, more or less often. Your individually tailored cream will usually come with either a dispensing syringe with 1 ml gradations on it or a 1 ml spoon, so you can accurately measure and control how much you're using.

Some doctors think the creams don't work when the hormone levels don't show a rise in future tests, but this is not necessarily a problem with the creams but rather the method of testing.

Most hormones love fat rather than water. When they're in the bloodstream, they'll bind to red blood cell membranes rather than stay in the watery liquid. If your blood sample is centrifuged, the blood cells and the hormones are removed prior to testing! Hence, blood testing can show no improvement yet saliva tests will show improvements within just a few hours.

Troches or Lozenges

The idea of troches is to hold them in your mouth for about thirty minutes while they dissolve, to allow the hormones to be absorbed through the mucous membranes. The problem is a lot of the troche gets swallowed rather than dissolved and absorbed. This means the hormones don't bypass the stomach and liver as planned.

Plus they can have a strange aftertaste. Some compounding chemists use aspartame to mask this.

The doses for troches are often similar to oral capsules (which are intended to be swallowed) so there's not really an obvious liver sparing effect.

Theoretically, troche dose should be around the normal physiological dose (e.g., 10 to 20 mg per day for progesterone). In practice, the dose of progesterone in troches is usually between 100 to 200 mg per day, which suggests a lot of the dose isn't being absorbed or is being swallowed.

The release of hormones from troches is fast compared to creams, which can cause a seesaw effect. In other words, the blood levels can go up fast and then go down again within four or five hours. This means they usually need to be used more than once per day.

There are two different types of troche.

Hard troches use PEG (polyethylene glycol) in the base. They are associated with allergic and sensitivity reactions and can cause lining of the mouth and gums to get inflamed. Hard or PEG base troches are not ideal for people with chemical sensitivities or high toxicities, such as leaky gut people.

Soft troches use gelatin. This is less likely to induce sensitivity; however, because the gelatin is water loving, the fat-loving hormones can clump together when made in high doses. This can decrease absorption from the troche into the body which means more gets swallowed (not ideal) rather than absorbed (this is what you want).

Hormone testing should be done via blood rather than saliva if you use troches because residue in the mouth can give inaccurate results.

Pellets

A pellet containing bioidentical hormones can be inserted under the skin. They are most often used for estradiol. They usually last about three to six months.

Progesterone doesn't come in pellet form because they would have to be huge to supply the doses needed. For example, forty times the size of an oestrogen pellet. Hence, progesterone creams are more suitable.

Pellets release a consistent dose (which is good), bypass the liver, and don't increase the risk of blood clots.

The pellet is usually inserted under the skin in a fatty area, such as the abdomen or buttocks. They don't need removal because they are totally dissolved within the body.

Many pellets include PVP (Povidone). Sensitive people should ask for PVP-free pellets to avoid reactions.

Leanne's Story

Leanne knew she needed help. She'd always been health conscious. She was particular with nutrition, loved to exercise, and took any prescribed herbs or supplements diligently. Even so, she was losing her menopausal marbles. Her memory was kind of funny or inconvenient depending on your perception. Her model figure was getting thicker around the waist and her fuse was getting shorter.

She was already looking after herself better than most people she knew, and had done so for decades. Nevertheless, she was starting to struggle. Her joie de vivre seemed to be in hiatus.

She wasn't content to hang up her smile just yet, so she hit the books and learned about bioidentical hormones. She searched around to find a doctor to test her and a compounding pharmacist to make up the prescriptions she needed. She hasn't looked back.

16

Hormone Testing

Limitations

The usual hormone tests are done via blood, saliva, and urine. The idea being to see if the levels are within "normal" range. But what's normal?

What if the hormones are within the so-called average range but not in the optimal ratios with each other?

The standard ranges are referenced by the average population rather than what might be optimal for excellent health for an individual. Just because something is common in a society, doesn't mean it is normal.

What if the "average" levels of a population are nothing like what you need?

What if you're in the low end of normal according to the statistics, but you're really deficient according to your symptoms and system functions?

One way to work with this is to make certain your levels are in the top third of the range.

It is common for postmenopausal women to have low oestrogen, progesterone, testosterone, and DHEA levels. That doesn't mean it is normal!

It's also common for these women to have weight gain, osteoporosis, diabetes, memory issues, heart disease, low libido, depression, etc. Being common doesn't make it normal.

Doesn't it make sense to have reference ranges which maintain healthy hormone levels which prevent these so-called age-associated illnesses?

If you're told your tests are normal and you still have symptoms, get another opinion from a practitioner who takes a more holistic approach.

Hormone testing can shorten the time taken to get you back on track. Symptoms alone can be misleading. For example, if you're having hot flushes, some may assume you need more oestrogen whereas they might be from high cortisol levels. By giving you oestrogen, it could make you worse rather than better.

How Can You Test When Hormone Levels Vary so Much During the Menstrual Cycle?

It is normal for hormone levels to rise and fall throughout the month in accordance with a normal menstrual cycle. (Postmenopausal hormones, adrenal hormones, and thyroid hormones don't fluctuate throughout the month.)

If you're still menstruating, it's best to test during the luteal phase of the cycle. In other words, around day 21. This is when progesterone levels normally peak, plus it avoids the mid-cycle oestrogen surge.

Timing Tests with Your Last Dose

Baseline hormone testing is usually best done in the early morning before breakfast.

In menstruating women, testing is best done between days 19 and 23 (ideally 21). This is when progesterone levels are normally at their peak.

Men can get tested on any day.

If you're using creams or capsules, get tested eight to twelve hours after the last dose.

If you're using troches, get tested four hours after the last dose.

For thyroid testing,
- If you're on T4 therapy (Oroxine), get tested eight to twelve hours after the last dose.
- If you're on T3, get tested one and a half to four hours after the last dose.
- If you're on thyroid extract therapy (armour thyroid), a combination of T3 and T4, get tested four hours after the last dose. Sooner can show a peak of T4 and later can show a drop-off of T3.

17

The Effect of Your Bowels

It took many years of floundering before I realized the importance of the bowels in hormonal health. I had an emotional investment in not seeing the link because I was in no rush to give up my week of chocolate each month, even though I was a devout puritan for the other three weeks.

Eventually, my desire to feel good outweighed my desire for chocolate. Plus the discovery that taking magnesium powder regularly puts an end to chocolate cravings was a doorway into a whole new world. I discovered that when my magnesium levels were at optimum, I didn't even want chocolate. When my magnesium levels dropped, I would crave it according to the degree of deficit.

It was so good for my self-esteem to realize I wasn't caving into the munchies because I had no will power or lacked self-mastery; it was simply a biochemical imbalance setting up the craving. Yes, the biochemistry was a result of emotional imbalances and faulty thoughts, and these clearly needed addressing also; however, the downward spiral needed a stopgap in order to restore balance.

Everything is connected to everything.

It doesn't necessarily matter where you start as long as you do and as long as you keep going. If you stop, things don't stay the same; they deteriorate.

Just like brushing your teeth or painting a house, it's not enough to do it once. Regular maintenance is required, and if you don't do it, deterioration will follow soon enough.

Your bowel and brain are reflexly connected.

If you took your brain out and put it on the table, and took your bowel out, scrunched it into a pile, and put it next to your brain, you'd see they look alike. They've both have grey rugations (folds with folds in on themselves). These rugae are directly related to each other. In other words, when a part of the bowel is irritated, inflamed, or damaged, it affects the corresponding part of the brain, triggering irritation, inflammation, and damage in the matching area, and vice versa. In other words, when a part of the brain is irritated, inflamed, or damaged, it affects the corresponding part of the bowel.

What does this really mean?

This means that when you eat foods your bowel is sensitive and reacts to, a corresponding part of the brain also reacts. This triggers irritation; faulty thoughts, beliefs and behaviours; and perpetuates old patterns. This blocks you from creating new pathways that are more aligned with your true self and direction.

This reflex connection between bowel and brain works in both directions.

This also means that when you have negative or restrictive beliefs, think toxic thoughts, or align with behaviours that don't serve you well, a corresponding part of the bowel also reacts, triggering desire for foods that are not good for you, sensitivity, inflammation, and damage.

It doesn't matter where you start to sort out your imbalances—at the bowel and food end or the brain and thoughts and beliefs end—as long as you do. They go hand in hand, so you'll need to realign both anyway. Just get started and keep going.

Digesting It All

The digestive system or gastrointestinal tract (GI tract) is a complex structure which needs multiple organs to work together in symphony.

The ultimate job of the GI tract is to absorb the nutrients you need to keep your body healthy and simultaneously reject and excrete the substances that are toxic. To achieve these important roles, the membrane that lines the entire GI tract acts as a selective barrier so it can let through what is "good" and reject what is "bad."

The three key steps of digestion are:
- absorption. This occurs across the bowel wall and into the bloodstream as food makes its way through the intestines.
- assimilation. This is when nutrients enter the cells of your body.
- elimination. This is where the body gets rid of waste products.

The GI tract uses one-third of the overall blood flow from the heart because it takes a lot of energy to get the digestive job done properly.

Normal Gut Flora

The GI tract has its own internal ecosystem. It is home to over four hundred species of bacteria. Most of these are beneficial.
- They produce nutrients essential to digestion (especially short chain fatty acids).
- They produce nutrients through bacterial fermentation of food.

These bacteria are considered normal or friendly and they number in the trillions. Healthy adults have two to four kilos (five to eight pounds) of friendly bacteria living in their bowel.

Absorption of Nutrients

It doesn't matter how much good food you eat or how many quality supplements you take; if your bowel isn't absorbing them properly, you aren't going to get the nourishment you think you are.

You may not absorb your nutrients very well because of
- food sensitivities. This sets up an immune reaction in your bowel and distorts absorption.
- clog. If your bowel is clogged with old waste, then the new food can't get through to the bowel wall to be absorbed.
- poor nutrient content in the food. If the nutrients aren't in the food you're eating in sufficient quantities, then obviously you can't absorb enough. You can't absorb what's not there.

- candida overgrowth. If you have yeast infections in your bowel, they will interfere with your digestion, make you crave sugar, and upset your hormonal harmony from all directions.
- disease processes in the bowel. In conditions such as celiac disease, the intestinal villi are diminished and often incapable of absorbing nutrients. This situation gets even more exaggerated by the consumption of wheat products.
- spinal subluxations. When you have misalignments of your vertebrae that interfere with the nerves that control the function of your bowel and digestion, the messages to and from the brain will be affected, resulting in bowel malfunction. This will also cause ovary and uterine malfunction.
- navel chakra congestion. When you have poor personal boundaries, it affects your navel chakra, and this will result in aberrant bowel function.

Your bowel is a long-term project. You need to be both consistent and persistent with it. I have always been particular about diet, except for during that premenstrual phase when all hell would break loose. This time of feeding frenzy was enough to do a lot of damage.

I figured that if I was out of control when I was premenstrual, it was even more important to be clean the rest of the time. Ultimately, I got to the point where I learned some tricks about managing what went in my mouth the whole month, because trying to use will power alone just wasn't doing it. I learned to:

- have protein with most meals, and especially early in the day, so I didn't get sugar cravings. Prevention is easier than wrestling with craving desire.
- As a rule of thumb, you need a serving of protein approximately the size of the palm of your hand with each meal daily.
- take betaine hydrochloride when I ate protein if I was stressed, to help digest the protein.
- take chromium and vitamin B complex supplements to assist keeping the sugar cravings at bay. Plus eat more pepper and celery, which are high in chromium, and meat, which is high

in vitamin B. Tricky since I'd been indoctrinated that being vegetarian was good. Too bad it wasn't good for me back then.

- take magnesium to stop the chocolate cravings. Plus eat more greens, which are high in magnesium.
- drink lots of good fresh water to keep hydrated. Sometimes, I thought I was hungry when I was actually thirsty, evidenced by spinal subluxations which interfere with the nerve messages to and from the brain.

It is proportionate. The more balanced I was in my life, the less dosage I needed to keep myself on an even keel.

The Gentle and Effective Detox Program

If you've been living on a Western diet laden with artificial colourings, preservatives, flavourings, and other food and water additives, you can be fairly safe in assuming your bowel is toxic and in need of regular cleansing.

There are many detox diets that do the rounds, but as with all things, some are better than others. I found this one to be gentle yet very effective. Keep in mind that your body is made of living tissue and you don't want to do harsh things to it. Gentle and effective is a good way to go.

Every time I've followed this detox program, I've lost excess weight and my energy has returned, as well as bringing me back towards hormone heaven instead of hormone hell.

Choose an amount of time you intend to follow this program for. I suggest you do it for one week and then re-evaluate. It'll be easiest to stick to the program without struggling if you choose a time when you don't have too many social commitments. It's far easier to do your own thing at home rather than having to work around restaurant meals and other people's opinions.

You can use the principle of this program as an ongoing maintenance routine.

As best you can, use fresh, organic fruit and vegetables either as juice, raw, or lightly steamed. Avoid potato and sweet potato, as they are starchy and tend to stick to your bowel wall. If it sticks to your teeth, it'll stick to your bowel, and you don't want this.

You can drink caffeine-free herbal teas, such as peppermint, chamomile, nettle, and liquorice root. You can also drink green tea. Even though it is caffeinated, it is particularly high in antioxidants.

Most people can easily stick to this and feel quite satisfied for one to two weeks. If you are doing it for extended periods, you may want to add some boiled brown rice after the second week. Of course, boil it in filtered, rather than chlorinated, water.

If you have medication or supplements that you can't do without, continue to take them even while you are detoxing. Take a break from anything else that is not absolutely essential and reassess your requirements after your cleanse. Hopefully, you won't need as much to get the same results. Always consult a qualified and experienced health-care practitioner.

It's an excellent opportunity to meditate more frequently and do forgiving and releasing techniques simultaneous to your bowel detox so you are cleansing your emotional and mental pollution as well as the physical sludge.

After your cleanse, ease back into other foods gently.

You have honoured yourself for a given period of time, so don't go full swing into nutritional abuse again. Everyone I know that follows this program wants to eat nutritiously and is more inclined to think clean thoughts with pure intention afterwards, simply because they feel so much better.

The Program

Do not follow this program if you are under fifteen years of age or pregnant.

Sort your attitude out before you start. It's much more empowering to do things because you want to rather than because you feel you should or have to.

- 2 tablespoon (40 ml) aloe vera juice. Take this first thing in the morning on an empty stomach so it is absorbed easily. Aloe vera barbedensis helps free the stored toxins and impacted waste in your bowel as well as helping heal your bowel wall.

- 1 teaspoon organic green barley grass powder in pure water (or apple juice) three times per day. This will detox, soothe, and help repair your bowel wall so you will absorb vitamin B more efficiently. You can take this supplement in-between meals as a satisfying and healthy snack. It is excellent for putting an end to food cravings.
- 1 teaspoon (1–2 g) vitamin C powder. Make sure it isn't artificially sweetened. Sweetened with the herb stevia is OK.
- Vitamin E. If you are prone to tender breasts and cellulite, take 1,000 IU vitamin E as well.
- 1 capsule (400 mg) cascara sagrada. Don't overdo it. This herb is particularly strong. You'll be on the toilet all day if you have too much cascara. In this case, less is better than more! This is a powerful herb which helps with constipation. If your bowel gets too loose, take a lower dose.
- Probiotics. Take a good acidophilus and bifidus supplement to restore your friendly bowel bacteria and prevent more holes forming in the bowel wall. In other words, prevent leaky gut syndrome. It is better to have a few doses regularly during the day when your stomach is at its emptiest, rather than one large dose. Store it in your refrigerator to maintain its potency.
- 1 teaspoon (2 g) glutamine powder. This helps heal your bowel wall and improves your mental concentration. It is especially useful if you have food sensitivities.
- Glutamine heals the holes in the bowel wall and stops the "too large" food particles from going through and triggering the immune response.
- 1 tablespoon liquid bentonite. This is like drinking liquid dirt but is fantastic at removing heavy metals. It's well worth the temporary disgust. Most of us have been victims of amalgam dental fillings and immunizations which have provided us with a surfeit of heavy metals. Plus a large quantity of the world's fish is now also contaminated with heavy metals. The fish eats the heavy metals, and then we eat the fish and get them too.

- 1 teaspoon psyllium husks dissolved in a full glass of pure water and then followed immediately by another glass of water. It is essential to take psyllium with plenty of water, else it will set like concrete inside you! This is not only not fun; it can be dangerous. In other words, it can seriously block your bowel if you don't drink plenty of water with it.
- It is very filling so it is good to have this midafternoon if you tend to get hungry. It is an excellent source of fibre which will bind and remove excess hormones and toxins from your bowel. It also provides a lot of bulk for your stool and will give you very satisfying evacuations!
- 33 ml of pure water per kg of body weight. Consider buying a good filter which removes
    - Chlorine
    - Heavy metals
    - Inorganic fluoride
    - Bacteria, such as cryptosporidium and giardia
    - Herbicides and pesticides

It will end up far more economical than constantly buying bottled water. Most bottled water comes in plastic, which kind of defeats the purpose.

- no coffee or black tea. Instead of coffee and black tea, drink plenty of water; or chamomile, peppermint, nettle, or green tea; or one part lemon to nine parts water.
- colonic irrigation/colonic lavage. This is the process of washing the bowel out with purified water from your rear end.

    Make sure you go to a professional clinic with a good reputation, and make sure you replenish your friendly bacteria with good-quality probiotics afterwards.

    A trained assistant will insert a fine tube in your anus and flush a quantity of warm water into your bowel. The water is usually treated with ultraviolet light to kill any bacteria it may have had in it. The trick is to be able to hold the water in for as long as you can before letting it go each time. This will enable you to clean farther around your bowel rather than just the last segment. The farther you can allow the water to travel, the greater distance of bowel you will cleanse. Even so, it will only clean your large bowel and not your small bowel because the water will only go as far as your ileo-cecal valve in your appendix area. When the ileo-cecal valve is working correctly, it prevents waste returning from the large bowel to the small.

The water washes free all the old and impacted matter that has been clogging your pipes for years. For as long as you have had hormone problems, you have more than likely also had toxic bowel problems because they go hand in hand.

Jump in. This is the current daddy of bowel cleansing, and once you feel the benefits, you will wish you hadn't baulked for so long. This is a particularly thorough way to clean the large bowel and it is a lot less revolting than you might think.

You can have colonic irrigation or colonic lavage without having to be on a detox diet at the same time. However, you'll probably get longer lasting benefits and feelings of well-being if you lighten your diet at the same time.

If you have trouble getting or staying motivated, it may give you a kick-start to have a colonic first.

Ileo-Cecal Valve

The ileo-cecal valve is designed to let waste go from the ileum at the end of your small bowel through to the cecum at the beginning of your large bowel. It should open to allow the waste to go through, and then close so the toxic waste can't come back into the small bowel.

One of the major problems with stress is it can cause your ileo-cecal valve to leak. A leaky valve allows toxic waste from the large bowel to re-enter the small bowel and poison your system.

What can cause your ileo-cecal valve to leak?
- stress
- coffee
- excess fibre
- stone fruits
- alcohol
- straining to pass stools

- Western toilets (compared to squatting)

A leaky ileo-cecal valve can cause
- tiredness
- bloating
- headaches
- migraines
- bad skin
- bad breath
- tenderness in the appendix region
- referred pain to your right shoulder
- referred pain to your neck. Sometimes, this can even result in a torticollis or wryneck.

After a Colonic

- It is really important to drink the appropriate amount of water for your body weight after colonic lavage (i.e., 33 mls per kilo of body weight) and to take high doses of probiotics, such as acidophilus and especially bifidus.

  Acidophilus helps your small bowel and bifidus helps your large bowel.

  Taking these supplements will help restore the natural balance of healthy bacteria in your bowel rapidly so the tendency to return to toxicity is lessened.

- If you are particularly toxic (have cellulite, headaches, hormonal imbalances, or emotional or anger issues) it is recommended you have a series of lavages. Perhaps weekly and then gradually spread them out to monthly. I never had anywhere near this frequency but still had excellent results. I always feel really vulnerable after a colonic as if stripping away the waste leaves the emotions I've been trying to suppress close to the surface. I refer to it as "feeling raw." If you're a sensitive person, it might be a good idea to plan to rest immediately afterwards rather than have to go back to work or doing anything that compels you to suppress those feelings again. You've gone to all the trouble of uncovering them, so acknowledge them and let them go rather than stuff them back down all over again.

- Of course, you need to stop doing all the things you did that caused the problem in the first place.

  If you have stuck waste in your bowel, it is also an indicator that you are stuck somewhere in your life and need to take steps to move things along. Whenever you have a physical imbalance, there will be a concomitant emotional imbalance and an outdated mental belief that goes with it. Your body and its symptoms are a gift to you, because it will constantly give you reminders about when you need to look at something that is happening in your life.

- It is essential to be relaxed and positive, drink pure water, eat appropriate foods and chew them well, have a good balance between work and play, exercise, have fun, meditate, have good self-esteem, and take any supplements you need to maintain biochemical balance in your body.

The good thing is you will feel better, look better, look younger, and think more clearly. I was amazed at how instantly my thoughts became clear—evidence of the link between bowel and brain.

Best to stop eating whatever causes your brain fog in the first place. If your thinking gets foggy or indecisive, do an immediate inventory of what you have eaten and notice the pattern. For me, it is sugar, dairy, and wheat. When I eat an excess of these foods, my clarity of thought suffers proportionately to how much I have consumed. When I have adequate doses of probiotics, glutamine, and green barley, however, it reduces the side effects dramatically.

It's important to realise that avoiding trigger foods and taking supplements aren't dealing with the emotional issues and faulty thinking that caused the imbalances in the first place. Even so, they are a good support for your physical body as you heal.

Often there is an underlying theme of self-doubt, self-criticism, and lack of healthy boundaries with patterns like this. Ultimately, this has to be addressed for true healing rather than just bandaging to occur.

Post-Ganglionic Reflex for Your Bowel

You can use the bowel post-ganglionic reflexes to help your bowel function whether you have a tendency to constipation or diarrhoea. It is simple and best done daily or even more often if you are having acute symptoms. The better your bowel functions, the more efficiently it can eliminate excess hormones and prevent them being reabsorbed into your system.

This does not replace the need to have your spine adjusted to remove interference to the pre-ganglionic nerves; however, these are wonderful techniques you can integrate into your self-help ritual.

Post-Ganglionic Reflex to Detox Your Bowel and Ease Constipation

- Lie comfortably on your back.
- Rest your *left hand* high on your *right shoulder* where your shoulder meets your neck.
- Use your right hand to gently massage your ileo-cecal valve/appendix area in your lower right pelvis, in a head-wards direction until the tenderness eases, either on the skin or through your clothing; it doesn't matter. Don't go in a foot-wards direction over the ileo-cecal valve because you don't want to upset its ability to open and close correctly.
  You may have a bit of bowel gurgling associated with this.
- Your *left* hand rests in place to maintain the circuit while you massage head-wards with your right hand.
- When the tenderness over the ileo-cecal/appendix region has eased, gently massage farther and farther around your bowel in *a clockwise direction*. In other words, come up from your ileo-cecal/appendix area towards your liver (under your right ribs), massage across your body from right to left just below your ribs, and then down the left side of your abdomen towards your left hip and pubes. This is the natural flow of waste through your bowel and you are assisting it.

If you are constipated, it increases the likelihood of toxicity because the stagnant waste becomes a breeding ground for pathogens.

Help yourself by working this reflex each day. Definitely repeat more often as required.

This post-ganglionic reflex is particularly good to do if you are constipated.

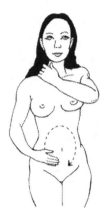

Bowel reflex for detox and constipation.

The more inflamed and blocked your bowel is, the more tender spots your right hand will find. Be gentle. You want to assist your body's natural ability to detox and repair itself, not punish it and add unnecessary pain or stress.

Pay attention to how the foods you eat affect you. Notice how the more food and drinks you consume that don't suit you, the more tender your bowel becomes.

Post-Ganglionic Reflex to Ease Diarrhoea

If your bowels are loose or you have a spate of diarrhoea, you can use the technique above in reverse to help yourself recover faster.

- Lie comfortably on your back.
- Rest your *right hand* high on your *left shoulder* where your shoulder meets your neck. Once again, your right hand rests in place to keep the circuit while you massage with your left hand.
- Use your left hand to gently massage your bowel in a reverse direction. In other words, intentionally go against the natural direction of bowel movement to slow the evacuations.

Start in your lower left pelvis and gently massage head-wards towards your left rib cage, progressing farther and farther around your bowel in an *anti-clockwise* direction. In other words, come up your left side, massage across your body from left to right just below your ribs, and then down the right side of your abdomen towards your right hip and ileo-cecal valve/appendix area. This is against the natural flow of waste through your bowel and you are intentionally inhibiting it. Only do this if you have diarrhoea. Other than this, go in the normal direction that helps elimination of your wastes.

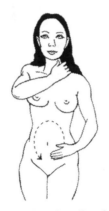

Bowel reflex for diarrhoea.

Candida and Parasites

Candida albicans, or candida for short, is a strain of yeast that is a normal component of a healthy bowel. Candida is ever-present everywhere. Under normal healthy conditions, it does not cause health problems; however, if the delicate balance is tipped, candida can grow out of control and create a myriad of mild to extreme health disorders. This is known as candidiasis, candida infection, or thrush. Thrush, oral thrush, yeast infection, and fungal infection are all candida infections.

Candida normally lives on your mucous membranes of your digestive, urinary, and reproductive systems. Its role is to help your digestion and nutrient absorption, but when there's too much, it breaks down the walls of your bowel and enters your bloodstream, makes toxic by-products, and causes leaky gut syndrome. This can cause a range of health issues from hormonal imbalances, digestion issues, and even depression.

Tipping the Balance

When an overgrowth of candida, parasites, or pathogenic bacteria replace the friendly bacteria that line the GI tract, it causes inflammation.

Plus it can release part of its fungal wall as debris which also causes inflammation.

Long-term inflammation can, amongst other things, disrupt the surrounding environment of breast cells. Hence, adverse changes to normal gut flora (such as long-term antibiotic use, sugar consumption, spinal subluxation, hormonal imbalance, etc.) can double the risk of breast cancer.

No wonder the prevention of breast cancer lobby are so against sugar. In other words, sugar feeds the candida, allowing for overgrowth which creates inflammation and increases the risk of breast cancer (as well as diabetes, suppression of the immune system, depression, and most modern diseases).

Candida grows out of control with changes in
- sugar levels
- pH
- temperature
- hormones
- the amount of other bacteria which normally keep it in check (e.g., acidophilus and bifidus)
- diet, such as
  - alcohol
  - carbohydrate
  - yeast consumption

When there is an overgrowth of candida, it inflames the mucous membrane and makes holes in the bowel wall, creating a condition known as leaky bowel or leaky gut syndrome. This means the fungus as well as larger, undigested particles of food can go through the bowel wall into the bloodstream and causes immune problems and food allergies.

Candida thrives if you
- have a high stress lifestyle
- have a high-sugar or high-carbohydrate diet—these feed the candida
- drinking chlorinated water
- take antibiotics
- take the pill
- take cortisone drugs

In these circumstances, candida wins the war against the friendly bacteria, such as acidophilus and bifidus, and continues to multiply and release toxins through your bloodstream, affecting your entire body. You know that something is wrong because you never feel "quite right."

Candida and Oestrogen

Candida growth flares with high progesterone.

Candida produces oestrogen-like compounds (in an effort to counteract high progesterone), which can obviously disrupt normal hormone function.

Meanwhile, other organisms can provoke hormone changes by binding oestrogen which makes it unavailable, causing the opposite problem than excess.

Symptoms of Candidiasis (Candida Overgrowth)

- tiredness and even chronic fatigue
- bloating, including being pot bellied
- diarrhoea
- irregular menstruation, endometriosis, PMS
- low libido
- headaches
- aching muscles
- food sensitivities
- seasonal allergies
- itchy ears

- itchy anus indicates parasite infections in general
- vaginal itching or infection
- urinary tract infections
- sugar cravings
- mood swings, anxiety, and irritability
- depression
- white coating or spots on tongue or inside cheeks
- brain fog and poor memory
- poor concentration and ADD
- skin and nail issues (e.g., infections, rashes, tinea, hives, eczema, psoriasis)
- PMS
- endometriosis
- painful breasts
- hormonal imbalance
- autoimmune diseases (e.g., scleroderma, psoriasis, Hashimoto's thyroiditis, rheumatoid arthritis, ulcerative colitis, lupus, multiple sclerosis)

Testing for Candida Overgrowth

The symptoms are reasonably definitive; however, you can also have specific testing done to back up suspicion.

- blood test
  High levels of IgG, IgA, and IgM candida antibodies indicate Candidiasis.
- stool test
  A comprehensive stool test needs to be ordered rather than a standard test. This test can also indicate the species of yeast overgrowth.
- urine
  A urine dysbiosis test detects D-Arabinitol, which is a waste product of candida. Hence, an elevated level of D-Arabinitol indicates an elevated level of candida.

How to Effectively Treat Candida

Using diet alone can take a lot of determination and three to six months to get definitive results. Hence, you'll get quicker and better results if you apply all the treatment steps at the same time.

1.   Stop feeding it.
     Stop consuming sugar, yeast, mould, processed and fermented foods totally. This includes large amounts of fruit and juice. It's essential to reduce your stress levels so you won't want these foods to begin with.

2.   Kill the candida.
     Take Saccharoymyces boulardii (a yeast which kills other yeasts), Pau d'Arco, echinacea, artemesia, garlic, and caprylic acid. (This comes from coconut oil and puts holes in the yeast wall, causing it to die.)
     Some people recommend oil of oregano, but this kills the friendly bacteria as well, which kind of defeats the purpose.

3.   Replenish the friendly bacteria.
     Take good-quality probiotics which contain acidophilus, bifidus, and caseii (friendly bacteria). A therapeutic dose is forty billion so anything less than this isn't going to get you the results you want. Probiotics are heat labile, which means they deteriorate in heat. Make sure you keep them in the fridge to maintain their quality and quantity. They are best taken first thing in the morning on an empty stomach so they aren't competing with your food.
     The good and bad bacteria balance in your body is crucial to efficient biochemistry and good health.

4.   Heal your gut wall.
     Healing your gut wall keeps the candida in the bowel where it belongs and prevents it entering your bloodstream.
     Eliminate the toxic thoughts and foods that inflame your bowel (any negative attitude and typically gluten and dairy).
     Add positive thoughts, beliefs, and nutrients that aid absorption (typically slippery elm and aloe vera juice).
     Taking enzymes can help keep candida growth under control.

- Digestive enzymes taken with meals help break down your food, making it more easily absorbed and therefore less available to feed the yeasts.
- Systemic enzymes/proteolytic enzymes or protein digestive enzymes are taken on an empty stomach so they're easily absorbed. They digest the toxins released by dying candida cells.

Digestive enzymes are taken with food, and systemic enzymes are taken away from food.

Giardia

Most first-world countries pride themselves on their standards of water supply. Even so, the parasite Giardia lamblia seems to be taking the world by storm.

Symptoms vary from mild to severe diarrhoea and gas, bloating, foul-smelling stools, and abdominal pain.

Water supply is the common way to be infected by Giardia cysts, but food and hand-to-mouth contact can also be culprits.

Ten grams of goldenseal per day for ten days has proven effective to rid Giardia infection. Other beneficial herbs are grapefruit seed extract, black walnut, wormwood, and ginger.

Parasites

When I was learning about parasites at chiropractic college in the seventies, I thought it was one of those things like AIDS that was rare in our community and I wouldn't have to worry about seeing it. Incorrect. Over the past decades, both have developed into mainstream problems.

Diagnosis is more accurate now, plus there are a higher number of people suffering problems. Live blood practitioners can tell by looking at a finger prick of your blood through a microscope if you have parasites.

It's not a pleasant thought that you may have parasites; however, it's a far more common than may be realized, guesstimates being anywhere from 20 to 80 per cent of the population.

Needless to say, parasites are a problem. They can cause a variety of blatant and obscure health issues.

It's not just about hygiene. Even sharing a yoga mat or using a shopping trolley is all it takes if your immune system isn't up to par.

Definitions

A parasite: is any living thing that lives on or in another living organism. They often interfere with body functions, cause irritation, destroy the host's tissues, and release toxins into the bloodstream.

A host is the organism which harbours the parasite.

Two Main Types of Parasites

There are large parasites usually called worms and small parasites that need a microscope to be seen.

- Round and flat worms (large parasites called nematodes and heminthins) can travel through your bloodstream before they're developed and infect any organ, gland, or part of the body. Depending on the type of worm, they can grow from a few centimetres to metres long.
  They can lay from a thousand to millions of eggs each day.
  The eggs stick to the walls of our intestines.
  The fish tapeworm is the largest of human tapeworms and can grow up to ten metres long.
  Beef and pork also have tapeworms.
- Protozoa (small single-celled parasites) travel through your bloodstream, reproduce, and can invade any cell in the body just like bacteria.

Intestinal parasites are most often due to constant negative thinking, insufficient immune system, deficient personal hygiene, poorly washed foods, or polluted water.

Parasites are undesirable invaders which take nutrients from the body; excrete toxic waste; destroy, injure, or irritate the body. Hormonal imbalances, allergies, arthritis, digestive disorders, asthma, and even nerve disorders can be directly linked to parasite infections.

- Mild infections can be asymptomatic, which does not make them any less harmful; it just means the problem is under your radar.
- Heavy infections can cause abdominal pain, diarrhoea, and appetite fluctuations.
- Very heavy infections can cause weight loss, appendicitis, blood loss, anaemia (Chronic anaemia can be from hookworm infestation. It attaches to the lining of the intestines and bites into blood vessels. It can drink enormous amounts of blood daily), and even death.

The moon plays an intricate part in the worm cycles just as it does humans. In other words, worms go rampant leading up to a full moon. Hence, if a person is extra anxious at the full moon, they may have parasites.

Worms also love sugar, acid environment, and constipation. More evidence that sugar is the scourge of our era.

Parasites often go undiagnosed because
- They may not be common in the region; however, with so many people travelling to exotic places, geography isn't a limitation anymore. Even if you haven't travelled far, it's likely the people around you have.
- Practitioners are busy and don't always get a full picture of your symptoms.
- Symptoms are similar to other conditions (e.g., hormone imbalance, flu, and chronic fatigue syndrome)

Unless we change the way we run our lives, we will continue to have growing problems.

Parasites can multiply in your body from
- ingesting raw or poorly cooked, meat, and fish
- contact with animals, such as patting a cat or dog and transferring the parasites to your mouth when you eat. Hence, the reason for washing your hands after handling animals.

- not enough friendly bacteria in your bowel. For example, from antibiotics, if your friendly gut flora is wiped out by antibiotics, the parasites are left with no competition and thrive. Unfortunately, if your gut flora levels are inadequate, holes can form in your bowel wall and allow the parasites to travel to other sites in your body, such as your liver and brain. Hence, the importance of balance in your gut bacteria is becoming more and more obvious.
- drinking contaminated water
- through open wounds
- burrowing through bare skin on the feet

Our food, cleaning solutions, and personal-care products (e.g., shampoo and body lotion) are high in solvents. The two most common are

- benzene
- propyl alcohol

These solvents cause the microscopic eggs from parasites to hatch quickly.

They can be passed sexually, by shaking hands, walking barefoot, eating or drinking from another's utensils, swimming in polluted lakes, rivers, or streams, and even by going to the beach.

In days of yore, before we used these chemicals, the parasite eggs would pass through our bodies, leaving us safe.

Don't use this information to feed fear and avoid these activities. Simply keep your sugar intake low, immune system high, and do whatever supports you to maintain healthy balance.

Symptoms of Parasite Infection

Symptoms usually depend on the type of parasite; however, the symptoms are often widespread, prolific, and similar to other syndromes. Such as

- chronic unexplained tiredness
- grinding teeth at night
- menstrual irregularities
- insomnia

- waking between 2 and 3 a.m.
- drooling while asleep
- bed wetting
- If you wear a gold ring and it discolours your finger, this is an indicator of chronic parasite infection in your small bowel.
- unexplained aches and pains
- nervousness
- picking the nose
- itchy anus
- itchy ears
- allergies
- digestive disturbances, such as
  - diarrhoea
  - constipation
  - excess gas
  - food sensitivities
- anaemia
- skin problems, such as
  - rashes
  - eczema
  - itching
- depression
- poor memory
- brain fog
- unsuccessful candida program and still crave carbohydrates (including bread and fruit), sugar, and alcohol
- white raccoon eyes
- white above the lips

The Lost Art of Deworming

In the past, it was commonplace to take castor oil, mineral oil, or a type of herbal mix to clear parasites every six months or with the change of seasons.

Each culture had its favourite approach. Is this where the six or twelve month medical check grew from?

Parasite Cleansing Programs

The best parasite-cleansing programs involve
- a periodic cleanse of the whole body expelling the parasites
- ridding what they feed on (toxins and sugar)
- ridding the toxins they create
- preventing re-infestation

Herbal Mixture Magic
Typical modern medication only kills a select group of parasites; however, the right blend of herbs can kill many birds with one stone, so to speak.

The three main herbs are
- wormwood (artemesia). This kills developing and adult parasites.
- cloves. This kills the eggs.
- black walnut. This kills developing and adult parasites.

These three herbs need to be used together to kill both the eggs and mature parasites.

Best you work with a trained herbalist to get the right mix, quantities, and time frame for you and your family.

In other words, you want the right blend often enough to do the job, but not so much it knocks your socks off.

Artemesia or Wormwood
Artemisia is particularly effective against parasites. I also use it as a preventative against malaria when travelling. The Chinese also use it to treat cancer.

Castor Oil
Castor oil comes from the castor bean (Ricinus communis). It has been used for centuries in multiple cultures as an excellent tool to clean the colon and help to remove parasites. It is also known as Palma Christi or the "Palm of Christ."

- Mix one tab spoon of organic castor oil in some hot water and sip slowly. (If you're extra brave and within ongoing close proximity of a toilet, you can also add one tablespoon of flaxseed oil).

* This is not recommended during pregnancy, breastfeeding, and menstruation or for long-term use.

Colloidal Silver (50 ml per litre of de-ionised water)

Colloidal silver can be used to kill pathogens by taking 5 mls in 250 ml of water four or five times per day.

Hydrogen Peroxide

Most harmful bacteria and cancer cells are anaerobic. This means they die in the presence of oxygen. Hydrogen peroxide is a strong oxidizer and hence kills pathogens. For oral use, it's best to use food-grade hydrogen peroxide under the supervision of a trained health professional.

Olive Leaf Extract

Olive leaf extract is antibacterial, antiviral, and antifungal. Take 5 mls four to five times per day.

Garlic

Garlic is an amazing herb. It contains
- nearly eighty sulphur compounds which are reputed for fighting infection and promoting healing.
- allicin which kills bacteria, fungi, and protozoa. In other words, it's nature's broad spectrum antibiotic and, unlike pharmaceuticals, it doesn't affect friendly bacteria.

Aloe Vera Juice

Aloe vera juice is antibacterial, antiviral, antifungal, and laxative. Take 25–50 mls twice per day on an empty stomach. First thing in the morning is standard.

Lactobacillus and Bifidus

Probiotics such as these are friendly bacteria, which make it harder to parasites to take hold.

Pumpkin Seeds

Chewing pumpkin seeds is a traditional Native American treatment for deworming. Plus they're a fabulous natural source of zinc, which is required for immunity, hormone, and enzyme functions.

Grapefruit Seeds

Chewing grapefruit seeds releases its antifungal agent and helps produce beneficial bacteria.

Pineapple

The enzyme bromelain in raw pineapple destroys parasites. It can destroy the protective coating around the parasite cysts and also the larvae inside. This is why raw pineapple is traditionally served with pork products, to counteract potential parasite infestation from the meat.

Gentian Root

Gentian root is *not* gentian violet dye (methylrosaniline chloride).

It rids parasites, kills bacteria (great for urinary tract infections), starts menstruation, stimulates the circulation and appetite, strengthens muscles, and counteracts poisons.

If you're a home-remedy person, be certain you identify gentian correctly because many have mistaken the highly toxic white hellebore (Veratrum album) for gentian and accidentally poisoned themselves instead. Oops.

Cramp Bark

Cramp bark is regularly used for regulating female imbalances. As the name suggests, it helps relieve cramps. In other words, it relaxes the ovaries and uterus including the after pains of childbirth.

Black Seed (Crystalline nigellone)

Black seed is antibacterial, antifungal, and anti-parasitic (antihelminthic). It enhances T-cell production in the immune system. As well as these good deeds, it regulates blood pressure and enhances bile, breast milk, and sperm production (not in the same person).

Thyme

Thyme is a strong herb. It is kills worms and fungal infections (including athlete's foot and lice) and is used for mastitis, suppressed menstruation, anaemia, lung problems and tooth infection.

Lugol's Iodine

Lugol's iodine is made from iodine (can be toxic) and potassium iodide (non-toxic). It is antibacterial, antifungal, antiviral. As well as helping rid parasites, it helps with the die-off symptoms that can occur as some parasites are culled.

It is often used in emergency when there's a radiation leak to block radioactive iodine uptake.

Plus it is used as a guide to vagina and cervical cancer detection. Normal vagina cells have a high glycogen content and stain brown by iodine. Cancerous vaginal tissue doesn't stain brown. This is how they know where to take biopsies from (Schiller's test).

Fennel Seeds

Fennel seeds help with female disorders as well as parasites. Not surprisingly since they're found hand in hand. It also helps digestion, lung and mucous problems, suppresses the appetite, and rids excess fluid and wastes.

18

The Gut-Thyroid Connection

Your gastro-intestinal tract (GI tract) has multiple roles and functions for your health including

- digestion
- nutrient absorption
- elimination
- detoxification
- hormone metabolism
- energy production

Seventy per cent of your immune system resides in your gut.

Ninety-nine per cent of the neurotransmitters in your body are actually created in the bowel. Every brain neurotransmitter can also be found in the bowel.

Twenty per cent of thyroid hormones need to be converted into its active form in the GI tract. In order for this conversion, there must be healthy colonies of beneficial bacteria in the GI tract. Hence, dysbiosis (imbalance in the good versus bad bacteria ratio) can lead to low thyroid function. This explains why so many people with digestive problems also have thyroid hormone imbalances.

Do You Have Digestive Problems?

Most people easily recognize the symptoms of digestive problems, such as

- bloating after eating
- gas
- pain

- poor and inconsistent stool formation
  - loose stools
  - constipation
- burping
- heartburn

Plus you can do the simple and easy transit time test in the comfort of your own home.

Transit Time Test

It is normal for food to pass through your intestines within eighteen to twenty four hours.

If it takes longer than this, there is something wrong.

- Purchase a product called "activated charcoal" which is a harmless substance and will turn your stool either black or dark grey.
- Swallow four capsules with a meal and record the day and time.
- Observe your stools to see when the black or dark grey stools appear. Record the day and time.
- Record the time lapse between taking the capsules and when the dark stools appeared.

If it took longer than twenty-four hours, you have work to do on your digestive tract.

Equally, if it took less than eighteen hours, there may be a problem, such as irritation or inflammation of the GI tract, causing increased peristalsis or gut motility.

Stool Analysis

An unpleasant idea, I know. The thought of providing a stool sample for testing is enough to put the feint hearted off. However, if you're sick enough, you'll do whatever it takes to get well again. (Unfortunately, that's not necessarily true for the general population. Research has shown that only one in nine people diagnosed with life-threatening illnesses make changes to their lifestyles).

A complete stool analysis will determine if there are problems in your digestive tract. It's my suggestion that if you're at the stage of even considering stool analysis, you already know you have a problem.

Complete analysis can tell if you have
- infections (which can also affect the thyroid gland)
- yeast overgrowth, parasites, fungus
- dysbiosis (imbalance between the friendly and non-friendly bowel colonies)
- irritable bowel syndrome (IBS)
- gluten intolerance
- how well you're digesting your food
- how well you're absorbing your food

The Four R's for Bowel Repair

1. Remove. Remove potential food allergens (e.g., dairy, wheat, nuts, eggs, soy), alcohol, caffeine, and NSAIDs (non-steroidal anti-inflammatory drugs).
2. Repair. Spinal adjustments at the nerve levels that control bowel-brain communication (especially Thoracic 10, Lumbars 1, 2 and 4), aloe vera, slippery elm and L-Glutamine all help repair the gut wall.
3. Replace. Replace digestive enzymes to help digest food give support while you heal.
4. Re-inoculate. Probiotics (e.g., lactobacillus and bifidus) restore friendly bacteria colonies. Forty billion is a therapeutic dose. Anything less than this per day isn't going to do the job.

Adrenal Hormones and the GI Tract

When we think of the GI tract, we usually think *digestion*. However, it has an essential role in immunity.

The mouth, throat, and GI tract provide an important defence against infection including bacteria, virii, parasites, fungi, and invasive forms of yeast.

The key to this defence are protective antibodies in saliva and the mucus throughout the digestive system. These antibodies are called secretory IgA (sIgA). They are the first line of defence as they block invasion by pathogens. SIgA levels decrease with adrenal deficiency.

As stress goes up, DHEA goes down and cortisol production in the adrenals goes up. This is a natural response by the body trying to adapt to the stress. DHEA goes lower and cortisol goes higher in people with IBS (irritable bowel syndrome) than those without it.

Cortisone is a steroid drug (a synthetic form of cortisol) often prescribed for people with IBS. It's essential to address why the inflammation is there in the first place, why the adrenals can't keep up with natural cortisol production and amend this, else disease and coping have to ensue rather than healing.

Female Hormones and the GI Tract

Oestrogen and progesterone have significant influence on the GI tract. Imbalance here upsets the movement of food through the intestines either by speeding it up, causing diarrhoea, nausea, and abdominal pain; or by slowing it down causing bloating and constipation.

The bowel moves waste along by a series of ripple or wave-like contractions called peristalsis. Progesterone is a muscle relaxant. Hence, high progesterone makes it harder for the bowel muscles to contract and harder to move waste along.

Candida growth flares with increases in progesterone.

The liver makes bile and the gallbladder stores it so when we eat fatty foods it is released to digest it. When oestrogen is high (due to low progesterone, birth control pills, HRT, liver congestion, spinal subluxation in particular at thoracic 8 and lumbar 3 and 5), bile thickens and can lead to gallstones.

In a healthy woman, excess oestrogen is excreted through the bowel. However, when the bowel is under par, oestrogen that should be excreted can be reabsorbed into the bloodstream, creating an excess. In other words, dysbiosis (imbalance of friendly and non-friendly bacteria) creates an excess of beta-glucuronidase enzyme which reactivates oestrogen and prevents its excretion, raising oestrogen levels.

Thyroid Hormones and the GI Tract

Low thyroid function can lower stomach acid and digestive enzymes and slows digestion in the stomach and intestines. Chronic constipation is a typical symptom of hypothyroidism (low thyroid function).

Melatonin and the GI Tract

Melatonin is mostly produced in the pineal gland and is famous for its role in our sleep-wake cycles; however, some is produced in the stomach and regulates the formation of stomach acid, the enzyme pepsin, and the movement of food through the stomach.

Melatonin production by the pineal is enhanced by darkness and inhibited by light (especially blue light, hence increasing issues since the advent of technology that involves screen staring).

19

The Good Oils

Pure essential oils are natural aromatic compounds extracted from plants. If you've ever enjoyed the aroma of a rose, kaffir lime leaves, or walked through a garden of flowers, you have experienced the beautiful and powerful qualities of essential oils.

If you squeeze the peel of a lemon, the fragrant residue on your hands contains essential oils.

The essential oil industry caters to the needs of aromatherapists, food flavouring, perfumeries, and the pharmaceutical industries. Hence, there's a wide variation in standards of essential oils, and price is usually a good indicator of quality between the same oils.

Comparing prices between different oils, however, can be misleading. For example, rose and frankincense oils are far more expensive than tea tree and eucalyptus due to availability, the amount of oil per kilo of plant, and the extraction processes.

The quality of essential oil required for food flavouring and industrial uses is not suitable for aromatherapy and healing. Buy the best quality you can afford.

I use aromatherapy practitioner grade pure essential oils in all the products I make.

My love for essential oils came after doing two courses in Melbourne in the mid 1980s followed by another two in Sydney in the 1990s. All of the courses inspired me and whetted my appetite to learn more.

The first course was two and a half days per week for ten weeks and covered essential oils, herbs, flower essences, and nutrition. This gave me a broad based knowledge of a range of oils, the various ways to use them and the importance of quality.

The second concentrated on the medical properties of essential oils. I'd always been strongly influenced by aroma and my mother was a keen gardener so the concept that aromatic plants were useful for healing and not just for looking and smelling good fascinated me.

The third also focused on the medicinal properties of essential oils as well as their use in perfumery. This was a formal certificate course with a lot of technical detail at Nature Care College in Sydney. I really only did this course in case I needed to have a certificate one day that officially said I knew something about essential oils. Even though I enrolled with this purely tactical approach, my depth of knowledge was extended even further. The course was so extensive it actually bordered on information overload. It certainly deepened my respect for what the oils do and how they do it. An added bonus was all the really nice like-minded people I met in the classes.

Naturally, I treated myself to a field trip to the south of France to see the lavender fields and distillation plants first hand. Many thanks for being my teacher and guide, Remy Bontoux.

The fourth was a cosmetic making course. This was outrageous fun as well as learning how to make moisturizer and soap bases as a natural foundation for administering oils easily. It was so easy to immerse in this course I could have stepped away from the rest of the world and experimented making natural cosmetics for the rest of my life.

In-between all these courses, I spent a great deal of time studying how to use essential oils with Chiron healing and the master diamond blueprints for the body. Some people refer to these as the etheric pattern or etheric body. In this system, I learned how to use specific oils on specific points of the body (minor chakras or mother points) rather than the broad-based approach of aromatherapy massage. Mother points are the same as the minor chakras discussed in many Eastern healing and yoga philosophies. They are the energy centres that feed all your organs.

My depth of knowledge expanded with my passion and I became more experienced in knowing which oils were best to use for what problems.

These days, it is very trendy and normal to use essential oils in oil burners, baths, and products; however, back in the eighties, people were conservative and even suspicious. Thank goodness, we've come a long way in a relatively short time.

As well as widely used in homes, most corporate offices now know and use the benefits of pure essential oils to help staff and clients focus and feel happy, and of course, it adds to the aesthetic appeal of their establishment.

Aromatherapy has now become such a popular term that even the soap industry is cashing in on it.

This makes it essential for you to be a discerning consumer because there's a vast difference in quality and the concentrations of oils used in products.

If the label doesn't say 100 per cent pure essential oil, then it is not.

If it says fragrant oil, you're getting synthetic or man-made oils which are manufactured to mimic the aroma of real oils. They don't have the healing qualities of natural, pure essential oils. Don't waste your time and money. Purchase the real thing wherever possible.

Initially I only used essential oils in burners and on the mother points; however, after I was divorced, I was blessed to have excess spare time on my hands. Even though I was still running a busy practice and managing my home for myself and my then nine-year-old daughter, I had so much spare time compared to before that I put it to good use—by soaking in the bath with gorgeous oils every chance I got!

People began commenting on how much younger and happier I looked. My skin looked amazing for my years in spite of me being an Aussie sun worshipper, and I was having moments when I actually felt relaxed. This was new!

The regular use of oils was balancing my hormones and moods as well as benefiting my skin.

I recommend you don't wait for external circumstances to change your life. Make the changes you want for yourself now. Create time to light some candles and soak in the bath with your oils of choice, regularly. You'll feel much better, your life will go smoother, and you'll have the illusion of having more time.

I look forward to an oil bath soak now. If I'm stressed, that's where you'll find me—de-stressing. It's a standard joke amongst my friends. In other words, if you can't find me, I'm probably in the bath.

I acquired a large range of oils because I needed a large variety for my patients in the clinic. Justification aside, I have a large range of oils because I think they're beautiful and I'm fascinated by their therapeutic effects.

I had a few favourites even though some were expensive; however, I had no trouble rationalizing the expense.

If I could use ylang-ylang and clary sage to transform me from one of the seven hormonal dwarfs—itchy, bitchy, sweaty, sleepy, bloated, forgetful, and psycho—into an angel, then every cent was money well spent in my opinion.

Because they're dispensed by dropper, a 10–15 ml bottle can last a long time. In comparison to the medication and psychotherapy I could have needed if I wasn't using them, it was an absolute bargain.

What Are Essential Oils?

Essential oils are the part of the plant that gives it its characteristic aroma. Some people have referred to them as the hormones of the plants.

The oils are collected from various parts of the plants including
- flowers
- leaves
- stems
- roots
- fruit peel

The more oil glands or ducts a plant has, the higher the yield of essential oil obtained from it. Generally speaking, this means the cheaper the oil and vice versa. Hence, the difference between the relatively low price of eucalyptus oil which can yield approximately 10 per cent and the high price of rose oil which only yields around 0.03 per cent.

What Are Fragrant Oils?

Essential oils like lavender and eucalyptus are readily available at reasonable prices. Therefore, they're not usually duplicated in laboratories. Jasmine and rose are a different story. Because it takes so much plant to get the oil, it is common for these to be made synthetically.

Given the high demand from the perfume industry, imitations of these oils can be really good with respect to aroma. However, the synthetic fragrance does not have the therapeutic properties of the essential oil.

Essential Oil Safety

Pregnancy
First up, when in doubt, don't.

What is absolutely fine for you may be a massive overdose for a growing baby. Do your research first.

Don't use the following oils if you are pregnant:

(They may have a risk of miscarriage or simply be too concentrated for a growing baby).

- aniseed
- basil
- clary sage
- cedarwood
- cypress
- fennel
- jasmine
- juniper
- marjoram
- myrrh
- nutmeg
- peppermint
- rosemary
- sage
- thyme

Sensitivity to Essential Oils

Some people are sensitive to essential oils just as they are to foods. The most likely of the common essential oils to cause skin sensitivity are

- thyme
- tea tree
- fennel

Obviously, if you are sensitive to an oil, don't use it. Also, if you are sensitive to one oil, be a bit mindful that you may be sensitive to others that have similar constituents in it. The most common reactions to oils are skin reddening and headache.

Photosensitivity

If an oil is photosensitive, it means it will react to sunlight and it's a good idea not to wear it if that area of your body is going to be exposed to the sun.

Bergamot oil is reputed for this.

When I did my first course studying essential oils, one of the things they had me do was place a drop of pure bergamot oil over my thymus gland on my chest each day. The desired result of releasing anger sure worked. I was as irritable as any hormonal woman could ever be, for weeks. All that locked-in anger was sure being released.

I didn't know to keep the area covered because bergamot is photosensitive and reacts to sunlight. The end result was I had a major burn the size of a fingernail on my chest while the rest of my skin was unaffected. This burn left a visible permanent brown mark on my skin. As the years went by, this discolouration actually moved up my chest. It was quite fascinating because I was well and truly past my growing years. (I didn't really grow much even when I was in my growing years.) As the brown mark moved farther head-ward and increasingly noticeable above my necklines, I had it removed.

Don't be overly cautious and restrain yourself from using the photosensitive oils when you need them, but do be respectful of them and don't expose your skin to sunlight if you have them on.

Photosensitive oils
- bergamot
- lime

Less so
- orange
- grapefruit
- tangerine
- mandarin

It doesn't mean don't use them. It just means don't put them neat on your skin and go out in the sun.

A rule of thumb is to wait for twelve hours after application.

Which Oils Are Used for What?

What oils should you use? There is a reasonable amount of overlap with many of the oils with respect to the benefits they provide, which is great because it gives you some leeway and variety to play with. Be prepared to experiment and find the ones you personally get the best results from.

You can use the oils individually or make a blend of two or three different ones that please you. I keep a selection in the bathroom so that I can make a combination of whatever I fancy at the time.

Some are light and bright and others can be quite strong and overpowering if you overdo it. You'll soon get to know which ones you can use more of and which ones to be conservative with. Allow your nose to be your guide. If it smells appealing to you, it's a good sign, and if it smells repulsive, then you'll probably want to refine your mix.

The Main Players on the Hormone Help Stage Are

Ylang-Ylang

When talking hormones, this is my hands-down favourite.

It has a deep exotic aroma which balances moods, is an anti-depressant, and also an aphrodisiac. It's especially good for when your confidence drops and frustration rises.

It'll lighten you up, especially if you've been working too much and start taking yourself and the world too seriously. I use this one a lot. We're excellent friends.

As well as bathing in it, I put a drop on my third eye when I get the warnings I might be a bit touchy.

There are four grades of ylang-ylang.
(Each has its own grade of quality and price.)
- extra. When ylang-ylang is distilled, the first and best quality collection is called "extra."
- first. This is the next grade that is produced and so on.
- second
- third
- complete. You can also purchase a "complete" ylang-ylang which is a blend of extra, first, and second grade.

There are no agreed-upon standards for ylang-ylang, so there can be a big difference in grading from one supplier to another.

Generally speaking, the sweeter the aroma, the higher the grade, and the harsher the aroma, the lower the grade.

Clary Sage

Clary sage is excellent to lift your mood and has a reputation for being euphoric.

I find it simply makes me feel better; however, I know people who feel so elated after using it they won't drive.
- Clary sage is a great oil to put in your burner to create an uplifting atmosphere if you are having guests over.
- It helps you open up to your partner and also to your children.

- I've seen women who have tried everything to combat post-natal depression and it's been clary sage that has done the trick for them.
- 1 drop in your naval eases menstrual cramps beautifully. You can use it with reasonable regularity, as in four or five times per day.
- If you put a drop on your forehead, it will help you to feel better about whatever is happening.
- It helps light periods to flow.
- Clary sage helps with fear, paranoia, and delusions; hence, it helps you get clear if your thinking is scattered or unrealistic.
- Even though it is an oil not to be used in pregnancy, it is very useful in labour because it eases the pain, speeds up the labour, and helps relaxation.

Clary sage has a fairly strong aroma, so it's probably better to be conservative if you are prone to aroma headaches.

Geranium

I love to blend geranium with other oils. By itself, it is quite distinctive, but when it is blended with the others, it takes them from nice to exotic.

- Geranium balances your adrenal glands so it's excellent for balancing stress hormones and, in turn, reproductive hormones.
- It is very good if your period is too heavy.
- It's a bit of an all-round helper for hormones because it also helps depression, fluid retention, and menopausal symptoms.
- I've also found it is excellent for soaking in the bath when I've overexerted myself and my muscles are aching. It gives almost instant relief.

Lavender

Even people who have no experience of aromatherapy at all are usually aware of lavender. It is pretty much the essential oil panacea of all ills.

It helps with an extensive list including
- pain relief (analgesia)
- insomnia
- oestrogen deficiency

- depression
- headaches
- migraine
- high blood pressure
- hysteria
- wound
- burn healing
- helps with light periods
- late periods
- helps you accept painful situations and move on from them (No wonder it is so popular.)

On my field trip to the lavender fields in the south of France, I was very fortunate to spend time at an essential oil farm learning about the different types of lavender. Personally, I prefer the aroma of lavender to the stronger spike lavender and lavandin.

Lavandin is a sterile hybrid of lavender and spike lavender. I'm sure growing lavender can be as beneficial as using its end products because the natural environment it grows in is absolutely stunning. The vista of whole mountains covered in lavender is simply divine. Finding the places up skinny little mountain roads with an inadequate map, signs in French, and a car with left-hand drive is another story though ...

Rose

If your bank balance allows you to buy Rosa damascena (Bulgarian rose, Turkish rose, or Rose otto) or Rosa centifolia (French rose, rose maroc, attar of rose, or rose absolute), I thoroughly recommend you do so. These are the world's best.

It takes approximately thirty roses to make one drop of oil or 4,000 kg to make one litre, so you sure don't want to waste any!

The rose has been referred to as the queen of flowers and the oil has such a divine aroma you can feel your heart healing as you breathe it in.

Like lavender, it is a panacea of all ills helping an array of difficulties, such as

- heavy bleeding
- irregular periods

- cramps
- infertility
- anxiety
- stress
- grief
- unforgiveness
- high blood pressure
- heart arrhythmias
- liver
- gall bladder problems

You can buy rose oil in a more affordable form when it is diluted in jojoba oil. Approximately 5 per cent in jojoba is standard.

I love adding rose oil to products for a touch of exquisiteness. I'll often put a drop over my heart because I'm convinced it opens my heart chakra and helps me let go of betrayals, both real and imagined.

Rosemary

- One of rosemary's claims to fame is its ability to help bad memory. The only thing is you have to remember to use it.
- It clears your head.
- Helps with aching muscles.
- Depression.
- Low blood pressure.
- Liver problems.
- Spleen problems.

Rosemary is excellent to use to improve quality of sleep, especially if you are prone to unusual dreams and waking in the night.

Lavender helps you to get to sleep and rosemary helps you to stay asleep.

This is an excellent oil to add to your shampoo and conditioner to help hair regrowth.

Juniper

Juniper has an unusual aroma. It is fabulous for

- balancing fluid
- balancing blood sugar
- Traditionally, it is used to help kidney, bladder, and diabetic problems.
- brings on and regulates periods
- relieve menstrual cramps
- It is very useful as an emotional cleanser, especially if there are things from your past that you feel shameful or embarrassed about. It also helps bring up hidden issues from the past where you may not have made the connection to your current issues.

Gin is made from juniper berries. This is why gin drinkers often end up crying as their emotions are freed.

Roman Chamomile

Roman chamomile helps with

- irregular periods
- PMS
- regulating temperature
- gently eases pain and inflammation

German chamomile tends to be used more in skin care because it has stronger anti-inflammatory properties compared to Roman chamomile.

Sandalwood

When I was a child, it was common to store sheets and blankets in a sandalwood chest so they would be imbued with its aroma and be disinfected.

Physically, it is excellent for:

- respiratory infections
- urinary tract infections
- aphrodisia

Spiritually, sandalwood is known as a protector because it helps stop you absorbing everyone else's negative energy. Traditionally, you place a drop on your third eye and a drop on the nape of your neck.

You will still have to stop making your own negative energy though.

Essential Oil Notes

Every colour has a shape, every shape has a smell, every smell has a sound, and so on.

The Frenchman Piesse was able to utilise this principle and classified essential oils according to notes on the musical scale. People often take this into consideration when blending oils with the aim of achieving perfectly balanced chords and harmonics.

- Top note oils tend to come from the top of the plant, the fruit, or flower.
  Top notes tend to evaporate first, and this is often the first aroma you will detect in a blend.
- Middle note oils come from the middle of the plant, the stem, or leaves.
  They evaporate next, so these are the next aromas you will detect.
- Base note oils come from the root or bottom of the plant.
  They are the last to evaporate and are usually deeper and longer lasting.

Because the oils of different notes evaporate in different orders, you will have different aromas from the same blend at different times.

The blending of the different oils can be a delicate balance to get a pleasing effect. Generally speaking, it is good to have oils from each one of the notes so they form a pleasing chord.

A common rule of thumb for balanced blending is
- Top notes: 15–25 per cent
- Middle notes: 30–40 per cent
- Base notes 45–55 per cent

Top Note Oils
- citrus
  - bergamot
  - orange
  - lime
  - lemon
  - mandarin
  - neroli
- lemongrass
- peppermint
- thyme

Middle Note Oils
- geranium
- lavender
- rosewood
- rosemary
- petitgrain
- marjoram

Base Note Oils
- sandalwood
- patchouli
- myrrh
- frankincense
- cedarwood
- vetiver

How to Use Pure Essential Oils

Oil Burner
This is one of the easiest ways to use your oils.

I recommend you choose an oil burner with a large bowl so you don't have to keep topping it up with water all the time. When they boil dry, they don't smell pleasant and are hard to clean. They make a mess in the dishwasher, so it's best to hand scrub.

I usually add pure warm water to the bowl rather than having to wait ages for the tea light candle to bring cold water up to a temperature where the gorgeous oil is going to evaporate. If you use hot water, however, the oil will evaporate too fast.

Add approximately five to seven drops combined amount of essential oil, depending on the size of your room. This means five to seven drops of oils in total, not of each oil in your blend. The smaller the room, the less drops and vice versa.

Some oils are stronger than others are, and the top note oils will evaporate before the middle and base note oils, so experiment and discover your personal preferences.

Bath

Use six to eight drops per bath for adults.

The rule of thumb is to use half the normal adult dose for children and the elderly.

Nurture yourself and "do it all."
- Turn the phone to silent.
- Close the bathroom door to the world.
- Light your candles a safe distance away from your hair.
- Add your beautiful blend to your nice warm water.
- Hop in and duck your head under the water so the skin on your face and your hair get the benefit of the oils as well. Be careful not to get any in your eyes.
- Soak, relax, and allow the oils to work their wonders.
- Enjoy every bit of it!

This is an excellent time to gently close your eyes and meditate. Some people like to play ambient music as they soak; however, I personally like silence.

Experiment and discover your own preference.

When you hop out, give the bath a good rinse because the oils can coat it and make it a bit slippery for unsuspecting future bathers.

Massage

I am fortunate that being a practitioner, most of my friends are practitioners as well. For years, I have been totally spoilt and had regular massages. I thoroughly recommend them.

Everyone has a different touch, so try different therapists and styles of massage so you can experience a variety and choose what you want according to your mood and needs.

There can be a substantial difference between a soothing aromatherapy massage and a remedial or therapeutic experience.

Essential oils are never used neat for massage. They are too expensive and too concentrated to use over a large body area. It is usual to dilute them in good-quality "carrier oil," such as almond, apricot kernel, grape seed, olive, or jojoba. (This is technically a wax rather than an oil.)

Some massage therapists don't use essential oils in their oil. Possibly because of expense, but they may not be trained in their use.

It is common for them to have a favourite oil which they buy in bulk and use repeatedly. If you wish to add some of your own essential oils to their carrier, take them with you because most therapists will be open to it as long as you approach them with respect. Say something like, "Would you mind adding these essential oils to your carrier, because I've found they really help me with my PMT/moods/endometriosis/hormone balance/sugar cravings/menstrual cramps …"

It may even open up an informative and beneficial discussion where they can share some extra tips with you.

Rule of thumb for adults: use half as many drops of essential oil per mls of carrier oil.

- For 50 ml of carrier, add up to twenty-five drops of essential oil
- For 100 ml of carrier, add up to fifty drops of essential oil.

Halve the amount of essential oil for children and the elderly.

Shampoo and Conditioner

I began blending my own shampoo and conditioner because the more I read about the effects of the chemicals in the products I was buying, the more alarmed I became.

Your hair follicles are portals for easy absorption, so make sure you are absorbing good products and not a cocktail of chemicals into your body.

These days, you can readily purchase sodium lauryl sulphate and propylene-glycol-free shampoo and conditioner bases and simply add your own blend of oils.

Use a 1–5 per cent dilution of essential oils.

In other words, for 100 ml of shampoo or conditioner, add 1–5 ml of essential oil. (A standard teaspoon is 5 ml.)

Creams

Choose a base cream that is water or aqueous based. If you use a petrochemical base cream, you are simply adding to your toxicity, which is counter-productive to what you're trying to achieve.

Add your essential oils in a 1–5 per cent dilution.

In other words, for 100 g of base cream add 1–5 ml of essential oil. (A standard teaspoon is 5 ml.)

If you are using the cream on your face, use the lowest dilution.

The essential oils will help you smell and look beautiful while they help you heal and get more out of life.

Which Oils Are Best for Which Conditions?

Labour

Lavender is consistently the most chosen oil in labour. It reduces anxiety, pain, and lightens the mood.

Peppermint helps vomiting and nausea in the later stages of labour.

Clary sage helps increase contractions, but most women then want lavender again to ease the anxiety.

PMS

To reduce depression and irritability: ylang-ylang, clary sage, bergamot (this can bring the anger "out" in some women), Roman chamomile, and lavender.

To decrease fluid retention: juniper, rosemary, and geranium.

Dysmenorrhoea

Menstrual pain can be relieved with clary sage, lavender, peppermint, jasmine, cypress, and chamomile.

One drop of clary sage in the navel works wonders as long as the skin isn't sensitive to having neat oil on it.

Menopause

Hot Flushes: clary sage, geranium, sage, lemon, evening primrose oil
Night Sweats: cypress, sage, grapefruit, apricot kernel oil
Fluid Retention: sweet fennel, juniper, lemon, geranium, apricot kernel oil

To Improve Moods: ylang-ylang, clary sage, bergamot, Roman chamomile, and lavender.

N.B. Sweet fennel is natural plant oestrogen.

Thrush/Candida

Antiseptic and anti-fungal oils: tea tree, German chamomile, geranium, lavender, myrrh, lemongrass.

The traditional way: blend a combination of these oils, add three drops to a large bowl of warm water, and sit in it twice a day.

The Radical "Let's Get It Gone" Way

Anyone who has had thrush, however, knows you just want it gone. Ditch the sugar and yeast from your diet you already know to do and sprinkle tea tree oil over a tampon and insert it for as long as it feels comfortable. This gets the oil to where it needs to do the job, plus when you remove the tampon, a lot of the infected material will come out with it.

If it burns too much, this is not for you.

20

Flower Essences

Back in the 1980s, a friend of mine was organizing a flower essence course and asked me to help her with the logistics.

I had never heard of flower essences before. I didn't know what they were or what they did, but she was a close friend and colleague and I wanted to help her out. What a good decision that was.

The course was facilitated by Ian White, the founder of the Australian Bush Flower Essences. His introduction included the structure of the aura and the energy bodies that surround us, and I was immediately interested. I had already been studying the master diamond blueprints and Chiron healing and had witnessed my patients experiencing miracles. My knowledge was now being expanded to include the healing effects of flowers and how they influence our energy.

Flower essences help you balance your emotions. Emotions are "energy in motion." When your emotions are balanced and your energy is moving in the right direction, your physical body can heal.

As well as helping with negative emotions, flower essences can be used to enhance your positive emotions.

The good news is they're inexpensive, easy to use, and usually in a dilute brandy base so they taste pleasant.

What Are Flower Essences?

Flower essences are vibrational remedies made from flowers that can help you with your emotions by harmonising and healing your negative feelings and belief patterns.

They are *not* essential oils.

The remedies from different flowers can help with the myriad of different emotions you express and suppress.

Flower essences are not new. Even the Aboriginals and Egyptians used them to restore emotional balance. Sadly, a lot of the old knowledge has been lost, but in modern times, Dr. Edward Bach rediscovered the mind-body assistance from English flowers and Ian White from Australian flowers.

How Are They Made?

These are the raw steps to making flower essences; however, the real truth involves more ritual and displays of respect to the plant and nature spirit kingdoms.

Flowers are gathered from pristine environments that are free of pollution and man-made impositions such as power lines.

The flowers are placed in a bowl (not plastic or synthetic) of pure water and left in direct sunlight (i.e., no shadows over the bowl) for a number of hours so the water is imbued with the essence of the plant.

The flowers are removed from the bowl and the solution they were in is kept.

Pure brandy is added to the water to ensure nothing unintentional grows in it.

This is called the *mother tincture*.

The mother tincture is diluted to stock potency and this is diluted yet again, to attain the appropriate therapeutic concentration referred to as *dose* strength.

Which Remedy Helps What?

Although there is an extensive range of remedies, the ones I found myself using repeatedly to successfully help with hormone related issues were

- billy goat plum

  This essence helps you stop judging and hating your body and any aspects of it. If you have feelings of shame or self-loathing, or feel dirty about sex, this remedy will help.

  It helps you accept and love your body exactly as it is.

- black-eyed Susan

  Are you impatient? Do you get overcommitted? This essence will help you stop running around and to centre yourself long enough to hear your inner voice.

- bottlebrush

  Bottlebrush helps you brush out the past and move on.

  This essence especially helps females in times of transition or change, such as going from adolescence to adulthood to motherhood to selfhood to grandmother-hood.

  It helps you let go of unresolved mother issues and helps bonding between parents and babies.

  It helps you clean out and let go the residues of your past and move into your bright future.

  This also helps when you do bowel cleanses.

  If you have love handles, this is your body's way of telling you to start now.

- bush fuscia

  This essence helps you access your intuition. Yes, this is supposedly a woman's domain; however, when the hormones kick in, the intuition can get kicked out. It integrates your inner feminine and masculine, right and left brain, logic, and creative. It especially helps with being able to speak up.

- crowea

  This essence helps when you just don't feel right, when you're out of balance. If you find yourself continually worrying, this will help you restore peace and calm and help you sort your feelings out.

- dagger hakea

  This essence helps you let go of resentment. Resentment is "re-send-ment"—thinking the same thoughts over and over. Resentment is often not displayed but kept hidden.

  Use this essence to help rid yourself of habitual negative thoughts that keep coming back even when you don't want to think them. If you have grudges against family members, old lovers, or friends, this remedy is for you.

  It will give you the opportunity to think new thoughts.

- five corners

  This essence helps when you have low self-esteem, poor self-confidence, and a self-love deficiency.

- mountain devil

  This essence helps you let go of anger as well as deal with hatred, jealousy, and rage. It helps you trade suspicion for love and acceptance.

  If you tend to hold grudges and have issues with boundaries, this essence is for you.

  If you've got thunder thighs, this is your body's way of showing you that you have stored anger to resolve.

- mulla mulla

  This essence is traditionally used for issues to do with fire. For example, fear of fire, recovery from burns, and distress in the heat. Many women find it useful to deal with hot flushes.

- old man banksia

  This essence helps when you're feeling tired and disheartened. It will help peel the covers off your enthusiasm and restore your joie de vivre.

- peach-flowered tea tree

  This essence helps with sugar balance and mood swings.

  If you lose enthusiasm for projects for no obvious reason, don't follow through on your goals, get bored easily, or fear getting old, this essence is for you.

  If you have a sweet tooth or flabby fat on your upper arms, these are indicators to use this.

- pink flannel flower

This essence helps when you're feeling ungrateful, taken for granted, and can't see anything good happening in your life. It will help you to open your heart and see what you can be grateful for which will in turn help you to manifest your desires.

- she-oak

  This essence helps with hydration and fertility—especially the inability to conceive for non-physical reasons. The fruit from the tree even looks like an ovary.

  If your skin or hair is dry, then chances are your reproductive organs are dehydrated too.

  As well as taking oral doses of she-oak, you can also put a squirt in your water bottle so your body utilizes the water you are drinking more thoroughly.

- sturt desert pea

  This essence this will help you let go of feelings of deep hurt, grief, sadness, and emotional pain.

- waratah

  This essence helps when your feel like you're going through the "dark night of the soul." When you're in despair, it helps give the courage to cope. When everything seems hopeless, it can help buoy your faith while you gather your resources to resolve your issues.

- wisteria

  This essence will help you when you don't feel like sex or don't like the feel of sex. If you're uncomfortable about sex or intimacy, this will help you relax and be more open.

  This is the remedy to help you get back to your centre and back to allowing yourself to give and receive pleasure.

  If you have any history of sexual abuse, take this remedy to help release the remnants of mental and emotional residue.

How Do You Use Flower Essences?

You can use the essences individually or in a mixture at the same time if they're addressing a common issue. A standard program is to take seven drops under the tongue each morning and night for two weeks.

The essences help heal different parts of yourself and you will have your favourites that get you out of trouble when you feel like you're sinking.

Remember to also use them to expand your positivity and take you to higher ground, not just to cope with negativity.

21

Essential Tests You Should Know

It has been drummed into us enough to seek the advice of qualified and experienced health-care practitioners when we need them. This is obviously good advice. However, it doesn't mean you should hand over the responsibility for your health to anyone else.

> Your practitioners are responsible for your health care,
> but you are ultimately responsible for your health.

There's a lot of simple signposts you can learn to interpret that will help guide you and your practitioners along the simple and easy path for your healing and maintenance of well-being.

Use these signposts to your best advantage and adjust your thoughts, words, and lifestyle accordingly.

Chromium Deficiency Indicators
- sugar cravings
- dandruff
- mood swings
- acne
- weight gain

Dark Circles under the Eyes
- black circle: weak kidneys and food sensitivities
- brown: liver congestion

Cracks at the Corner of Mouth
- Vitamin B2 (riboflavin) deficiency
- Iron deficiency

Essential Fatty Acid Deficiency
- dry skin
- dry hair
- excess wax in ears
- poor concentration
- low moods
- food cravings

Eyebrows
Loss of hair at the outer third of your eyebrows: thyroid hormone deficiencies

Inappropriate Fat Accumulation
- waist: too many androgens and small bowel problems
- lower thighs: enzyme deficiencies
- upper thighs: oestrogen and progesterone imbalance
- under arms: excess blood sugar
- love handles: large bowel problems

Hair Analysis
Hair analysis gives an accurate recording of not only your mineral levels but also toxic heavy metals, such as lead, mercury, and cadmium. The testing company will give clear instructions about where to snip the hair from and how much is needed.

The closer to your body the hair sample is taken, the more indicative of recent conditions in your body. In other words, if you have long hair, sending the trim off the end is not much use because it will indicate what was happening in your body a long time ago rather than recently.

Iron Deficiency
- want to eat ice
- tired
- headaches at the back of your head

- more hair loss than normal
- pale on the inside rim of your lower eyelid
- pale skin
- fainting and dizziness
- sore tongue
- breathless

Magnesium Deficiency
- PMS
- cramps
- twitching eyelid
- chocolate cravings
- sugar cravings
- insomnia
- mood swings
- dental cavities
- confusion
- depression

Nail Indicators
- chipping and splitting: Poor protein digestion. Needs hydrochloric acid (betaine hydrochloride)
- longitudinal ridges:
  - mineral deficiencies due to lack of digestive enzymes. You may need to supplement minerals as well as enzymes because they won't be absorbed adequately while the enzymes are low.
  - eczema
  - rheumatoid arthritis
  - peripheral vascular disease
  - lichen planus infection
- white spots: zinc deficiency
- concave: iron deficiency
- splinter haemorrhages:
  - injury
  - severe anaemia

- o infective endocarditis (inflammation of the heart muscle)
  - o rheumatoid arthritis
- discolouration: Healthy nail plates are pink and the nail looks white as it grows off it.
  - o nail polish staining
  - o nicotine stains from cigarettes
  - o infections
  - o injury affecting the nail bed
  - o medication: antibiotics, anti-malarials, chemotherapy
  - o melanoma
- lifted nail: If the nail plate lifts off bed, it will appear white.
  - o rough manicure or pedicure
  - o nail varnishes which contain hardening chemicals (e.g., formalin)
  - o rough removal of artificial nails
  - o psoriasis
  - o tinea or fungal infection (watch for diabetes or lowered immunity)
- thickened nails: This affects toenails more than fingernails.
  - o fungal infection
  - o injury
  - o poor circulation
  - o arthritic toes
  - o faulty gait (walking pattern) creating abnormal pressure
  - o poor fitting shoes
  - o psoriasis
- brittle nails that break easily: thyroid imbalance
- pits, grooves, or crumbling are associated with skin and systemic autoimmune diseases, such as psoriasis, eczema, lichen planus, or lupus.

Rash on Chin

Excess sugar gives a red rash on your chin. Children will typically lick this rash and exaggerate it when they have excess sugar.

Saliva Testing

Saliva testing has proven to be very useful in testing hormone levels. It is also cheaper and painless. Saliva testing may actually be more accurate than testing blood levels, because in the blood, many of your hormones are bound to proteins, so even though they are there, they can be functionally useless. In other words, it depends on the way the lab does the tests as to the usefulness of the results.

Another valuable piece of information the biochemist can tell from testing your saliva is its pH. This will give insightful information about the initiation of the digestive process in your mouth. Combining the information from saliva testing and urine testing will often give them even more insight into the status of your biochemistry.

Stool Appearance

- floats and is hard to flush. You're eating too much fat or your liver and gall bladder are congested and having trouble keeping up with its digestion.
- sticky. Too much mucous in your bowel. Stop eating foods you're sensitive to. Typically, this is dairy and wheat.
- food present. Need digestive enzymes and chew your food properly
- dry. Need more water; fresh fruit, and vegetables; exercise; probiotics; let go emotions from the past that you are hanging onto. Do the post-ganglionic reflex for constipation each day.
- loose. Modify diet; probiotics; rtemisia; set some goals and achieve them. Do the post-ganglionic reflex for diarrhoea each day.
- ribbon-like. Your bowel is congested and you need to do a cleanse or have a colonic. Do the post-ganglionic reflex for constipation each day.
- sheep droppings. Your liver is congested which is upsetting your bowel. Do a cleanse and take St. Mary's thistle, psyllium husks, and drink plenty of water. Do the post-ganglionic reflex for constipation each day.

Tongue Indicators

- coated white
  - excess mucous in your body. Stop eating foods you're sensitive to. Typically, this is dairy and wheat.
  - candida. Take acidophilus, bifidus, Pau d'Arco, and garlic. Let go all victim consciousness.
- coated yellow
  - congested bowel. Do a bowel cleanse and take acidophilus, bifidus, and aloe vera. Do the post-ganglionic reflex for constipation each day.
- crack down the middle
  - HCL (hydrochloric acid) deficient
  - Don't drink carbonated/fizzy drinks
  - Chew your food properly
- red tip
  - emotional imbalance
- sore tongue
  - iron deficiency/anaemia
  - vitamin B deficiency

Urine Testing

Urine testing is cheaper, totally painless, and less invasive than blood testing. It can be used to test variations in levels during the day.

It can be used to test urine levels of

- carbohydrates
- pH
- cellular debris
- salts
- nitrogen wastes
- ammonia wastes

You're likely to need to expertise of a biochemist to interpret the results and know what to do to correct the imbalances, but that usually comes with the report. They can give you valuable and measurable information that helps you heal yourself.

Vitamin B6 Deficiency

If you crave peanuts or peanut butter, you have a vitamin B6 deficiency. It's your body's way of trying to replenish it.

- vitamin B6 deficiency test. If you're vitamin B6 deficient, it will be harder than normal to curl your fingers comfortably into the palm of your hand.

  Hold both arms outstretched from the sides of your body with your palms facing up and fingers extended (so you look like a standing T).

  Without bending your wrists or your palms at all, curl your fingers to touch the outer edge of your palm where your fingers meet it. This is not making a fist. Do not bend your palm.

  If you can touch your fingers to the border of your palm easily, you do not need more B6. If it is restricted in any way or impossible to do, then you need more B6.

  Take a B complex supplement so that you are getting the balance of the B's together.
- fluid retention
- PMS

Vitamin C Deficiency

- bruise easily
- bleeding gums
- immune deficiencies and infection
- nuisance infections (such as needing to blow your nose)
- vision problems leading to cataracts.
- cellulite

If you take too much vitamin C at a time, you will get loose in the bowels, so it's best to spread the dosage out during the day.

Vitamin E

- sore breasts
- cellulite
- high cholesterol
- atherosclerosis

- PMS

Thyroid
Do It Yourself Thyroid Screening

You can do an easy test to screen for low or high thyroid function with a thermometer at home. Simply take your underarm or oral temperature first thing upon awakening in the morning.

Take these temperatures while you are still in bed.

To test your underarm temperature, you need to leave the thermometer in place for ten minutes.

To test your oral temperature, you need to leave the thermometer in your mouth for two minutes.

The normal range is 97.8 F to 98.2 F or 36.1 C to 37.8 C.

If your temperature is below this range, it is an indicator of hypothyroidism or low thyroid function, and if it is above this range, it is an indicator of hyperthyroidism or overactive thyroid.

Of course, if you have an infection at the time, this will be inaccurate because you naturally raise your temperature to fight infection.

Also, your resting pulse rate should be sixty-five to seventy-five beats per minute. Below this is an indication towards low thyroid function, and above this is an indication towards high thyroid function.

Finger and toenails tend to be brittle and break easily with low thyroid function.

Zinc Deficiency
- white spots in your nails
- liquid zinc test: can't taste it. (It tastes significantly unpleasant when your zinc levels are adequate.)
- acne
- fatigue
- infertility
- lowered immunity and infections
- cracks behind your ears

22

What Vitamins and Minerals Come from Where?

In a perfect world, we would gain all our nutrients from our foods. Unfortunately though, our food isn't what it used to be. The nutrient value has declined as foods are force grown and then transported and stored. Even the flavour of the fruits and vegetables of our grandparents' era is not what it is today. Sadly, we're sorely lacking.

In the last century, our food became increasingly more tampered with in the name of new flavours and varieties, greater yields, increased pest resistance, consistent size and shape, better transporting qualities, longer shelf life, and aesthetic appeal. Needless to say, natural isn't necessarily natural anymore. A natural apple is now increasingly more likely to be a hybridized, irradiated, or waxed variety.

Fortunately, the public demand for organic and good-quality food is increasing which makes it more viable for farmers to grow it, which in turn makes it more available to consumers.

This usually means produce is seasonal rather than available all year round, which is more aligned with what our bodies need. If a food doesn't grow naturally in a particular environment or season, then maybe there are other foods that are better for you to eat at that time.

We are beings of nature, and the more we align with its cycles instead of exerting our will over them, the healthier we will be and the smoother our paths will be. Doesn't it make innate sense to eat salads in summer and hot foods in winter?

When you are in tune with your body and listen to its needs, you'll naturally be attracted to the foods you need at that time.

Calcium
- green barley grass
- wheat grass
- alfalfa
- dairy foods. I don't recommend this as a source. No other species on the planet naturally consumes the milk of another species and no other species on the planet consumes milk past weaning. It is mucous producing and prevents the absorption of valuable nutrients from other foods.
- fish
- nuts
- dried fruits
- vegetables

Chromium
- celery
- black pepper
- whole grains
- yeast
- chilli
- oysters
- cabbage
- banana
- carrots
- green beans
- egg yolks

Essential Fatty Acids
- fish
- seeds and oils, including flax, evening primrose, olive, sunflower, sesame, pumpkin
- avocado
- nuts

Fibre
- whole grains, including rice, oats, wheat, millet, corn, rye

- psyllium husks
- fruit
- vegetables
- lentils

Iron
- chicken
- meat
- eggs
- dark-green vegetables
- dates
- beetroot

Magnesium
- green vegetables (the darker the green, the more magnesium it contains.)
- nuts
- whole grains
- seafood

Potassium
- tomato
- banana
- potato
- leafy green vegetables
- raw fruit
- whole grains

Protein
- meat
- fish
- eggs
- cheese
- nuts

Selenium
- fish

- broccoli
- garlic
- Brazil nuts

Sulphur
If it smells, it probably has sulphur in it.
- broccoli
- cabbage
- brussels sprouts
- garlic
- onions
- cauliflower

Tryptophan
Tryptophan is an essential amino acid needed to make serotonin. It helps with sleep quality and duration and decreases appetite. It's a good guy.

It is also a precursor of niacin (vitamin B3).

"Essential" means your body doesn't make it so you have to consume it.
- cashews
- all complete proteins

Vitamin A
- Yellow fruits and vegetables
  - apricots
  - carrots
  - pumpkin
  - sweet potato or kumara

Vitamin B
- fish
- meat
- eggs
- whole grains, including brown rice
- yoghurt
- mushrooms
- peanuts

- yeast (Don't take if you have candida problems.)

Vitamin C
- raw fruits
- raw vegetables

Vitamin E
- whole grains
- cold pressed vegetable oils
- avocados
- seeds
- nuts
- leafy green vegetables

Vitamin K
- cabbage
- leafy green vegetables
- vitamin K is also manufactured in your bowel by bacteria.

Zinc
- oysters
- shellfish
- fish
- pumpkin seeds (Munching a handful *every day* is adequate for most people.)
- beans and pulses
- whole grains
- nuts

23

Fibre and Food Sensitivities

As you now know, if you don't eliminate oestrogen via your bowel fast enough, you increase the chance of it being reabsorbed into your bloodstream and escalating any oestrogen dominance problems. The more efficiently the waste is removed from your bowel, the better.

Your diet obviously impacts on the ability of your bowel to remove wastes. A large factor in this is the amount of fibre you eat in your diet.

It's the fibre in your diet that binds oestrogens and other toxins in your bowel and then transports them out of your body. When you don't eat enough fibre, this contributes to the build-up of excess oestrogens and toxins in your bowel and being reabsorbed back into your body. This is especially prevalent if you have "leaky gut syndrome," which is when the bowel wall is more permeable than it should be and allows substances to be reabsorbed back into your body that should normally be excreted.

Your bowel wall can become more permeable because of food sensitivities.

The Synergy Between Fibre and Cholesterol

There are two types of fibre.
- Soluble fibre dissolves in water and becomes soft and gel, like cooked oatmeal. This type of fibre slows down sugar absorption, which will help keep your blood sugar levels even and help lower cholesterol.

  Not that high cholesterol is bad in itself. It's the high blood sugar that is bad, which raises cholesterol to try to deal with it.

In recent decades, cholesterol has been given a lot of unjustified bad press. Cholesterol builds up in arteries where there is inflammation and damage. It does not cause the damage. It is there trying to fix the damage. To blame cholesterol is like blaming firemen for fires. Firemen are consistently seen at fires. They are there trying to put them out. Blaming the firemen for the fires is unjustified.

Cholesterol is consistently seen where there's inflammation in arteries. It's trying to put the inflammation out. Blaming cholesterol for the inflammation is unjustified.

Sugar, gluten, free radicals, and other food sensitivities are known culprits to cause inflammation.

Hence, soluble fibre can help lower cholesterol because it lowers the blood sugar and inflammation and therefore the cholesterol doesn't need to be there anymore.

- Insoluble fibre is dense, fibrous, and doesn't absorb water as in vegetables and bran. This stimulates bowel movements and helps eliminate wastes from your body.

  Insoluble fibre provides bulk, which helps trigger bowel movements and hence helps the elimination of wastes.

What Is Food Sensitivity?

Food sensitivity is when you have an immune system response initiated by food.

Technically speaking, it is when an antigen-antibody complex is formed in response to food which triggers your mast cells to respond.

This means there is an immune reaction to a food. This can be anywhere from mild to severe. In other words, it can be a mild discomfort, a life-threatening allergy, or anything in-between.

Why Does Food Sensitivity Happen?

- Overload of a food and lack of variety in your diet.

Some people dismiss food sensitivities as an issue through faulty logic. They think that because they've eaten a particular food their whole life, it can't possibly be a cause of their problems. They think that if it didn't cause obvious symptoms for the last twenty years, then it's not an issue now.

Incorrect!

It's because they've eaten the same food repeatedly for years that the immune system has become exhausted trying to deal with it. In other words, food sensitivities can arise from eating too much of the same thing for too long. For example, if you've eaten wheat regularly for years, you can develop an intolerance to it.

When you consider the high wheat content in most Western diets, it is easy to understand how this can happen.

How Often Do You Eat Wheat?

- Do you have toast, croissants, pastries, or wheat cereal for breakfast?
- Do you have sandwiches or bread rolls for lunch?
- Do you have pasta or meals with wheat-thickened sauces, or bread on the side, for dinner? Do you eat cookies, crackers, or cakes?

You may be surprised at how much and how often you consume wheat and wheat products.

Read the labels because it is even added to things that seem unrelated, such as soy sauce and potato crisps. (Tamari is a wheat-free substitute to soy sauce.)

How Often Do You Eat Dairy Products?

- Do you have milk on cereal?
- Do you have milk in drinks?
- Cream in cocktails?
- Do you eat cakes, cookies, custards, omelettes, or frittatas?
- Do you eat butter, cheese, cream, ice cream, cream cheese, or yoghurt?
- Do you eat chocolates?

How Often Do You Eat Eggs?
- o Do you have eggs for breakfast? This is an excellent source of protein to start your day—as long as it isn't day after day for decades and you aren't sensitive to them.
- o Do you eat quiche or frittata?
- o Do you drink egg flips or egg nog?
- o Do you eat custard, ice cream, or cake?

How Often Do You Eat Nuts?
- o Do you individually nuts or trail mixes?
- o Do you eat peanut butter, Nutella, or praline?
- o Do you eat sundaes, chocolates, cookies, or cakes with nuts?

- emotional stress and oversensitivity
  As within, so without.
  If your body is reacting to sensitivities, it corresponds that your personality is also reacting to someone or something.

  Who or what are you sensitive to?
  If you are reacting against your food, you are also reacting against yourself and others.
  - o Where are you irritated by what is happening or not happening in your life?
  - o Where are you irritated by what others are doing or not doing?
  - o Where and when are you irritated by what you are or are not doing for yourself?
  - o Where haven't you set boundaries or have set boundaries that are inappropriate?
  - o Where and when do you doubt yourself?

  Set firmer and more appropriate boundaries for yourself. Support you and trust yourself.

- leaky gut syndrome
  When you have an overgrowth of candida in your bowel, this leads to larger than normal particles from your food going into

your bloodstream. This in turn sets up an immune response and sensitivity against these abnormal particles.

Gluten also makes the bowel wall more permeable, which in turn allows other proteins to cross into the bloodstream that shouldn't be allowed through. This means the immune system has to stage a constant war against foot soldiers that shouldn't be there in the first place.

- liver problems
  If the liver is overloaded, you can't digest your food efficiently, which can create an overgrowth of candida, food sensitivities, leaky gut—and the spiral continues.

Indicators of Food Sensitivity Include

- fatigue and sleepiness (e.g., feel tired and sleepy after eating sandwiches for lunch). Teachers have known for decades to teach subjects that require concentration and memory in the mornings because students' attention span can deteriorate rapidly after lunch.
- bloating
- diarrhoea
- poor digestion of foods (e.g., unbroken down food particles evident in the stool)
- lack of absorption of nutrients. In other words, needing to take higher doses of supplements even when the diet is nutritious and balanced. This can also lead to weight gain as your body craves more the nutrients which it isn't receiving because of poor absorption.
- dark circles under your eyes
- sinusitis
- loss of concentration
- loss of motivation
- confusion
- mood changes (e.g., irritability, aggression, uncooperative)
- depression
- headaches

- stiff joints
- Alzheimer's
- schizophrenia

The Most Common Foods People Are Sensitive to Are
- wheat
- dairy
- eggs
- nuts
- sugar
- also soy, potato, tomato, chocolate, wine

Wheat Sensitivity

We have come to rely on our educated knowledge and brains more and more in order to compensate for losing touch with our intuition and innate awareness of nature and her cycles.

Ancient civilizations that ate grain in their diets ate corn to open themselves up psychically and spiritually.

Leading up to their dedication ceremonies, typically with the changes of the seasons, the oracles of the villages would eat a meat-free diet of corn and simple vegetables or broth. This allowed them the lightness of body and energy to tune into their inner voice to advise the villagers of such things as when to plant or harvest or when to prepare for invasion, drought, or war.

After these seasonal rituals, they would eat wheat to shut themselves down and anchor themselves back into their body again. If their intuitive antennae were receptive and active all the time, they could easily lose touch with reality, so this closing down was essential.

As time went by, wheat went from being a post-festive tool and a treat to being used as an everyday indulgence. Instead of eating corn daily and wheat occasionally, we came to eat wheat daily and corn occasionally. Hence, a large part of our natural intuition has been lost because we are unknowingly shutting ourselves down. In other words, wheat shuts us down psychically.

Plus when you eat the same foods constantly, you can set up sensitivities just because of the overload. Wheat products for breakfast, lunch, and dinner day after day is overload in anyone's language.

Wheat shuts our bowel function down physically by making the bowel wall more permeable than it should be. This allows larger particles to go into the bloodstream than should be allowed. Hence, the immune system is constantly overworked fighting these foreign particles that shouldn't be there. This sets up inflammation in the brain, which affects its function. Just like an arthritic knee gets red and inflamed, that's what happens to the brain.

This also sets up inflammation in the arteries where the foreign particles are, leading to atherosclerosis. Plaquing is a healthy response to try to protect and prevent more inflammation.

It also sets up inflammation in the bowel itself, as the immune system tries to halt the invasion across the bowel wall, which leads to a destruction of the bowel villi, which further disrupts absorption. In this context, this is good because you don't want more absorption of particles that shouldn't be being absorbed in the first place; however, destruction of the villi means it's harder to digest everything, not just gluten and its cohorts.

In the Midwest of the United States, nutritional problems from eating excess corn is as prevalent as nutritional problems from eating excess wheat elsewhere in the world.

It is common in Western schools for the attention span and focus of children to drop after lunch. This has been attributed to the constant wheat content of their lunch food, such as bread, cookies, cakes, and bars. Extreme cases also fall asleep. Some teachers tell me it's not just the children who fall asleep!

Skip the grains.

If you have an intolerance to wheat, don't eat it at all. Eliminate it totally from your diet.

Skip the carbs.

Go with protein and vegetables as your staples.

There are many alternative grains to wheat products now. You can easily purchase corn, rice, spelt or buckwheat bread, flour, and pasta.

Be aware that many supermarket corn flours are not actually corn. Read the labels diligently because many corn flours are actually wheat. If the label says "made from wheaten flour," it is not corn.

However, carbohydrates of any description are inflammatory, so best to skip these too.

You can steer towards the simplicity and reliability of using hazelnut or almond meal instead of flour in cakes; however, this is no use if you are sensitive to nuts as well. Using hazelnut or almond meal makes a dense and delicious cake which is filling and satisfying. Most people will be content to have just one small or regular size piece and enjoy the added bonus of protein and natural oils from the nuts.

You can break free of having a dob of cream on the side because these cakes are excellent all by themselves or even with a few berries—or a lot of berries—which are high in vitamin C as well as taste.

Dairy Sensitivity

**Be aware: non-dairy simply means less
than 0.5 per cent milk by weight.**

Dairy is one of the most common food sensitivities in the world. So much so, I can't help but think that cows' milk was meant for baby cows rather than people.

- Humans are the only species on the planet who consume the milk of another species.
- Humans are the only species on the planet who consume milk past weaning.

Drinking cow's milk has been linked to breast and prostate cancer, heart disease, diabetes, and learning difficulties. Cheese and butter can be exemptions for some because the rennet in cheese changes the casein molecules to be more digestible, and butter is casein free.

The harder the cheese, the more rennet it has and therefore the less likely it is to cause a reaction.

The French eat a lot of cheese and still have low cancer and low heart disease.

There are so many good-quality soy, rice, nut, oat, and goat milk products readily available that it is really easy to find cow's milk substitutes. Some people are sensitive to soy as well, so it is important to work with what is best for you rather than simply follow a trend.

If you are dairy sensitive and really want to persist drinking cow's milk, you can purchase lactase enzymes and add it to the milk prior to consumption so it is somewhat predigested for you.

Some people who are dairy sensitive can get away with eating good-quality yoghurt every now and then. If you seek them out, you can purchase good-quality natural yoghurts made with live cultures. The live cultures help your bowel to function by restoring good bacteria levels and help prevent indigestion.

If the yoghurt you have purchased has fruit in it, it also contains additives because the enzymes in the fruit break down the yoghurt and make it watery. Consumers don't like to purchase watery yoghurt so the manufacturers modify it with thickeners to make it more appealing and saleable.

I've never enjoyed drinking milk. I grew up in the era of having to drink it at school because of a well-meaning government scheme where it was provided to all primary schoolchildren. God bless Wendy White for drinking mine whenever we could arrange it.

To consume milk as an adult would leave me bloated, in pain, and looking newly pregnant. The mucous reaction in my body to prevent its absorption also prevented the absorption of essential vitamins and minerals leaving me with a loss of motivation and feeling flat and depressed. This didn't please me or anyone else around me.

If I didn't have dairy at all and then only a small amount every now and then, my body could handle it—kind of. But if I crossed the threshold into whatever my body considered to be overload at the time, it let me know. I see this as a blessing because I didn't have to guess whether it is right for me or not. It's clearly not.

Symptoms of Dairy Sensitivity

The most common symptoms are
- gastrointestinal: pain, gas, vomiting, diarrhoea, constipation, infantile colic, mucous
- dermatological: skin rashes, hives
- respiratory: runny nose, wheezing, mucous
- headache or migraine
- tachycardia

The symptoms can occur within only a few minutes or sometimes hours later in delayed reactions.

What're the Differences among Milk Allergy, Milk Protein Intolerance, and Lactose Intolerance?

A food allergy is an immune reaction to a protein that is normally harmless to a non-allergic person. Hence, milk allergy is an immune reaction to milk protein.

Milk protein intolerance (MPI) is a delayed reaction to milk protein. Milk protein intolerance produces a non-IgE antibody and is not detected by blood tests. The symptoms of milk protein intolerance are similar to milk allergy symptoms but usually less severe.

Lactose intolerance is a non-allergic food sensitivity due to a lack of production of lactase enzyme, which is needed to digest the principal sugar in milk.

What're the Guts of It?

- If you have a lactose problem, you'll only get the gut symptoms.
- If you have a casein or milk protein problem, you'll get whole-body symptoms.
- If you have a lactose problem, lactose-free milk is OK.
- If you have a casein or milk-protein problem, lactose free milk is *not OK* because the protein is still present.

- If you have a casein or milk protein problem, you might be OK with A2 milk but not A1.

Milk Proteins

There are two main types of milk proteins.
- casein (αs1, αs2, β, and k caseins), which is found in the solid or curd part of milk. In other words, the part that curdles.
- whey, which is found in the liquid part of milk that remains after milk curdles.

Casein makes up about 80 per cent and whey about 20 per cent. Other low-level proteins are antibodies and iron-carrying proteins.

All cows make beta-casein. There are two types of beta-casein.
- A1
- A2

Most fresh milk brands contain both A1 and A2 beta-casein.

A2 milk comes from cows which produce A2 milk at the exclusion of A1 milk.

(A2 milk still contains lactose. Therefore, if you're lactose intolerant, drinking A2 milk will not avoid your digestion problems.)

A2 milk has been identified as the original form of beta-casein that would have been produced by cows thousands of years ago. At some point, dairy herds across Europe (except France) began producing A1 milk.

Guernsey cows have the highest frequency of A2 genes and therefore produce milk with the highest levels of A2 milk. Jerseys produce A2 milk, though not as high levels as Guernseys. Holsteins and Friesians carry A1 and A2 genes in about equal proportions.

People with milk sensitivity or allergies can be reactive to one of dozens of the proteins in milk. The most common one is alpha S1-casein.

Alpha S1-casein differs between species. This explains why someone with a sensitivity to sheep's milk can't drink goat's milk but can drink breast milk without a reaction.

Milk Carbohydrates

Cow's milk contains several different carbs.
- lactose (which is made up of glucose and galactose)
- glucose
- galactose
- other oligosaccharides

It is lactose which gives milk its sweet taste.

Lactose Intolerance

Lactose intolerance happens when the person can't digest lactose. In other words, they don't have enough lactase enzyme to break down lactose into glucose and galactose, which can result in abdominal pain, bloating, gas, diarrhoea, nausea, and even vomiting.

Most mammals naturally stop producing lactase after weaning. Some human populations (mostly Europeans) continue to make lactase in accordance with their lactose consumption.

It's common sense if you're fine and then you consume lactose and you're not fine anymore that lactose intolerance is present. However, many people worship at the shrine of science and need more than common sense to tell them what's what, so here are some back-up tests to tell people what they already should know or have been able to work out.

Hydrogen Breath Test for Lactose Intolerance
Fast overnight then drink 25 g of lactose in water.

If there is lactose intolerance, the lactose can't be digested and the gut bacteria will metabolize it and make hydrogen and methane. If so, this can be detected on the person's breath with a gas chromatograph or compact solid-state detector. This test takes about two or three hours.

Blood Test for Lactose Intolerance
Fast overnight then provide a blood sample.

Drink 50 g of lactose in water the provide blood samples at thirty minutes, one hour, two hours, and three hours. If lactose can't be digested (i.e., if lactose intolerance is present), the blood glucose levels will rise by less than 20 mg/dL.

Stool Acidity Test

This test is especially useful for babies where other forms of testing are impractical.

The baby is given a lactose drink. If the lactose is digested, it is absorbed in the small intestine. If it is not digested, it will travel to the large intestine, where the bacteria and lactose cause acidity in the stools.

In other words, if the child's stools are acidic (less than pH 5.5), it is lactose intolerant.

Avoiding Lactose Products

It can be a bit of trial and error for people to discover how much lactose they can handle. Personally, I question why we would consume the milk of another species, especially past weaning—until someone waves a delicious panne cotta or crème brulee under my nose and my theories fade into delicious oblivion. Even so, it makes sense that our bodies are better off without it.

Lactose is present in two main food categories.
- dairy products
- food additives (in both dairy and non-dairy products)

It's common for milk or milk derivatives to be added to processed foods, such as bread, crackers, cookies, cakes, manufactured meats, soy cheese, soups, gravies, chips, margarine, and products labelled "non-dairy," such as whipped topping and creamer.

It is also common for milk derivatives like casamino acid to be in vaccines.

In some cases, heating the dairy product (baking) can denature the proteins. Only the ingredients that are chemically reacting will denature.

It is important to note that many processed foods that do not contain milk may be processed on equipment contaminated with dairy foods, which may cause an allergic reaction in some sensitive individuals.

Lactose is water soluble, not fat soluble. This means if a dairy product is low fat or fat free, it's likely to have higher lactose content. In other words, if the fat and hence lactose-free content is lowered, the lactose content is relatively raised.

Hence, butter (high fat and low water) has less lactose but still has some unless the butter is also fermented (clarified butter) which contains very little lactose and is OK for most lactose intolerant people.

Some people can handle traditionally made yoghurt better than milk because the bacteria used to make the yoghurt also makes lactase which breaks down the lactose into glucose and galactose. Frozen yogurt can be similar; however, many commercial brands add milk solids, which in turn increases the lactose content.

Fermented, aged, and high-fat cheeses have less lactose. Commercial cheeses, however, don't have the same lactose-reducing properties.

Traditionally soured cream may have less lactose, but most commercial brands add milk solids, which raises the levels.

Lactase Supplements

You can purchase lactase enzyme to add to milk prior to consumption or take it with dairy foods to assist digestion.

Lactase, which is similar to human lactase (b-galactosidase), can be produced commercially from fungi (genus Aspergillus).

Timing is everything. It's no good to take the lactase on an empty stomach because the stomach acid will denature it; however, it has to reach the small bowel at the same time as the dairy food, else there's no point.

Most lactose-free commercial products contain lactase from yeast (genus Kluyveromyces). This must be thoroughly mixed throughout the product and is destroyed in acidic environments.

What to Do if You Have a Food Sensitivity

- Stop eating the trigger food until you have healed your sensitivity. To keep eating it is only going to overload your already struggling system further.

- Set boundaries in your everyday life. If you don't decide what is OK for you, someone else will. This can lead to feeling irritated by what you are doing or by what you aren't doing, which reflects in your digestive tract getting irritated as well.

- Chew your food *well* and only eat when you are relaxed.

- Detoxify and heal your bowel. If you don't restore normal digestive function, you're going nowhere.

- Take Astragalus (Astragalus membranaceous) to help regulate your T helper cells in your immune system. Most long-term inflammatory conditions are set off by an imbalance in the ratio and activity of T-helper lymphocytes (Th1 and Th2). These are in a constant state of balance like a seesaw. When one is increased, the other is decreased and vice versa. With allergies, there is a Th2 excess, which also leads the body open to infections because of the relative Th1 decrease. Check with your herbalist for your correct dosage of Astragalus.

- Take probiotics, such as Lactobacillus acidophilus and Bifidobacterium lactis, to help restore and maintain the balance of beneficial bowel bacteria.

- Take L-glutamine and aloe vera juice to help repair the mucosal lining of your gut wall.

It is essential to sort out your diet and food sensitivities in particular, if you want to enter hormone heaven.

Your body is literally made from of the food you eat. If you're not happy with the balance of your biochemistry, then change what you are eating and the way you are eating it.

Foods to Eat More Of

As well as eliminating the foods that create your imbalances, add in the foods that you know to be beneficial to your hormone health, such as

- broccoli and the cruciferous vegetables. These contain sulphuraphane and calcium d-glucorate which take the excess oestrogens out of your body.
- fish and eggs provide you with essential fatty acids and protein which help your hormones, moods, skin, and hair.
- soy products. Soy is pro-estrogenic for your brain and bones and anti-estrogenic for your breasts and uterus due to its effect on the beta receptors. This is a clever food matched to a clever body.
- sprouts. Sprouted seeds provide protein, enzymes, antioxidants, and phytoestrogens.
- seaweed. These are very high in calcium and iron.
- flax seeds help sex hormone binding globulin and therefore help high androgens and especially polycystic ovaries.
- cold pressed extra virgin olive oil for essential fatty acids.
- whole grains, such as brown rice for fibre.
- fresh fruit and vegetables for fibre, minerals, antioxidants, and a natural sweet fix.
- clean water. Drink plenty of it.

Choose fresh and organic foods as much as you can and even consider growing your own. Interestingly, this generally means you eat food that is appropriate for the environment you live in too.

It's very satisfying to watch seeds sprout and grow into healthy produce. I've also noticed that I am far less wasteful with home-grown produce when I have actually put work into propagating the garden myself rather than just picking items up at the market. It's as if you gain an added level of respect for the cycles of life when you see all the growth stages firsthand. Children will often willingly try eating varieties of fruit and vegetables they have watched grow that they may baulk at from the shop.

24

How Do You Resolve Your Issues?

Enough with the academics, the whys and wherefores.

When you've got to the point where you realize you've created your own reality and your present circumstances are the combined result of everything you've thought, said and done to date, the next logical step is to do something about it.

- Take the appropriate vitamins, minerals, and herbs you need. Use the natural hormone creams or troches that support you.
- Exercise, stretch, meditate, and contemplate to bring yourself into a place of peace and alignment as much as possible in your current world.
- Remove the toxins and xenoestrogens from your food and environment as much as is practicable. And resolve the thoughts, words, and deeds that underpin everything that is going on for you.

It takes a high degree of self-responsibility to look at the emotional and mental causes of diseases and in this case hormonal imbalances. It can appear easier to just pop a pill, smear a cream, or suck on a troche and continue along your own merry way.

If the way was merry, then this in itself would be fine. However, the way is often not merry because the body and its symptoms are a conduit to you for messages from your soul. In other words, when your soul wants to bring your attention to something so that you will rethink and redirect what you're doing and how you're doing it, it will get your attention as best it can by

- giving you specific body symptoms related to the issue
- bringing you a life experience highlighting the issue
- drawing to you other people with similar symptoms and life situations that mirror what is going on for you. If you're missing what your own body and life are telling you, there'll be opportunities to see the problems and solutions in the lives of the people around you. The trick is to notice where and why this is relevant to you and then take the steps to re-calibrate the faulty beliefs, thoughts, emotions, and actions that result from it.

Taking supplements, medications, and doing exercise programs to bring your hormones back into balance will help prop you up. However, this does nothing to alleviate your soul's directives to change what you are thinking, saying, doing, and believing that is causing your hormonal imbalances in the first place.

When you're hormonal because you're angry or hormonal because you're depressed, it's essential the underlying causes of these need to be addressed.

I'm not suggesting it's bad to use supplements, medications, and exercise programs—quite the opposite. They are incredibly useful as long as you don't miss the point and not correct your faulty beliefs, thoughts, emotions, and actions as well.

When you accept your hormonal imbalances are a natural body response to the beliefs and circumstances you've been supplying, then the following meditations and belief-changing exercises can go far to resolving your issues and helping you restore alignment with your soul and life purpose.

I'm also not suggesting you need to go it alone. It can be a tough gig resolving some of your deepest, darkest thoughts, fears, and beliefs. That's why they're deep and dark—we hide them from ourselves because they can seem all to confronting. However, confront them we must, if we want balance, freedom, and health and soul alignment as our core.

I offer you a variety of ways to skin this feline. All of them work, to the degree that you'll open your heart and allow yourself to shift the energies that have been holding you stuck.

My experience has been that a method will work particularly well for a while and then not seem to work anymore. It's nothing to do with the method and everything to do with how you apply it, or not.

I've found that once I think I know how to forgive and release my issues, the method doesn't work so well. While I focus on opening my heart and feeling the forgiveness and release rather than thinking, the methods work absolutely brilliantly. It's nothing to do with the method and everything to do with your willingness to accept, forgive, and release.

Thinking alone isn't going to get you there. If it was, you'd be fine by now. The feeling and allowing have to be hand in hand with the thinking.

If someone hurts your feelings and they say sorry without the hand-in-hand feeling, nothing gets resolved. If you don't believe them, you won't accept their apology. The situation may even escalate because the apparent crimes can be deemed to compound.

It's exactly the same for you resolving your unresolved issues from your past—your karma.

If you just do the exercise from a mental level, your brain and mind might be very happy but your heart and the rest of your cells won't get on the bus. The feeling has to match.

> Heartfelt forgiveness has to be present for
> you to get the results you desire.
> The method itself doesn't matter.
> They are just techniques to help you get to the feeling.

How many times do you need to do a technique before you get resolution at a mind, body, and soul level?

If someone killed your nearest and dearest, how many times would they need to apologise to you before you could let it and them go?

That's how many times!

In other words, if they can openheartedly apologise to you one time with the acceptance and responsibility for what they have done, then that may be enough for you to let it go.

If they need to apologise a bunch of times until you both can allow the resolution, then that's how many times it takes.

Hence, if you can access the level of acceptance and responsibility for what you have thought, said, and done in the past that has created the consequences you have now, and openheartedly apologise in the way your soul can know, feel, hear, and believe you, then it can all be released in the moment.

If you need to layer your way into finding that level of acceptance, responsibility, forgiveness, and release, then however many times it takes you to get there is how many times it takes.

It has nothing to do with trying. You either do it or you don't. A person is either pregnant or they're not. You either forgive and release wholeheartedly or you don't.

Use the following techniques as often as you like and in any order you wish. They are the means to the end. They are useful steps to get you to the feeling and allowing, to the letting go. It's not the techniques that work as such, as your willingness to love and forgive and surrender your past. However, it's the techniques that can help get you there.

How Do You Know What to Forgive and Release?

How Do You Know Which Beliefs, Thoughts, Emotions or Behaviours Are Causing Your Hormonal Imbalances?

This has the potential to be as easy or as hard as you want to make it. It can be really simple or it can be really difficult, depending on how prepared you are to accept responsibility for what you've created and how willing you are to stop hiding it, judging it, justifying it and totally and completely let it go on all levels.

Everything that is happening in your life and your body is a consequence of the decisions you've made in your past. The key is to know what they were so you can resolve them and also not propagate them any further into your future.

If you find yourself resisting, justifying, blaming, or the like, pay even closer attention. These are the armoury of the ego. Your ego does not want you to resolve your past. It wants to keep driving the show.

Here's the thing: do you want your ego to keep driving the show, or would you rather be healthy and happy?

Are you delighted with where you have ended up or have you decided to listen to your soul, the symptoms of your body, and your situations so you can realign with the highest vision for yourself and move on in health and peace?

Exercise

Decide what you're going to have.

Please note I didn't say, "Decide what you want." The mind responds to direct instructions. Tell it what you want and it will obey your command and have you keep wanting it—indefinitely. In other words, never getting it but keeping wanting it. For example, if you want to lose weight, you'll get to keep wanting to lose weight. However, if you decide to weigh whatever kilos or pounds, then all your systems will help get you there—as long as you allow it.

That's the next tip—allowing it.

For example, if you've decided to weigh a specific amount but somewhere in the past, in such as a time of deep hunger, you stated something like "I'll never go hungry again" or "I'm going to eat whatever I want no matter what," it won't matter how many diets you go on. You'll never be successful until you either cancel the original command or override it so strongly and constantly with what you've decided instead that the original statement or vow can't sabotage you anymore.

For example, if you've had the responsibility of too many children in the past and vowed, "I'll never do this again," this will be the predominant program. This can be a devastating sabotage for an infertile person wondering why they're not conceiving. The low sperm count, the hormone deficiency, and the inhospitable uterus are all consequences of the direct command from the past to never do this again.

The old programming needs to be cancelled and replaced with new programming—just like a computer upgrade.

First up, decide how your body, life, and career are going to be. The trap for young players is to immediately make a list of the finer points.

For example, house on the hill, prince or princess for a partner, career in the United Nations, and so on. Have clear goals, and write them down.

I'm not saying don't make goals. I am saying make certain you include the bigger canvas. Rather than listing a partner who brushes his teeth twice daily, takes the rubbish out without having to be clouted physically or emotionally, and loves kids, open it up to your equal love of your life partner and relationship.

Here's the thing (if you're delicate, cover your eyes and ears because I'm about to blaspheme): the universe can be a b--tard. It will bring you what you have asked for, not what you think you have asked for. If you ask for your divine, sacred marriage partner, you may very well get a very difficult relationship even though you think you've asked for something ideal. The universe's idea of ideal might be anything that makes you grow into a more divine expression of yourself. How will it help get you there? Often through challenge and adversity. Is that really what you want in your primary relationship? It might be far more peaceful and fulfilling to ask for your love-of-your-life relationship. Even better, apparently, to call for your equal-love-of-your-life relationship. Yes, you guessed correctly. I stubbed my toe on this one.

Yes, include the details as well. If it's a deal breaker for you that your partner smokes, is married to someone else, isn't fluent on your language, or has more than a twenty-year age difference, then you need to be clear about it. The universe will bring you what you've asked for not what you think you've asked for.

Let's backtrack a little to see how easy it is to trip ourselves up. For me to say the universe can be a b--tard is not useful. The universe has no option to be a b--tard if that's what I state. Our words are our wands. If we make a statement such as that, then that's what we'll get.

Obviously, it's best to not make statements like that in the first place; however, I wanted to make a point. It's imperative to cancel, clear, and delete such commands as soon as your thought police pick up on the treason; otherwise, life turns in to a b-stard and you might not remember why. You now know though, and the follow-up steps are what to do about it.

Cancel, Clear, Delete

When we think or say negative thoughts or words, complain, worry, or indulge in victim mentality, it's imperative to cancel, clear, and delete them immediately.

Thoughts are things. They are a command to your brain and nerve system to bring into reality what you thought or said. It is not discerning. It doesn't know if you're joking, serious, or just letting off steam. It just obeys orders.

If you have a bad relationship and vow, "I'm never doing that again," it will block you having future relationships. The universe or god is not against you; it's your own thoughts, vows, and agreements that have established the circumstances of your life.

It is common for humans to complain. It gives voice to anger, fear, frustration, and cries for attention. It can even be used un-usefully as a way of sharing misery to bond with others. This is completely unhealthy and detrimental. The more energy you spend on complaining, the more you create it in your life and attract others to support and add to your misery.

This is the same for self-deprecation and negatively based humour.

Focus on what you do want and stop feeding what you don't want. What you feed has to grow.

Physical stimulants, such as caffeine, nicotine, and sugar, can add to this by making your mind race or worry. Eliminating these from your diet will help calm and clear your mind so you can more deliberately choose words that take you towards what you desire rather than perpetuate old patterns and paradigms.

How Do You Cancel a Negative Thought?

Get your thought police on the job. As soon as you catch yourself saying anything negative, even if it's in humour,

- Stop.
- Hold your hand up like you do when you mean stop, in order to push the energy away from you.
- Say, "Cancel, clear, delete."

- Say the positive command you choose to replace it with.

This is similar to pressing control-alt-delete on your computer. It deletes everything giving you the opportunity to start again.

It is not enough to just think a new thought over the top of your old one unless it's markedly strong enough to override the previous commands. If you plant a seed, it is likely to grow. If you planted weeds, pull them out and replace them with flowers before your garden is overridden with things you don't want.

Gillian's Story

Gillian worked with males. She learned to cuss and express with the best and worst of them. When she realised how much her language was affecting her life, she resolved to change it; however, it was a strong habit to tackle. She began by cancelling, clearing, and deleting like a professional while she retrained herself to not swear in the first place.

How Do You Forgive and Move On?

It can be easy to say, "I forgive you." We can understand the necessity because it makes sense. If you don't forgive and let go, it's a magnet for you to attract more of the same.

Most people know their word is their wand—you get more of what you think about. If you keep regurgitating in your mind the issues and events that have caused you pain or grief, you'll not only perpetuate them but feed them and give them even more fuel than they started out with.

Clearly, we need to forgive and let go for our own sakes as well as everyone else involved. The thing is you need to really mean it on all levels of your being.

There's a big difference between knowing there's a need to forgive and let go and truly managing to do it on a heart and cellular level. As we know, just because someone says they're sorry doesn't mean they wholly mean it.

I'm going to give you a bunch of forgiveness techniques to help you free yourself and move on.

Why do you need more than one technique?

You don't—unless you have old thoughts, beliefs, and emotional investments in not letting go.

There's the catch. If it was easy for you to let go, you would have already done so by now. The fact that you haven't means there's a "good reason" justifying it somewhere and somehow. The further catch is you don't necessarily remember the catch.

For example, if it's hard for you to speak up now because a parent smacked you every time you said something that didn't match their governing policy, even if you logically know you need to forgive them so you can set yourself free and speak your own truth regardless of whether others agree or approve, there's a catch. You don't want to give your honest opinion because your experience is you'll get hit if you do.

As an adult in the free world, that makes no sense, because you can think, say, and do almost whatever you want now. You may not even remember getting hit when your ideas didn't match your parent's. You may not connect the dots at all. All you really know in the present is you get nervous to speak up and give your honest opinions, especially if you know they're different from others'.

It's the feeling of forgiveness that lets you know when you're complete. In other words, when you've truly let go, not just wanted and hoped but actually been successful.

With all the techniques, it will help you to start by recalling a time when you felt great love. This expands your energy, opens your heart, and accesses the feelings you need to forgive. This is essential, because if you're contracting your energy you're resisting and holding on, whether you consciously want to or not.

Thinking won't get you there; however, it can certainly get you to the door. It can give you the understanding required to keep your mind happy, but it's your openheartedness that's required to get you through the door.

It's your heart's job to give and receive love. It's your hearts job to bestow forgiveness upon yourself and others. The sooner you clear your mind and its justifications out of the way, the sooner you'll set yourself free and move on.

This doesn't mean ignore your mind. It just means get the order right. Lead with your heart and have your mind take the action steps to create what you need. Have your heart and mind work together like two horses pulling a chariot: equal strength, intent, and going in the same direction. In other words, get the feeling of what you need to do, then use your mind to organize the action steps rather than let your mind brew up an idea and then try to force your heart happy with it.

Use the techniques however they suit you. If you have a favourite, stick with it. If you don't like the format, words, or anything else, keep working through until you find what you have an affinity with. We all have different personal philosophies, so go with the techniques you resonate with you the most.

If you're not able to access the feelings of love, forgiveness, and release, try another one and see if that can get you to let go and surrender to the depths required.

The Preparation Basics

Rather than repeat the set-up steps that are common to all the methods, I'll list them here so you can apply them with ease prior to each technique.

You're aiming for a place of contemplation, where you're super relaxed but still consciously aware of what you're doing and why you're doing it (you're still clear and focused on your intent) rather than deep meditation (where you're off with the pixies and not necessarily aware of what's going on).

1. Sit in a quiet comfortable place where you know you won't be disturbed.
2. Relax your body and gently close your eyes.
3. Slow and deepen your breathing.

4. Mentally send all negative energy that's with you (emotions, such as anger, jealously, impatience, frustration, irritation, demanding problems or situations, etc.) up to and bind them to the universal white light of source, up above your head.

    It doesn't matter if you created the negativity yourself or absorbed it from someone else. Focus and send it all to source so your energy is clean and free from interference.

    If someone wrote on your forehead that you're an idiot, you'd want to clean it off. Clean everything negative from you.

    * Tip: If you're out in space and you spill a drink, it just floats around. Energy is the same. If you don't bind it to source for transformation, you leave it floating around for someone else or even yourself to reabsorb all over again.

    * If it's difficult for you to visualize, you're possibly not focusing enough, simply need more practice, or low in B vitamins. If you don't visualize well or recall your dreams easily, it's likely you're low in B vitamins. Be patient with yourself and keep practicing with the intent to be able to do it easily and effectively.

    * If you have a preference for affirmations, you can include words like "I now clear all negativity affecting myself, raise it up, and bind it to the light." You can also add on for good measure something like "In the name of the Lord Jesus Christ/Lord Buddha" or whichever master of light you have an affinity with, if you like that sort of thing.

5. Keep breathing, and mentally surround yourself with the white light of positivity.

    * Once again, if you like affirmations, add in your words of protection, such as "I clothe myself in a beautiful robe of white light" or "I clothe myself in a robe of white light composed to the love, power, and wisdom of god not only for my own protection but so that all see it and come in contact with it are drawn to god and healed."

6. Ask for help from whatever is positive and aligned with your personal belief systems. For example, your higher self, spirit guides, angels, ascended masters, the creator, source, and God/Goddess. (If you do this, remember to give thanks afterwards.)

My experience with all the methods is I get better results (i.e., deeper and faster levels of forgiveness and surrender) when I say these words

- out aloud
- in nature
- repeat them three times

However, it is really common to awaken at all hours of the night when you need to release something. In which case I recommend you do it there and then rather than delaying until your next beach or bush walk.

At first glance, parts of these techniques can seem a little wishy-washy, new age or even a potential waste of time; however, I've both seen and experienced major shifts in myself and others by using these methods. The proof is in the pudding, so to speak.

I recommend you experiment with all of them and discover which approaches resonate with you best. I rotate them when I get too in my head and logical rather than freely accessing the feelings and allowing the whole truth of forgiveness to flow.

Let your results be your guide.

These techniques are offered for your own personal use and healing. They are not in any way offered as a means to treat others. Leave that to the professionals and seek professional help yourself as you need it.

EFT or Tapping

Do the preparation basics as previously discussed.

EFT (emotional freedom technique) or tapping has roots the branch of chiropractic called kinesiology and acupuncture. It works by saying aloud the causal issue while you repeated tap or stimulate specific energy meridian points in order.

There are many versions of varying complexity. I'm only going to outline the basics here (the tried and true method I use myself). If you wish to explore this method in more depth, I encourage you to seek out courses or practitioners with the appropriate knowledge and qualifications.

Do three cycles and re-evaluate. Keep going until you don't experience the issue in your life anymore.

As you continually tap the meridian points (listed below) keep repeating aloud, "Even though I ... (get moody and angry/feel depressed and defeatist/blame others/get confused/have this headache/have these menstrual cramps/crave chocolate, etc.) ... I deeply and profoundly love and accept myself."

(* This affirmation acknowledges the problem and creates self-acceptance despite the existence of the problem).

Do three rounds of saying this at each meridian point as you tap there. In other words, tap solidly but not forcefully, using the pointer and middle fingers of your dominant hand together, at each point for as long as it takes you to repeat the affirmation aloud.

It doesn't matter which hand you tap or use to do the tapping; however, most people are more efficient using their dominant hand to do the tapping.

The meridian points in order are
1. karate-chop point: between the top of your wrist and the base of your fifth finger (i.e., the part of your hand you'd use to karate-chop)
2. upper left (or right) chest. Feel the U-shaped notch at the top of your sternum or breastbone. Go down towards your navel about 7 cms (3 inches), then 7 cms (3 inches) to the left (or right). Within a small radius, you'll find a tender spot. This is it.
3. start of the inner end of your eyebrow. Just above and to one side of the bridge of your nose.
4. bone at the outside corner of the eye.
5. bone directly under the centre of your eye.

6. under your nose, between your nose and top lip.

7. under your bottom lip, between your bottom lip and the point of your chin.

8. where your clavicle (collarbone) and sternum (breastbone) meet.

9. the side of your body (under your arm) 2–3 cm (1 inch) below nipple height. For a female, this is approximately in line with the under fold of the breast.

Extra Points if You're Being Extra Thorough

10. outside edge of your thumb at the base of the nail.

11. edge of your index finger on the side closest to your thumb, at the base of the nail.

12. edge of your middle finger on the side closest to your thumb, at the base of the nail.

13. edge of your fifth finger on the side closest to your thumb, at the base of the nail.

14. karate-chop point again.

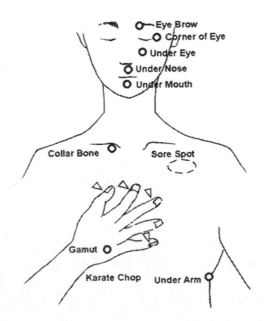

Forgiveness Technique 1

Do the preparation basics as previously discussed.

In your openhearted, slow-breathing, contemplative state, affirm with conviction three times,

> By divine decree and under the law of grace and my free will, I fully and freely forgive and release ... (my mother for raising me as a boy, the person who sexually abused me, myself for thinking I'm not good enough/giving up to soon/judging myself, etc.) ... all related beliefs and all that has gone to cause these from ... (e.g. a chakra or body part) and my entire mind, body, and spirit through all time, space, and dimensions now. So be it. (Keep breathing.)
> I call to Quan Yin and the karmic board and ask for karmic absolution from all that has gone to cause this from all levels. (Keep breathing.)
> I call to Quan Yin and the karmic board and ask for the total and complete cancellation of all contracts, vows, and agreements, both known and unknown to me, from all levels. (Keep breathing.)
> I call to Lord Michael and ask for the cutting of all cords, ties, and attachments. (Keep breathing.)
> I call to the Great Ladies and ask for the soothing and smoothing of all memories and the integration of them into my heart. (Keep breathing.)
> Thank you, thank you, thank you.

Forgiveness Technique 2

Do the preparation basics as previously discussed.

In your openhearted, slow-breathing, contemplative state, affirm with conviction three times,

> I call forth all contracts, vows, and agreements, both known an unknown to me, pertaining to ... (abandonment, my father, my mother, jealousy, etc.) ... and stamp them all cancelled, making

them all totally and completely null and void on all levels. I tear them all into shreds and burn them in the rainbow flames on all levels. (Keep breathing.)

Forgiveness Technique 3

Do the preparation basics as previously discussed.

In your openhearted, slow-breathing, contemplative state, affirm with conviction three times,

> By divine decree and under the law of grace and by my free will, it's my crystal-clear intent to totally and completely forgive and release and lift into the light all ... (unworthiness/betrayal/ revenge/punishment/judgement, etc.) ... all causes, cores, effects, records and memories both known and unknown to me from all levels, through all lifetimes, spaces, and dimensions totally and completely once and for all.
> I accept full responsibility for all that I've created.
> I have learned my lessons.
> I give 100 per cent permission for total and complete forgiveness, healing, and release on all levels.
> I choose to be totally and completely free and clear of these aspects, energies, structures, and patterns on all levels now.
> Yes, I forgive you. (Repeat three times.) (Keep breathing.)
> Yes, please forgive me (repeat three times.) (Keep breathing.)
> Yes, I set you free and I set myself free. (Repeat three times.) (Keep breathing.)
> I call upon Quan Yin and the karmic board and I ask for total and complete karmic absolution from all that's gone to create this on all levels.
> In the name of the mighty, I AM presence I AM I close all corridors completely and correctly on all levels now.

Forgiveness Technique 4: Hoponoopono

(This method is well known as the Hoponoopono Prayer.)

Do the preparation basics as previously discussed.

In your openhearted, slow-breathing, contemplative state, affirm with conviction three times,

> I'm sorry.
> Please forgive me.
> Thank you.
> I love you.

Susan's Story

Susan went through early menopause. She'd always had hormonal issues. It started out as heavy, painful periods as a teen and spiralled to fibroids and positive Pap smears and a hysterectomy. Even though she didn't have ovaries or a uterus anymore, she still had all the emotional symptoms and mood swings. She was not impressed. How could this be?

That was a good question to ask. Unfortunately for her, it wasn't asked years earlier. As she delved into the dark recesses of her hidden secrets, she committed to doing whatever it took to forgive her brother who had sexually abused her as a child. It was a confronting journey, but she took the steps and got the results.

Releasing the blocked emotions and issues freed her. The bioidentical hormones and spinal adjustments now supported her in keeping her stable.

Integrating Aspects

Through our myriad of experiences, we've experienced a gamut of different situations, beliefs, cultures, and situations.

We have loved, learned, hated, surrendered, resisted, succeeded, failed, judged, and much more.

Part of our healing and soul's journey is to reclaim the parts of ourselves that we have judged, shamed, and hidden from ourselves and others.

Whenever you judge yourself or someone else, you are blocking the flow of love, creating separation, and perpetuating the issues in your life. When you block the flow of love, fear and worry spread and spin you into a downward spiral.

Unresolved aspects can play out in your life as confusion, fear, worry, and sabotage of your life's purpose. When you doubt yourself, you know there's an aspect of you that needs reintegrating. It's trying to keep you safe from pain or failure but it blocks everything, including success as well as what it's trying to protect you from.

How do you integrate your aspects?

Do the preparation basics as previously discussed.

In your openhearted, slow-breathing, contemplative state,

> Lovingly accept responsibility for all misuse of power and karma you hold within you and for all relationships you are involved in that are karmic in nature.
>
> Call forth all your aspects pertaining to the issue you're working on, including those that create resistance and sabotage in your life or have unresolved memories.
>
> Call them into your heart. Reassure them that it's a safe place.
>
> Cancel all contracts, vows, and agreements that have created this situation.
>
> Forgive all these aspects on all levels. (You can use the Hoponoopono Prayer or any of the previous forgiveness techniques to help you access the intent and feelings of forgiveness required.)
>
> Ask them to please forgive you on all levels.
>
> Set them free and set yourself free.
>
> Use your sword of truth to cut all cords of attachment that have been holding this in place.
>
> Integrate these aspects of yourself back into you or into the universal white light.

25

Heal Your Wounds;
Heal Your Life

Instead of resolving the underlying cause of their issues, most people overlook the imbalances in their bodies and lives and find ways to either adapt or soldier on. We now have excessive use and abuse of medication, surgery, addiction, therapies, drugs, and quick-fix programs to cope with daily events.

Once you become aware that the imbalances are gifts, your whole perception of the world can transform. When your paradigm changes from one of suppressing pain and coping to looking for the gifts and being grateful for them, you start to steer your own ship again rather be a passenger. You still have to find your way across the oceans; however, you're in a position of responsibility again.

The greatest wounds you have will be recognized as your greatest gifts when you can find and accept the blessings within them.

Everyone comes into life with three wounds or challenges ahead of them. There is always balance in the universe—so equally that you will have three pleasurable events to the same degree as your difficulties or challenges. Remember to look for your fortunate events as well and not get swamped by the challenges.

Look for the gifts in your current challenges. Don't wait to look in the rear-vision mirror after you have resolved your issues to see what the gift was with your bright light of hindsight. Start noticing the gifts in the present moment.

Can't usually means *won't*. If you can't see the gifts yet, ask yourself why you won't. It's likely to be because you'll have to change something.

Most of us are keen to change everything except ourselves. It's far easier to blame others and circumstances for our situations, but the truth is that we created our circumstances with our past choices and actions, and only by changing ourselves will we have lasting change around us.

Nature doesn't go in a straight line. Rivers take a meandering course from the mountains to the ocean—twisting this way and that around, over, and through obstacles. Our paths follow a similar route. Rather than get frustrated with the rocks in your stream, find a way around, over, or through them. Keeping safe doesn't work! There are always going to be rocks!

If you have a disease or condition, be grateful for it. The location and nature of the illness will tell you what you need to resolve and change in yourself. What are you learning? Where is the gift in your issues?

Have you noticed that people reflect back to you what you hide from yourself?

What are you doing about it?

What do you intend to do about it?

Are you learning to give and receive love equally? Do you love yourself rather than give all your love to another in the hope they'll love you in return? Would you allow it if they did?

To be grateful is to be *great-ful*. When you're grateful, you're full of greatness!

Be discerning. What has caused your issues? Be and do who and what is required to resolve them, and move on. Rather than trying to get back to where you were, strive to move forward to higher ground. Restoring something back to where it was is no use, because that's where the problem started in the first place!

Stop trying to get your life back how it used to be!

Move forward to where you choose it to be from here on.

While acquiring the knowledge and skills to resolve your own issues and imbalances, you learn things that can also help other people on their journey.

It used to bother me that I had so many injuries from childhood sports and accidents and that I had to dedicate so much time, energy, and money learning how to heal the effects of them. I spent most of my adulthood healing the consequences my childhood! Conversely, it all turned out for the best, because I investigated and experienced many healing methods and philosophies. I learned what works and what doesn't and that's precious information—not just for me but also for the people who came to see me as a practitioner, because they were able to directly benefit from my pursuits. If I hadn't had all the injuries and consequent health challenges, I may well have become just another book-learned practitioner and teacher rather than living up to my name.

What are your issues? What have you learned because of them? What gifts have they brought you so far? Your challenges show you clearly and accurately what you need in order to love yourself, love others, and return to the oneness your soul desires. It's all yours in this lifetime as soon as you allow it.

Look for the gift. It's in the present, the now.

About the Author:
Joanne, *The Messenger*

Joanne Messenger is just the person to write *How to Balance Your Hormones: The Revolutionary Owner's Guide*

In the true sense of "the wounded healer," everything she had to learn and implement to restore her own health after fracturing her pelvis in a trampoline fall at age twelve is what she uses to help others.

Most people know her as a chiropractor and Chiron healer, but she also has over thirty years of experience as a public speaker and course facilitator and was Australia's best-known teachers of Chiron philosophies and techniques.

Dr. Joanne Messenger was born the youngest of seven children—all girls, except for six boys—in Pingelly, Western Australia. Her mother was a nurse, so right from beginning, she was immersed in health care.

At an early age, one of her brothers was diagnosed as terminal. Being a nurse in the 1960s, her mother followed the medical route but got no happy result. Cortisone was the only easer. After an arduous path, her parents took her brother, Chris, to a chiropractor, where he was given spinal adjustments to restore function to his nerve system.

A *modern miracle* resulted!

In 1978, Joanne went to chiropractic college in Melbourne to study this natural healing method that had worked wonders in her family.

Joanne was an excellent student, and her academic qualifications are impressive. She has a bachelor's degree in applied science (1982), a diploma from the National Board of Chiropractic Examiners (USA), an Excellence Award in Radiology, a diploma of sacro-occipital technique, practitioner and teacher certificates in Chiron healing, and a certificate IV in assessment and workplace training. She is a certified yoga (RYTA200) teacher, is certified in neurolinguistic programming (NLP) as applied to education, and has studied aromatherapy, Australian bush flower essences, essences of the ancient civilizations, Pleiadean light work, and pranic healing.

Dr. Joanne is one of the founding members of Chiron healing, past principal of the Australian Energy School of Chiron, past vice president of the International Association of Chiron Healers, Inc., and past treasurer of SOTO A/Asia Ltd.

Joanne studied firsthand with Master Chiron and compiled the manuals and teaching programs for Chiron healing. Philosophical differences led to a parting of the ways, and *Be in One Peace* and *Blueprint Healing* evolved.

Joanne has taught the philosophies and techniques of energy and healing throughout Australia and the world.

Index

Symbols

5 Hydroxytryptamine, *41. See* 5HTP: Serotonin

A

Absorption, *195*

Acupuncture, *3, 37, 292*

Adjustments, *136, 164. See* Subluxations

Adrenal Exhaustion, *45, 151, 152, 153, 155, 157, 159, 160, 161, 162, 169, 170, 173*

Affirmations, *23, 24, 25, 291*

Air, *xv, 27, 28, 38, 39, 57, 59, 61, 63, 76, 90, 92, 95, 96, 97, 130, 160. See* Breathe

Alcohol, *131, 134, 137, 201, 207*

Alignment, *27, 48*

Aloe Vera, *198, 210, 217, 223*

Aluminium, *75, 97, 99*

Amalgam Dental Fillings, *199*

Anger, *3, 47, 58, 68, 69, 71, 77, 78, 80, 127, 136, 180, 202, 232, 244, 248, 287, 291*

Anti-oxidants, *35*

Anxiety, *xiii, 12, 44, 45, 46, 47, 48, 53, 54, 60, 69, 80, 137, 147, 153, 158, 160, 170, 176, 209, 237, 243*

Aromatherapy, *8, 227, 228, 235, 242. See* Essential Oils

Artemesia, *210, 216*

Asanas, *43, 45, 47. See* Yoga

Assimilation, *195*

B

Asthma, *60*

Astragalus, *167, 279*

Atherosclerosis, *30, 139, 145, 154, 271*

Backache, *3, 68*

Bacteria, *17, 39, 61, 66, 67, 97, 102, 179, 186, 195, 199, 200, 202, 207, 208, 210, 212, 214, 217, 218, 221, 223, 224, 225, 263, 273, 276, 277, 278, 279*

Basal Metabolic Rate, *45. See* BMR

Beliefs, *22, 23, 24, 37, 44, 51, 58, 64, 65, 76, 78, 83, 98, 121, 152, 162, 194, 210, 282, 289, 295, 297*

Betaine Hydrochloride, *143, 196, 253*

Billy Goat Plum, *247*

Bio-Identical Hormones, *185, 186*

Black Eyed Susan, *247*

Blame, *16, 53, 58, 66, 72, 73, 74, 266, 293, 300*

Blood Pressure, *12, 13, 153, 154*

Bone Density, *86, 88*

Bottlebrush, *247*

Boundaries, *51, 196, 203, 248, 268, 279*

Bowel, *32, 33, 102, 103, 104, 118, 131, 137, 138, 148, 172, 186, 193, 194, 195, 196, 197, 198, 199, 200, 201, 202, 203, 204, 205, 206, 207, 210, 214, 215, 221, 223, 224, 247, 252, 255, 256, 263, 265, 266, 268, 269, 271, 273, 278, 279*

Brain, *xiii*, *12*, *21*, *24*, *28*, *29*, *34*, *35*, *42*, *43*, *44*, *55*, *62*, *63*, *75*, *121*, *123*, *132*, *148*, *153*, *155*, *160*, *164*, *176*, *177*, *185*, *193*, *194*, *196*, *197*, *203*, *214*, *221*, *223*, *247*, *271*, *280*, *283*, *287*

Breast, *1*, *3*, *38*, *41*, *63*, *75*, *87*, *88*, *96*, *99*, *140*, *142*, *207*, *217*, *218*, *272*, *275*, *294*

Breathe, *xv*, *38*, *47*, *54*, *236*

Bromelain, *218*

Bush Fuscia, *247*

C

Caffeine, *127*, *128*, *137*, *157*

Calcium, *33*, *34*, *103*, *260*, *280*

Cancel, Clear, Delete, *287*

Cancer, *17*, *60*, *61*

Candida, *137*, *147*, *196*, *206*, *207*, *208*, *209*, *210*, *211*, *215*, *224*, *244*, *256*, *263*, *268*, *269*

Carbon Monoxide, *58*

Cascara, *199*

Casein, *104*, *272*, *274*, *275*. *See also* Milk: Lactose: Dair

Castor Oil, *216*

Catalyst, *75*

Catecholamines, *12*

Central Nervous System, *21*. *See* Nervous System; Nerve System: CNS

Cerebro-Spinal Fluid, *28*. *See* CSF

Chakra, *68*, *181*, *196*, *237*, *295*

Chamomile, *238*, *244*

Chiron Healing, *8*, *9*, *228*, *245*, *303*, *304*

Chiropractic, *8*, *28*, *44*, *122*, *292*

Chlorine, *61*, *92*, *97*, *130*, *200*

Chocolate, *5*, *7*, *25*, *140*, *170*, *171*, *193*, *197*, *270*, *293*

Cholesterol, *12*, *13*, *29*, *139*, *140*, *144*, *145*, *148*, *153*, *257*, *265*, *266*

Chromium, *5*, *196*, *251*, *260*

Cigarette, *58*, *60*. *See* Smoking

Clary Sage, *230*, *234*, *235*, *243*, *244*

Colloidal Silver, *217*

Colonic Irrigation, *201*

Confusion, *3*, *298*

Constipation, *101*, *129*, *148*, *176*, *204*, *215*, *222*

Corn, *32*

Cortisol, *5*, *11*, *54*, *80*, *153*, *154*, *159*, *160*, *161*, *167*, *173*, *177*, *178*, *179*, *184*, *186*, *192*, *224*

Cosmetics, *xv*, *59*

Cramp Bark, *218*

Crowea, *247*

CSF, *28*. *See* Cerebro-Spinal Fluid

D

Dagger Hakea, *248*

Dairy, *6*, *32*, *33*, *96*, *103*, *106*, *133*, *203*, *210*, *223*, *255*, *256*, *272*, *273*, *275*, *277*, *278*. *See* Milk

Dairy Sensitivity, *272*, *274*

Dandelion Root, *148*

DDT, *xiv*, *63*, *92*

Deficiency, *5*, *6*, *11*, *17*, *36*, *85*, *90*, *102*, *133*, *137*, *138*, *139*, *141*, *142*, *145*, *154*, *169*, *172*, *224*, *248*, *252*, *253*, *256*, *257*, *285*

Depression, *3*, *45*, *47*, *49*, *53*, *54*, *69*, *86*, *153*, *154*, *155*, *159*, *173*, *191*, *207*, *235*, *244*

DES, *62*. *See* Diethylstilbesterol

Detox Program, *197*

DHEA, *84*, *153*, *154*, *159*, *160*, *161*, *173*, *186*, *191*, *224*

Diabetes, *2*, *30*, *139*

Diarrhea, *140*, *170*, *171*, *204*, *205*, *206*, *211*, *213*, *224*, *255*, *274*, *276*

dichlorodiphenyltrichloroethane.. *See* Di chlorodiphenyltrichloroethane

Diethylstilbesterol, *62*. *See* DES

Digestion, *12*, *36*, *101*, *147*, *221*

Dioxin, *76*